MOBILE AND MARGINALIZED PEOPLES: PERSPECTIVES FROM THE PAST

Mobile and Marginalized Peoples: Perspectives from the Past

Edited by

RUDOLF C. HEREDIA

SHEREEN F. RATNAGAR

Proceedings of a workshop held in December 1998 at the Ishvani Kendra, Pune organized by the Sontheimer Cultural Association and the Social Science Centre, St. Xavier's College, Mumbai with financial assistance from the Life Insurance Corporation, Pune

MANOHAR
2003

First published 2003

ISBN 81-7304-497-X

Published by

Ajay Kumar Jain for
Manohar Publishers & Distributors
4753/23 Ansari Road, Daryaganj
New Delhi 110 002

Typeset at

Digigrafics
New Delhi 110 049

Printed at

Lordson Publishers Pvt. Ltd.
Delhi 110 007

Contents

Contributors

R. CHAMPAKALAKSHMI, retired Professor of south Indian history, Jawaharlal Nehru University, New Delhi.

AJAY DANDEKAR, Senior Research Fellow, Social Science Centre, St. Xavier's College, Mumbai.

RUDOLF C. HEREDIA, Director, Social Science Centre, St. Xavier's College, Mumbai.

JAYA MENON, Lecturer, M.S. University of Baroda, Vadodara.

ARCHANA PRASAD, Fellow, Nehru Memorial Museum & Library.

SHEREEN F. RATNAGAR, former Professor of Archaeology, Jawaharlal Nehru University, New Delhi.

CHETAN SINGH, Reader, Professor, Department of History, Himachal Pradesh University, Shimla.

NANDINI SINHA, Lecturer, University of Delhi.

SUPRIYA VARMA, Lecturer, Panjab University, Chandigarh.

Introduction

SHEREEN F. RATNAGAR

During an event that we fondly remember as 'Pastoralism I' (Ratnagar, ed., *Studies in History*, vol. 7, no. 2, 1991), a modest collection of papers was put together that dealt with the role of pastoralism in the prehistory and history of South Asia, in a preliminary and admittedly patchy way, because that role is poorly inscribed in the epigraphic, literary, and archaeological record. A major focus of that volume was the environmental parameters of the semi-arid zone (set out by Rodgers), and the area covered cut a kind of swathe southward from Afghanistan and Baluchistan to western Rajasthan, Kathiawad, Maharashtra, and Andhra Pradesh. (In this study, which may be called the 'Pastoralism II' venture, a paper on the high Himalayan reaches of northern India takes the place of Afghanistan and Baluchistan, and there is a discussion on early Tamil Nadu instead of Andhra Pradesh. But we have also incorporated the thickly-forested hills of central India, well beyond the semi-arid zone.) The ecological facets comprised the relation between agriculture and pastoralism, including the importance of manure and cattle power in agriculture, and access to stubble, water, and pasture for herdsmen. Kavoori and Balland discussed the repercussions of the extension of agriculture. A second theme that emerged was the dimensions of mobility and the conditions under which the routes and the length of migration were altered. Also, two important papers (Audouze and Jarrige, Varma) discussed how we infer the existence of mobile pastoralism from the archaeological record. 'Pastoralism I' touched to a lesser extent on forest, agro-pastoralism, and linkages of nomads with urban society. Anil Gupta gave a theoretical paper on the rationality of the mobile pastoral economy and the room it affords for individual choice.

* The references to this introduction occur after the concluding summary to the book.

There have been important contributions to this general area of scholarship since then, and I refer here to a few of them. In 1999, one of the contributors to 'Pastoralism I', P.S. Kavoori, published an extensive analysis of pastoral migration in and out of western Rajasthan, its ecological basis, and its interrelation with agriculture; not only was detailed information on fallow systems and grass species and growth noted on field journeys made with pastoralists, but also important was the interpretation of the great adjustments that migration patterns have recently made within the context of the changing political economy. Taking a refreshingly new theme for study, V.K. Srivastava (1997) discussed the inner life, the religion of renunciation, amongst the camel-breeder Raikas of Rajasthan. Vasant Saberwal (1999), whose field studies were conducted in Himachal Pradesh, investigated the origins of the notion of impending environmental disaster caused by pastoralist land use, and found that these lay in the problems of forest administration and contestation over the control of forest resources. Saberwal points also to the contrast between predictions and the actual nature of environmental degradation, and to the fact that little is really known about causes and processes.

Klaus Ferdinand's voluminous and illustrated tome (1993) on the Bedouin of Qatar is a model documentation of pastoral everyday life and material culture. It incorporates a range of information on tents and clothes (and their social meanings), utensils, weaving techniques, hunting methods, diet, and so on. There are useful pieces of information on livestock-handling skills, such as details on attendance at birth and lactation, weaning, milking, and the castration of camels. More important, Ferdinand views the material culture as an apparatus of skills and knowledge without which Bedouin culture would not be viable.

Among other recent works on pastoralism are studies on the Bhotiyas (Sharma and Rikhari 1995; Farooquee and Nautiyal 1996), to which we will refer subsequently, and a thoughtful enquiry by P.K. Misra (1992) into the terms on which nomadic peoples may be incorporated into the national mainstream. There is also the work of Ruhela (1999) which discusses aspects of the nomadic life of the Gaduliya Lohar (iron workers) in Rajasthan.

However, none of these studies on pastoralism, nomadism, or pastoral groups focuses on the past. For a historical perspective we turn to other work, beginning with a collection of papers edited by Arnold and Guha (1995). Many of these papers are about irrigation, shifting cultivation, and the use of forest, with just two, by Chetan Singh and N. Bhattacharya, concerned with pastoralism and pastoralists. Colonial rule and the watershed it represents in terms of state policy and administrative attitudes towards nomadic peoples and the various categories of natural resources is a theme connecting many of those papers.

A volume edited by N. Bhattacharya (*Studies in History*, vol. 14, no. 2, 1998) is also on history. It has a fascinating historiographic theme, lucidly formulated by Bhattacharya: the recent swing away from the study of agrarian history and towards the study of the environment and nature, and the arguable notion of a disjuncture in the environmental history of South Asia said to have occurred in the colonial period.[1] There is a paper on forest in Ashoka's time, and two discussions of the extent of uncultivated land in the Mughal Empire. A paper deals with the culture of the cattle-raiding Bhils of central India in the nineteenth century. For the rest, the studies are concerned with forested areas in the colonial period. The contributors do not take much interest in pastoralism (the subtitle of the issue notwithstanding) and 'Pastoralism I', also published as a special issue of the same journal, finds no citation therein (justifying Dandekar's starting complaint in this volume). The reverse is, however, not the case, and some arguments there do have relevance to, and find mention in, this collection of papers. The reason for this last is our shift of emphasis, on which more below.

Sumit Guha's book (1999), which deals with forest and forest dwellers and tribal communities (tribal society is not specifically defined in the book) in the north-western Deccan and central India, takes an eight-century perspective up to the present, venturing also into archaeological interpretations of prehistoric times. Guha argues for repeated changes in the environment, in land use, and in social boundaries and identities. This is one of the most sustained and

[1] According to Skaria (1999), the hiatus between the Mughal and the colonial periods is of great importance for it was then that new state forms took shape, and changes occurred in the geography of forest use and of pastoralism; with the coming of the British, the wilderness was tamed and marginalized, and mobility was largely extinguished.

systematic arguments against the primordial nature of social identities and ways of life.[2]

The subject of this volume, archaeological and historical perspectives on pastoralism, is therefore a still neglected one in scholarly circles. We present a second small contribution to this topic, admitting again that the outcome is not spectacular. It is the past that is critical to an understanding of current problems such as the nature of change, how people coped with natural calamities and contested habitats and displacement, and the dynamics of group identity. We need to study land use in times when pastoralists were not hemmed in by world market imperatives, twentieth-century misgovernance and corruption, or unprecedented pressure on land and water resources.

Nevertheless, some adjustment to our approach has taken place since Pastoralism I. The trend in that volume was to distinguish pastoralism from agricultural production so as to give pastoralism a shape and content, and to establish its place in South Asian history. While such a contrast has analytical utility, however, it may not be correct to segregate land use systems as distinct/separate for any specific historical situation. As early as the 1970s, scholars had pointed out that communities are rare whose economies are based on the utilization of single resources. Although in Pastoralism I some mention was made of agro-pastoralism and the spectrum between sedentary agriculture and fully nomadic animal herding, and one paper discussed the great importance of trade among certain nomads, we are now more aware of the dangers of thinking in terms of hard and fast categories. To quote Waller and Sobania (1994:63) writing about African pastoralism, 'We see pastoralism as a variable adaptation unable to survive without the existence of complementary economic modes, and we view pastoral communities as embedded in regional networks of exchange and accumulation.' Kavoori's work (1999), one may add, is in much the same framework.

This is the background against which we requested the participation in the workshop of Prasad and Sinha, who do not work on

[2] Regretting the 'virtual absence of any historical context' in studies on pastoralism in Africa, Waller and Sobania (1994) also place stress on the major changes that have occurred in pastoral economy and ethnic identities. Moreover, the 'range and intensity' of the interaction of the Maasai pastoralists with traders and agriculturists 'belies any notion of pastoral isolation' (p. 53).

pastoralism but who have specialized in the histories of non-peasant and non-ruling class communities on the fringes of stratified society. Their work alerts us to the dangers of quick-fix labels. In the following pages, therefore, the discussion on rural settlement and depopulation, the dimensions and structural disadvantages of mobility, ecosystem change, and the craft production and trade of mobile peoples, including pastoralists, is enriched by considerations of flexible and composite livelihood systems and their integration into the larger society and economy by way of several kinds of linkages.

The essays in this book are varied in theme and rich in content; below I refer to them not to give accurate summaries, but to relate their contents to what has been discussed above. Thus the references to them below do not do full justice to the essays, and each has to be read in its own right.

There is one paper in this collection that does not discuss the historical dimensions of pastoralism or other non-agrarian livelihoods. Instead, it sets the present-day academic perspective for us. Rudolf Heredia is concerned with the ways in which processes of modernization victimize the already disadvantaged groups—often nomadic tribes—in India. Rather than engage with 'the vanishing primitive', he is concerned with the alienation of vulnerable groups in the name of national development. Scholarship about unequal relationships is never politically neutral, he says, and must show an awareness of the political context of academic debates, and of the ways in which power affects the production of knowledge. Academicians can never portray the cultures of other peoples as final and complete truths, and certainly not in a bird's-eye view. Contestations of portrayals are inevitable. Even so Heredia thinks that the study of other societies is an enriching experience when we create a 'dialogue' with those whom we study.

Empowerment is the end in mind; one route towards this is literacy and the enabling of people to write their own history and sociology. As for oral traditions, they are not simply narratives. Such narratives often define a group by tracing its origins to one or another place, social situation, and time; and this is the social construction of history that gives identity to a group (Waller and Sobania 1994:55-9). Moreover, there is also Misra's pertinent point (1992:216) that when a nomad culture makes the transition from the oral to the written, it 'tends to lose its autonomy and flexibility, and moves towards a social space where the technical order is dominant and the moral order becomes subordinate'. As Misra argues, with literacy comes standardization and an inevitable devaluation of the newly-literate culture.

In keeping with our accent on fluid categories and boundaries, Chetan Singh, while opening with the observation that nomadic pastoralism and tribal organization are different and separate from peasant society organized under the state, shows that the sheep-herding Kinnauras of Himachal Pradesh absorbed influences from caste society, and were ruled by a regional kingdom/chiefship. Having established the geography of migrant sheep-herding in the high mountain regions, and of agricultural-pastoral interrelationships, Chetan Singh goes on to show that pastoralism by itself is not viable within Kinnaur and that seasonal movement into lower-altitude pastures was essential. Thus neither geographic nor economic entities have neat boundaries. There is also the close association of sheep nomadism with the India-Tibet trade. In 1991, Balland had discussed the trade that the Afghan pastoralists brought annually into the Indian plains and the decline of that trade because of British policies and the new international frontiers established at Independence. In Chetan Singh's case study, the linkage with trade is not only the mobility of sheep herders, but also the loads that goats and sheep are made to carry when no other means of transportation will work on the steep slopes. Engagement with trade—which, the evidence suggests, was important to the pastoralists and to the region[3]—necessitated large numbers of these animals (which carry small loads) and hence skilled and specialized animal breeding. The trade with Tibet ceased years ago, and while Chetan Singh suggests no causation, we are reminded of Balland's finding (1991:225) that the Lohanis, dominant trader pastoralists of the nineteenth century, appear to have vanished as an ethnic group mainly because their trade came to an end and they had to disperse.

[3] Sharma and Rikhari (1995) in their detailed ecological study of Bhotia transhumance state that two trading trips were made each year to Tibet. With the closure of the trade and restrictions on grazing in many areas, flocks have dwindled and wool production has declined.

Even as we question separate or contrasting categories, we contend with Ajay Dandekar's findings here that rulers during the medieval period made hardly any land grants in the semi-arid zone of Maharashtra, whereas memorials to heroes who died on cattle raids (dating generally to AD 900-1300) are predominantly located *in* the semi-arid zone. Dandekar challenges the received wisdom that states emerge in 'nuclear' zones of high agricultural productivity, as if pastoral production and society do not count. In his 1991 paper he had, in fact, suggested that sheep-herding and the manure it provides almost made dry-zone agriculture possible in Maharashtra. Also, he had suggested that the pilgrimage and the annual herding circuits seemed to run on the same track and schedule. Here it is suggested that medieval dynasties may have had strong roots in pastoral economy and society.

We thus see that animal herders could have had a substantial social presence in the past, and not only that, they could have actually risen to dominance under certain historical conditions—and that not only as marauding or raiding groups. Gurukkal (1998:260-1) has argued that in early Tamilakam, as represented in the Sangam poetry, as chiefships and social stratification developed, the plundering cattle raiders of the *palai* or 'parched zone' were part of a political process in which cattle redistribution was integral to the office of the chiefship, and plunder was the main means of acquiring goods to redistribute. In medieval Maharashtra, however, cattle-raid chiefs may even have risen to positions of regional dominance. Considering that no one has yet refuted the absence of archaeological sites in inland Maharashtra for the period AD 400 to 1300,[4] Dandekar's hypothesis is a tempting one, even though it may require finer chronological tuning.

Anil Gupta's paper (1991) played a somewhat similar role in Pastoralism I as Heredia's does here. Taking a broad theoretical view rather than adopting a particular case study, Gupta had modelled the 'portfolio' of the activities of agro-pastoralists at various stages of the spectrum. In the model were variables such as distance of migration and the nature of access to common property resources, as well as craft production. Gupta was the only participant then to mention the

[4] This was first brought to notice by M.S. Mate; see Dandekar, this volume.

crafts of pastoral people, and Jaya Menon takes up the theme in this volume.

Menon's discussion has perforce to be cross-cultural and across the periods, for she is making a kind of first foray into the different kinds of artisan mobility and the kinds of craft production recorded amongst pastoral groups in general. (Comparative anthropology, it may be said, has come into its own and does not rest on finding a number of similarities between disparate cultures; it shows an awareness of the importance of form as well as meaning; it helps one to isolate causally or functionally related variables. See Holy, ed., 1987.) Pastoralists have developed craft skills in materials that they themselves produce. Mobility is a constraint not only on the range of craft items made, but also on the equipment and complexity of techniques. Also, time is a variable—the longer the sojourn in one place, at least in a few instances, the more ambitious is the work undertaken. However, mobility itself is sometimes a response to weak demand, and hence a symptom of disadvantage and not its cause.

Many other ideas come up in Jaya Menon's discussion, which will be mentioned in another context. For now we may refer to what Ferdinand has said (1993:359-60) about the material culture of the Bedouin camel keepers of Qatar, who regularly use oasis- and town-made products: 'These objects are just as "Bedouin" as the objects they make themselves.' For centuries there has been 'mutual co-operation and dependence between [Bedouin] encampment, village, and city. . . .' This, then, is another dimension of the openness of social and economic categories.

Supriya Varma's 1991 paper broke new ground by addressing itself to the question whether pastoral nomadism was important to the prehistoric economy of Gujarat. The problem was explored by formulating a tentative typology of settlement remains, and by analysing settlement-pattern changes down the centuries to the historic period. In that volume Audouze and Jarrige (1991) had focused an ethno-archaeological exercise in Baluchistan on the distinctive features of a pastoral camp as against a settled village, in terms of architectural remains, grain storage pots, traces of cooking places, and so on. Like Varma, these archaeologists too report that very meagre signs of sojourn are left behind at a pastoral camp site; they found that even animal bones are not left behind because dogs chew them or carry them away.

Here Varma attempts the interpretation of a long period when no archaeological sites are evidenced in Kathiawad. To conclude that the whole area was depopulated would be to read archaeological evidence literally. The possibilities explored comprise—besides major droughts and destructive warfare that lead to region-wide emptying out of villages—a major change in land use that brought about a different settlement pattern, one that did not contribute to mound formation[5] (i.e. visible archaeological remains). Land use variables considered by Varma are flexibility between animal herding and agriculture, recourse to hunting and gathering, and soil exhaustion.[6] Varma rightly avoids an approach that totally separates farming from animal herding. There is an interesting historical content to the paper (admittedly selective) and, at the same time, an awareness that mound stratigraphy can tell us just that much; we cannot always detect short-term abandonments or seasonal mobility, or piecemeal desertion of one region for another, even though environmental archaeology in some parts of the world is now coming up with inferences about shifts from agriculture to pastoralism over periods of three to four hundred years (Butzer 1996:145). Reference may here be made to Hardiman's evidence (1995) on the history of small dams in Khandesh. These fell into disuse after civil wars and raids that forced the peasantry to flee. Then followed the arrival of shifting cultivators in the area, who had no use for dams, canals, or terraces. Also pertinent is Kavoori's description (1991) of the dynamics of pastoral movement and the connectedness of newly-opened agrarian areas with new end points of shepherd migrations. Also, Kavoori pointed out, migration rhythms may change in response to the changing 'world' in such a way that herdsmen do not return annually to their

[5] For instance, the dispersed nature of the Bhil village is well known; neighbours live within hailing distance of each other and there are no clusters of houses, even though the Bhils practise agriculture. Moreover, there is a periodic fissioning of villages (Mann 1981:119; Deliege 1985: 87ff).

[6] I cannot desist from mentioning Madgulkar's novel, *Bangarwadi,* and its evocation of utter desolation when the stoic herdsmen, and then agriculturists, desert a village: 'The houses remained where they were. . . . But the men were gone, both good men and bad. What remained behind was a vacant, dull, silent, empty relic of human habitation' (p. 130). Ultimately the school teacher too is transferred out, and an old man, his daughter-in-law, and two sheep are left behind to their fate.

erstwhile home base. And the larger a flock, the longer the distances it has to move.

If Hardiman shows that Bhil occupation of the small river valleys of Khandesh was not one dating to 'time immemorial', Nandini Sinha in this volume shows that far from being isolated, Bhil society is best understood in a wider context: the history of southern Rajasthan and Gujarat, and especially their medieval kingdoms. Bhils appear in the historical record as hunters and gatherers and as shifting cultivators. But they also functioned as guards and watchmen, and provided indispensable militias for medieval armies. Also, they provided construction and mining labour, at least in Rajasthan.

Sinha, however, also distinguishes the nature of Bhil participation in the affairs of the kingdom of Mewar from that of Dungarpur (which was, like Mewar, ruled by the Guhilas, but which emerged comparatively late)[7] and the kingdom of Gujarat. The Bhils were in positions of greater or lesser subordination in one or the other of these kingdoms. In history of Dungarpur, actually, it is not impossible that they were the dominant group before the coming of Rajput rule. More important, Sinha finds that in Mewar the Bhils were 'in and out of actual territorial control' through the centuries. Also in the paper are valuable snippets of observation about the mutual influence between Bhils and Rajputs in traditions like the remembrance of heroes. As a very broad generalization we can suggest that whereas Varma deals with the advance and retreat of the agrarian frontier, Sinha discusses a kind of political and social counterpart to that process.

The contribution of Archana Prasad is an analysis of the subsistence systems of the forested hills of central India in pre-colonial and colonial times. Subtle shifts continuously took place within these systems between what we would classify as distinct modes: agriculture, hunting-gathering, and husbandry. Like Sinha, Prasad finds that shifting cultivator tribes had many kinds of interaction with the tribal and peasant groups around them. A historical exploration of the period after 1600 gives valuable insights about how Gond and Baiga life and livelihood could be transformed because of the interests of

[7] The Bhils made the *tika* in blood for newly installed rulers of Mewar, but not in Dungarpur. One may add that Srivastava (1997:15) found that in Rajput folklore, a Raika is often the trusted confidant of the Rajput hero.

peasant society at large; there was retreat, dispersal, displacement, taxation, and, in the oral memory of the oppressed, slaughter.

Sinha and Prasad both offer insights into the ways in which elites can emerge amongst tribal groups that are incorporated within states or form their frontiers. Prasad shows that all devastation cannot be attributed to the effects of colonial policies; there were also the depredations of the Maratha armies in the earlier period. Prasad's paper provides an academic link between this volume and earlier studies such as Arnold and Guha (eds., 1995),[8] Bhattacharya (ed., 1998); and Guha (1999); her work is also directly or indirectly a contribution to the latter two books. Prasad's attention to environmental and ecological detail calls to mind the model constructed by Munshi Saldanha (1990) of the ecological logic of *rab* and *dalhi* cultivation in the northern Western Ghats.

Champakalakshmi in this volume presents a description of the changing role of pastoral production and pastoral groups in northern Tamilakam, from the beginnings of the historic period to the rule of the Colas. Sangam poetry reveals pastoral activity—cattle keeping—in forested tracts not far from the areas of cultivation, and also in places that were crossed by west-east routes feeding the trade with Rome. Pastoralism, hunting, and shifting cultivation are attested to in the Sangam corpus as coexisting activities, bringing to mind the situations described for central India and western India for later periods by Prasad and Sinha. Most important, Champakalakshmi unravels the nature of the historical change: community pastures, transhumance and mixed flocks, cowherd settlements that were clan based, and chiefs making claims to high status appear in the early historical period, whereas sources of the period of the Pallavas attest to the processes of increased sedentarization and the extension of agriculture. More important, tribal pastoralist organization gives way to a larger agrarian and stratified order with herdsmen's villages forming the adjuncts to large villages and towns. Herdsmen's villages are no longer identified with individual clans, but are now part of the larger settlement system and have lost their autonomy. Champakalakshmi stresses that pastoralism was not eliminated as a form of

[8] See, for example, Pouchepadass' 1995 paper on shifting cultivation in the southern stretch of the Western Ghats and his reference to the regular exchanges of forest produce by the hill communities with the outside world.

land use—she refers to hero stones in the Pallava period—but it appears that ruling elites depended not on the military strength of mobile herdsmen, but on land grants and revenues from land and the emergent temple estate and its economy. Clear evidence for the absence of social separation in early Tamilakam are the figures of Bhakti 'saints' who began life as cowherds or guards. A major contrast is thus provided to the historical situation analysed by Dandekar in this volume. So too, economic and social developments were at work that never gave rise to a centuries-old hiatus in settlement evidence, as in Kathiawad. The reasons for such contrasts have yet to be worked out, but we can guess that the landscape played a major role.

Reconstructing Identity, Preserving Dignity: The Struggle of the Nomadic Pastoralists

RUDOLF C. HEREDIA

MODERNIZATION and development have everywhere been a threat to the cultural identity and the dignity of tribal peoples, even where in countries such as India there is an official policy of protection and promotion of tribal welfare. Among the oppressed, it is the nomadic tribes in particular who are the most vulnerable when change overtakes them. More than others, they are under threat of being assimilated into the bottom of the social strata, as even now they are being displaced from their traditional lands in the name of an unacceptable 'development' from whose benefits they are alienated.

Obviously, we need to restructure our economic development if it is to reach the people who need it most. But the structural violence that such 'development' inflicts on its victims is only part of the indignity to which they are subjected. For there is also an accompanying cultural hegemony that subverts identity, and in doing so undermines the very cultural resources which such groups would have collectively found in their tribal identity to mobilize against this dominance.

Challenging Inferiorized Identities

For any real mobilization of cultural resources we need a pedagogy that will help counter the cultural violence to which the agencies of socialization subject such people, whether these be the formal education system or the informal encounters of everyday living, whether in the mass media or the marketplace.

It is in these very areas of social life and social encounters that we need to resist the hegemonic 'pedagogy of violence' (Lele 1995) perpetrated by the dominant groups and replace this with a pedagogy of affirmation for struggling subaltern peoples. We need to break the 'pedagogy of silence' (Heredia 1996) which, by a pretended neutrality that cannot but perpetuate the status quo, allows such cultural violence to be internalized by society. It is only creative and relevant action that will shatter the 'culture of silence' (Freire 1972) in which people are imprisoned and isolated, and not misguided attempts to preserve their cultural inheritance, as one would for an endangered species in a protected environment.

Our endeavour, then, is not directed towards the preservation or 'museumification' of tribal culture, for our concern does not stop with cultural survival. Chetan Singh's discussion in this volume of polyandry and its subversion in modern times provides an apt example of a people caught between two worlds. Rather, our project must be one of empowerment, of enabling all people to grow as the subjects of their own history and not as mere objects in an alienating process of national development. As I have argued elsewhere (Heredia 1997), collective identities must be located within the social context and material history of a group, and problematized as a dynamic process in which a social unit produces and reproduces itself. It is precisely because such identities are constructed within a dynamic historical context that they can be challenged and reconstructed once again. To assume otherwise is to adopt an ahistoric and static perspective.

Moreover, we wish to distance ourselves here from the unhelpful controversies between the 'primordialists' and the 'instrumentalists', the 'survivalists' and the 'evolutionists', the 'maximalists' and the 'minimalists'. We shall instead position ourselves with those for whom ethnic identity is 'seen as a *historical phenomenon*, subordinated to existing class and centre-periphery contradictions, and as an element operating in cultural dialectics' (Devalle 1992:16) For there are three essential dimensions to be put together in describing any collective identity:

(1) an objective foundation for identity formation in the material history and existential group relations of that society,
(2) a subjective construction of this in the articulation and motivation of common myths and rituals, symbols and values, and

(3) a contextual recognition by others of this group differentiation, even if only to contest it.

We are by no means naive about the very real odds stacked against such attempts at social reconstruction and cultural empowerment in the contemporary circumstances; it is even possible that this collection of papers could be misread and misused. Yet we believe the goal we have set is both possible and even feasible. We recognize that this can ever be done in one big leap, but we believe that small steps can all add up. Thus, even something as basic as literacy can be a process to help one read the 'word' in order to read the 'world', and to become the subjects rather than the mere objects of history, as Freire (1972) would argue.

The kind of inferiorization to which the marginalized are subjected can only be reversed by collective movements that affirm ethnic identity. But first the groundwork for such a movement must be in place. We hope this workshop will be a contribution in this direction. The aim of this volume is not merely a rediscovery of traditional tribal identity, but also a reconstruction of it in creative and relevant ways.

The contributions to this volume cover considerable ground both in space and time, and across disciplines as well. In trying to set a more comprehensive context in which they can be read, and with ideological coherence, this paper will elaborate a three-fold context within which the project can be situated:

(1) the politics of anthropology, against which texts must be read
(2) the poetics of ethnography, in which they must be understood
(3) the ethics of cultural rights, for which they must be used

The Politics of Anthropology: Local Voices, Global Forces

In colonial times anthropology was very much a part of the colonial enterprise, and while it was often sympathetic towards the peoples it studied, it was still an attempt to know and understand subject peoples in order to administer and control them. Indeed, most colonial anthropology 'dichotomizes and essentializes its portrayal of others and . . . functions in a complex but systematic way as an element of colonial domination' (Clifford 1988:268). Colonial scholarship could not but be an expression of an unequal relationship. It inevitably was paternalistic even when benevolent, but all too often it was exploitative and degrading, even if unintentionally so at times. This was the tradition that the colonies inherited, and they have not put it to bed even after their independence. 'Interpretative anthropology' has still remained awkwardly 'colonial' even in a non-colonial academic context (Rabinow 1990:245).

It cannot be disputed that, besides being 'a process of empire', anthropology also began to emerge as a serious discipline, already in colonial times but more so in the post-colonial era. But no social discipline can be politically neutral, and indeed power relations are rife in anthropology (Manganaro 1990:26). After the end of the colonial period, the earlier 'civilizing mission' offering recipes for what Malinowski called successful cultural change began to give way to a concern with empowering the powerless to state their case. Anthropologists now began to speak for those who could not do so for themselves. This new perspective brought into sharper focus the questioning search that had earlier begun to contest some of the key concepts of Western civilization. But too easily it stood the older anthropology on its head and romanticized subordinate peoples while demonizing elites and officialdom, thus falling again into an essentialist and integrationist view of culture.

What is needed is a study of culture in its historical 'processes of resistance and accommodation . . . not without its own internal contradictions . . . [as] a product of struggle' (Marcus 1990:178). Indeed, 'there is a constant battle over relations of meaning, one which points to a more fundamental conflict over the relations of power' (Giroux 1981:307).

This politics of anthropology underscores the 'contradictory consciousness' that finally does make change possible (Gramsci 1996:333). For if all knowledge must be situated in the society that produces it, then it must change with changing social relationships. It is this dialectic that sets the context for the politics of anthropology. Our endeavour here is not to deviate into a discussion on the sociology of knowledge, but rather to contextualize this collection of texts in our contemporary situation.

Marcus (1990:165, n. 1) refers to two common modes of positioning ethnography in a historical context that prescind from such an endeavour. These are the 'salvage' mode and the 'redemption' mode. Both seem to assume a pure ethnographic subject that has to be either 'saved' before the deluge from the outside world, or 'redeemed' after its impact. While such an assumed subject is both ahistorical and apolitical, the theme of the 'vanishing primitive' is so pervasive in ethnographic writing that it implies a rupture in an unchanging tradition overwhelmed by rapid social change. This adds up to 'a rhetorical construct legitimating a representational practice: "salvage" ethnology in its widest sense. The other is lost in disintegrating time and space, but saved in the text' (Clifford 1990a:112). And 'redemption by textualization' is not our purpose.

Moreover, in a globalizing world with the dominant economic and political systems penetrating the remotest areas of local societies, isolationism can only be a pious wish rather than a social reality. There are no longer any islands of cultural forms in a world where 'human ways of life increasingly influence, dominate, parody, translate, and subvert one another' (Clifford 1990:22). For the inevitable linkages and interdependencies in a rapidly integrating world system only accentuate the tension between 'local voices' and 'global forces'.[1]

We need to give a place to these increasingly lost 'voices' before they are silenced by other forces.[2] Our presentations, then, are not meant to romanticize the tribal past but rather to critique it for the building of a new future. They are not meant to be read from an ahistorical or an apolitical position, but from one that is situated in the relevant contemporary context. Indeed, they are intended to be not a *source* to deconstruct a people's self-understanding and world-view so much as a *resource* to reconstruct their identity and self-respect in the present situation. Hence, this is not meant to be a detached exercise, but one that begins with academic commitment and leads eventually to social and political engagement. For we believe that real knowledge is not possible without true involvement.

While we take responsibility for the textual presentations made at

[1] Archana Prasad's paper in this volume on the Baigas handles this issue sensitively. And Chetan Singh's description of officialdom's biases against the Kinnaur pastoralists, already apparent in the nineteenth century, is also relevant to our argument.

[2] Some of the presentations in this collection do this better than others, particularly the papers by Nandini Sinha and Ajay Dandekar.

this workshop and the political beliefs on which they are premised, we are well aware that these studies will be inclined more to some reconstructions of identity than others, just as some texts allow certain interpretations more easily than others.

The Poetics of Ethnography: Text and Textualization

The contributors to this volume are ethnographers in the sense that they represent other cultures. While we can be clear about the need for a historical and political contextualizing of their texts, any claim to their representativeness is admittedly tentative. For one thing, 'no gathering in' of a cultural heritage can be definitive or final. The culture of a people is not a static system waiting to be recorded by someone claiming to have access to its final truth, but is instead fluid, diverse, and often contested. We can make no pretensions to a complete or comprehensive presentation of tribal culture. For another, we need to be sensitive to the subjective-objective dilemma, not by forcing a resolution of the issue but by allowing more positively for multiple interpretations to emerge and by avoiding both pejorative subjective assessments as well as pretentious objective evaluations.

We do, of course, realize that the political options we have implicitly exercised and the contextual choices we have explicitly made may well not be acceptable to, or affirmed by, all. We are also aware that 'recent anthropological writing has called into question the legitimacy with which we represent the "other" in cultural accounts' (Manganaro 1990:3). But we still hope we can approach each other's texts empathetically, and better yet, beyond such empathy, allow ourselves to be challenged by, and enter into a dialogue with, the texts of others' not only written tracts but also oral texts from traditions that have for too long been kept out of the dialogue. For only recently has the legitimacy and validity of oral history been conceded.

In other words, we seek to be sensitive about not imposing a monologue, but instead encouraging a dialogue in a continuous reconstruction of the cultural heritage of diverse groups, tribal or urban. Here we are but taking a few hesitant initial steps in what must be a continuing process if such a dialogue is to effectively reconstruct cultural identities and preserve human dignity. This, of course, assumes that the postmodernist 'death of the author' will not end in a postmodernist 'death of the reader'!

It has become a truism that reconstructing the history of the 'other' inevitably involves us in the project of reconstructing ourselves. For indeed 'every version of an "other" wherever found is also the construction of a "self", and the making of ethnographic texts . . . has always involved a process of self-fashioning' (Clifford 1990a:23). Furthermore, we cannot efface or eliminate ourselves from the texts. But hopefully the real living people will not be excluded or remain marginal to the reading of these texts, just as we must try to ensure that they are included, and that their concerns are made central, in our descriptions of them. Hence our ethnographic texts are not meant to add up to detached representations of any groups so much as they are intended as a participative discourse with, and among, those whom we study.

A conceptual shift in the compiling of texts is carried over to the reading of them as well. Only then will the starting ethnographic 'collage' have a chance of emerging into an 'organic whole' (Clifford 1988:146) in a continuous discourse within the enlightened limits of a 'communicative rationality' (Habermas 1983:8) Conceptually, such a changed perspective amounts to an almost 'tectonic' shift that destabilizes the terra firma on which we felt so much more secure and settled. There is no mountain-top overview from which to 'map human ways of life, no Archimedean point from which to represent the world' (Clifford 1990a:22). This now calls both the constructor and the reader to look 'at' as well as 'through' the text, as Geertz (1988:138) has argued.

In other words, it is not ethnography as representation, appropriating to itself the legitimacy of representing the other, that is the operative principle of understanding. Rather, what we want is to be empathetic and sensitive to the question of legitimacy, as also committed and concerned. This challenge can be met 'not by doing away with tropes, (which is not possible) but by appropriating and inventing new ones' (Pratt 1990:50). And hence in thus breaking with everyday speech, the text becomes essentially 'poetic'. Simone Weil, the secular mystic, once described poetry as the agonized effort to express the inexpressible. 'A poem is beautiful to the precise degree in which the attention whilst it was being composed has been turned towards the inexpressible.'

If poetry is that which is lost in translation, how does this affect ethnographic texts? It has long been suggested that all ethnography is translation across cultures (Lienhardt 1954), and this is surely more basic and more hazardous than merely a translation across languages. The textualization of experience is implicitly alienation, the more so when it is across cultures and especially when there are inequalities in the power relationships between these; and even more so again when this textualization is non-participatory and monologic. Hence, in the final analysis, the task of the translator is not just to 'carry across' a message and leave the points of departure and arrival unchanged, but to enrich and enhance cultural capacities on both sides of the divide that still persists.

The Ethics of Cultural Rights: Identity and Dignity

After the political and the ethnographic, the third and final contextualizing of our texts is now the ethical one of cultural rights. One can make a legal claim for these, and perhaps even more convincingly a political one. But such claims must be ethically grounded if these rights are to be more than a matter of political pragmatism and/or legal expediency. Here we make no pretense to spell out such a grounding at any length; we only wish to foreground the ethical dimension to the dialogic encounter/exchange that these presentations are intended to precipitate/facilitate.

Foucault (1980) has made us aware of the complex ways in which power permeates social relations and 'produces truth' within a given discourse. But to hold that a 'will to power' must irredeemably subvert the 'will to truth' is to fall into a dangerous irrationalism that can have disastrous political consequences, which Habermas rightly denounces (Habermas 1983). We want to distance ourselves from such ethical relativism here, as we have earlier done from an uninvolved political neutrality, for such non-commitment only reinforces the status quo. Thus, to give a less ambiguous example, we are not proposing to be non-judgmental; we do not accept the violence that a tribal group exercises against its 'witches'.

Individual rights are founded on a person's inviolable dignity, and cultural rights are grounded in a community's distinctive (ethnic) identity. What is experienced as a person-community tension in a society is carried over into the area of individual and community rights (Mendelsohn and Baxi 1995). Indeed, it could be argued by some that anthropology has been more sensitive to the group than the individual. However, our purpose here in focusing on the community or group is not to undervalue the human person. We would premise a complementarity of individual and community in terms of persons-in-community and/or a community of persons. What appears critical is that both human dignity and community identity are affirmed together and not against each other.

Besides individual-group tension, another level of tension in the exercise of cultural rights is between groups. There are no impermeable 'cultural boundaries' in a plural society, no 'neatly bounded and mutually exclusive bodies of thought and customs, perfectly shared by all who subscribe to them, and in which their lives and works are fully encapsulated' (Ingold 1994:330). This gives rise to 'fuzzy communities' (Kaviraj 1992:26), and allows for multiple or layered identities for group members. For communities subjected to rapid social change, this can be an especially problematic area.

Moreover, it is important that an encounter between groups, or between the self and the other, or the ego and the alter ego, be mediated by a third. Hence the need to extend the dyad into a triad. Whether the third party is a more specific agency, such as 'the nation-state, or simply the government' (Gupta 1996:11) or a more general frame of reference such as 'Chomsky's grammar, Levi-Strauss's "structure" or Marx's "mode of production", and Lacan's "Other" ' (ibid. 183), it is this triadic approach that makes for 'contextualizing human agency and culture in a dynamic holistic framework' (ibid. 139).

For us, in the Indian scenario the most significant third entity in the triad is the state. The Constitution of India recognizes 'the principle of equality between groups *qua* groups' (Sheth 1987:8). This is the foundation for collective rights with special consideration for the more vulnerable sections of Indian society, such as linguistic and religious minorities and socially and economically backward classes. And yet today there are powerful movements for homogenization within the same body politic. This then brings in yet another level of tension: between the group and the state. Our insistence is that identity and dignity must both prevail at all these levels to resolve the inevitable tension in a more pluralist and tolerant whole. We need a 'culture of rights' that will 'neither propagate an ideology of enforced homogenization nor seek violent methods of resolving conflicts of interest' (Bhargava 1991:171).

It is in the interstices of these three levels of tension, between the individual and the group, between groups, and between groups and the state, that we seek to reconstruct and affirm the identity and dignity of the individual and the collectivity. It is towards this ethical purpose that we hope this collection of papers will make a significantly useful contribution.

An individual's identity is never formed in a walled-in consciousness. Such solipsism can only be dangerously pathological and asocial. So too group identity is never constructed entirely from within the group but always in an engagement/relationship with others. Thus the importance of dialogue with other groups and communities; it makes group identity a dynamic rather than a static process. Indeed, because group identity is always in process, it can be reinvented and reshaped and reconstructed anew by each generation (Fischer 1990.195).

At the same time, there is always the danger and, depending on the power relationship involved, the probability of a group being engulfed and assimilated into its wider social environment to the point that it loses its distinctiveness. Only when difference becomes a positive value in a society is there a defence against such encompassment, especially for the weaker and more vulnerable peoples, for example, the tribes. Only a sustained commitment to tolerance guarantees equal treatment and dignity for all, very much as it does for individuals/persons. This is the Gandhian insight on which the praxis of *ahimsa* and *satyagraha* were effectively based.

An Optimism for Struggle

As Ricoeur is at pains to remind us, 'a text is more than a linear succession of sentences. It is a cumulative, holistic process' (Ricoeur 1971:548). Only when we grasp the inner dialectic of this process can we comprehend it as a whole. In fact, as Heidegger rightly points out, what we must first comprehend is not just the text or the discourse in which the text is set, but the whole project from which the discourse derives. Indeed, 'what we want to understand is not something hidden behind the text, but something disclosed in front of it' (ibid.:557). Then as the focus of our understanding moves from the hidden to the disclosed, from the background to the foreground, our comprehension of the text will advance 'from what it says to what it talks about' (ibid.:558). And here once again the role that oral traditions can play needs to be underlined.

This, then, is the hermeneutics we must pursue, and it is only in dialogue that we can enter into such a hermeneutic circle, from explanation to understanding and back again, from text to interpretation and back again. Further, it is only an enduring 'optimism of the heart' (Panikkar 1983:243), not just the 'logic from the head', that will sustain us in completing and reiterating such a cycle. We hope that the dialogue initiated here will help contextualize action effective for, and lives committed to, the tribal peoples who we have textualized in this workshop.

For settled people the nomad is the 'quintessence of otherness' (Greenblatt 1991:124). And yet our geographic and social mobility today is creating modern nomads, who might in the pastoralists of old recognize themselves and the other in themselves. I began this essay by challenging inferiorized identities, and end with an optimism for the struggle ahead, a struggle to reconstruct tribal identity and affirm the dignity of tribal peoples, a struggle which is so much the more urgent for vulnerable groups such as nomadic pastoralists. It is a struggle that will demand genuine 'organic intellectuals' to engage with committed and involved activists for an authentic Freirean 'praxis' to emerge. This workshop has attempted a dialogue between scholars committed to fieldwork and activists concerned with theorizing their experiences so as to go beyond an ad hoc or merely pragmatic response. Our hope is that this exchange will be as rewarding for those with whom we share it through this volume as it was for those who participated in the workshop.

REFERENCES

Bhargava, Rajeev, 'The Right to Culture', in K.N. Panikkar, ed., *Communalism in India: History, Politics and Culture,* Delhi: Manohar, 1991, pp. 165-72.

Clifford, James, *The Predicament of Culture: Twentieth Century Ethnography, Literature, and Art,* Cambridge, Mass.: Harvard University Press, 1988.

———, 'On Ethnography Allegory', in James Clifford and George E. Marcus, eds., *Writing Culture: The Poetics and Politics of Ethnography*, Delhi: Oxford University Press, 1990, pp. 98-121.

———, 1990a. 'Introduction: Partial Truths', in Clifford and Marcus, eds., *Writing Culture*, Delhi: Oxford University Press, pp. 1-26.

Devalle, Susana B.C., *Discourses of Ethnicity: Culture and Protest in Jarkhand*, New Delhi: Sage, 1992.

Fischer, Michael M.J., 'Ethnicity and the Post-Modern Arts of Memory', in Clifford and Marcus, eds., *Writing Culture*, Delhi: Oxford University Press, 1988, pp. 194-233.

Foucault, Michel, *Power/Knowledge*, New York: Pantheon, 1980.

Freire, Paulo, *Pedagogy of the Oppressed*, Harmondsworth: Penguin, 1972.

Geertz, Clifford, *Works and Lives: The Anthropologist as Author*, Palo Alto, California: Stanford University Press, 1988.

Giroux, Henry A., 'Ideology, Agency and the Process of Schooling', in L. Barton and S. Walker, eds., *Social Crisis and Educational Research,* London: Croom Helms, 1981, pp. 303-33.

Greenblatt, Stephen, *Marvelous Possessions: The Wonder of the New World,* Chicago: University of Chicago Press, 1991.

Gramsci, A., *Selections from Prison Notebooks*, eds. and trans., Q. Hoare and G. Smith, Hyderabad: Orient Longman, 1996.

Gupta, Dipankar, *The Context of Ethnicity: Sikh Identity in a Comparative Perspective*, Delhi: Oxford University Press, 1996.

Habermas, Jurgen, 'Modernity—An Incomplete Project', in Hal Foster, ed., *The Anti-Aesthetic Essays on Postmodern Culture*, Port Townsend: Bay Press, 1983, pp. 3-15.

Heredia, Rudolf C., 'Ethnicity, Class and Nation: Interrelationships in a Multi-Cultural State', *Economic and Political Weekly*, vol. 33, no. 19, 1997, pp. 1010-16.

———, 'Teaching as a Subversive Activity: Pedagogies for Change', *New Frontiers in Education*, vol. 26, no. 3, 1996, pp. 236-480.

Hartog, Francis, *The Mirror of Herodotus: The Representation of the Other in the Writing of History*, trans. Janet Lloyd, Berkeley: University of California Press, 1988.

Ingold, Tim, ed., *Companion Encyclopedia of Anthropology*, London: Routledge, 1994.

Kaviraj, Sudipto 'The Imaginary Institution of India', in Partha Chatterjee and Gyanendra Pandey, eds., *Subaltern Studies VII,* Delhi: Oxford University Press, 1992.

Lele, Jayant, *Hindutva: The Emergence of the Right,* Madras: Earthworm Books, 1995.

Lienhardt, Godfrey, 'Modes of Thought', in E.E. Evans Pritchard et al., eds., *Institutions of Primitive Society,* Oxford: Basil Blackwell, pp. 95-107.

Manganaro, Marc, 'Textual Play, Power, and Cultural Critique: An Orientation to Modernist Anthropology', in Marc Manganaro, ed., *Modernist Anthropology: from Fieldwork to Text*, Princeton, NJ: Princeton University Press, 1990, pp. 3-35.

Marcus, George E., 'Contemporary Problem of Ethnography in the Modern World System', in Clifford and Marcus, eds., *Writing Culture,* Delhi: Oxford University Press, 1990, pp.163-93.

Mendelsohn, Oliver, and Upendra Baxi, eds., *The Rights of Subordinated Peoples*, Delhi: Oxford University Press, 1995.

Panikkar, R., *Myth, Faith and Hermeneutics,* Bangalore: Asian Trading Corporation, 1983.

Pratt, Mary Louise, 'Fieldwork in Common Places', in Clifford and. Marcus, eds., *Writing Culture,* Delhi: Oxford University Press, 1990, pp. 27-50.

Rabinow Paul, 'Representations Are Social Facts: Modernity and Post-modernity in Anthropology', in Clifford and Marcus, eds., *Writing Culture,* Delhi: Oxford University Press, 1990, pp. 234-61.

Ricoeur, Paul, 'The Model of the Text: Meaningful Action Considered as Text', *Social Research,* vol. 38, 1971, pp. 529-62.

Sheth, D.L., 'On Communalism—The Communal Virus and the Problem of Reservations', *Lokayan Bulletin,* vol. 4, no. 1, 1987, pp. 4-17.

Between Two Worlds: The Trader Pastoralists of Kinnaur

CHETAN SINGH

NOMADIC pastoralism was for long the primary economic activity of societies in many parts of the world. There are, furthermore, numerous instances where it successfully combined with a tribal form of organization that is sometimes considered to be 'the political dimension of pastoral nomadism' (Tapper 1991:54).[1] Pastoralism, nomadism, and tribalism are, however, not always coterminous. We need not belabour the point that sedentary agriculture was (and still is) practised by a large number of tribes. Conversely, it can be argued that all pastoralists are not members of tribes. I will endeavour to show that in Kinnaur pastoralists were an integral part of a caste-structured society and supported a fairly complex non-tribal state structure. Nomadism as a way of life is commonly associated with pastoralism, because of the movement of people in response to the grazing requirements of their animals. Yet there are seasonal movements with flocks, classified as transhumance and semi-nomadism, which differ in nature from full-fledged nomadism.

In this volume, Heredia mentions the particular vulnerability of nomadic tribes to dominant communities during periods of modernization. If tribalism and pastoralism are frequently indistinguishable from each other, it is not because they necessarily enjoy a fundamental interdependence. It is their apparent *difference* from sedentary, non-tribal society that seems to mark them out. It is, at times, believed that the difficulty of establishing political and economic control over mobile groups and tribes prompted sedentary states to deal with them in

[1] Tapper argues that this thinking is deep-rooted in many parts of the Middle East.

similar fashion (Tapper 1991:54).[2] It has been argued about tribes that even if they functioned as political units, they were not closed, self-contained societies but, more likely, were part of a larger cultural world (Gellner 1983:536).[3] The long-term objective of sedentary states often sought the conversion of pastoralists to settled agriculture, but there are several exceptions to this rule. Enforced sedentarization would rarely be the policy in a state where settled agriculture, though crucial and predominant, gave modest yields, and pastoralism contributed substantially to revenue. Western Tibet was clearly one such region of the world, and the medieval Tibetan state was successful in harnessing the resources generated by pastoralists; it exercised control over them without forcing them to take to agriculture (Vitali 1996: 111).[4]

Pastoralism as we know it has been inevitably linked to, and even dependent on, non-pastoral economies and societies. That pastoralism must necessarily take cognizance of a larger non-pastoral world (both socially and economically) in order to define itself is now recognized. Even culturally there is perhaps a larger system within which pastoralism could be seen to be contained (Asad 1977:422).[5] In this

[2] This argument is repeated time and again in a large number of works on tribal societies and enjoys considerable acceptability.

[3] Gellner writes that '. . . tribes may or may not be cultural units, but they certainly are political ones. Their political role may perhaps not exhaust their essence but it is a central part of it. By contrast, their cultural role and differentiation though it exists, is not very marked. The tribe does not fill out the world, but it defines itself in terms borrowed from a wider civilisation. . . .' The Middle East tribes, Gellner argues, 'share the cultural styles and assumptions of the Muslim majority'.

[4] Vitali's work is a history of fifteenth-century western Tibet. In addition to the cultivated area assigned as a grant to the monastery at Tholing, it is noted that, 'since the nomads of the land have to give, from their own resources, salt and the equivalent of [such] field crops to the monks, no one can avoid these duties, which have been assigned . . .'.

[5] Asad observes, 'Contemporary pastoral nomads in Third World countries might not see themselves within a class context . . . but rather as a total society—a "tribe" or "people", a "nation". But there is no reason why the anthropologist should uncritically adopt the same viewpoint as his *analytical framework*. The point, surely, is to identify and analyse the nature of the total system within which nomads exist and reproduce themselves as a distinctive cultural, political and economic entity. It is not merely that nomads "interact" at different social levels with sedentaries, but that the social conditions of their existence are reproduced by the total system. . . .'

context, the significant question, as raised by Talal Asad, is not 'What are the spatial/social boundaries of (nomadic) society?' but 'What are the critical elements and limits of the system of reproduction of an ideologically defined social group?' (Asad 1977:424)

Yet another question that has attracted the attention of scholars is the possibility of identifying characteristics that distinguish 'tribe' from 'state'. Several distinctions can, perhaps, be made in this regard between the ideal conceptions of both 'tribe' and 'state'. Such an exercise might even be useful for examining theoretical possibilities. But in understanding social realities it could create complications of its own. Tapper notes that 'the "pure" tribe is an empirical impossibility' and 'the "pure" state is similarly impossible' (Tapper 1983:66, 67).[6] Any empirical study of the relationship between 'tribe' and 'state' would, therefore, have to deal with societies placed within a wide range of deviations from their theoretically conceived 'pure' state.

This is also true of pastoral nomadism. Pastoral societies around the world have exhibited such diversity that disagreement persists over what it constitutes. A rudimentary definition of it being the 'exploitation of the primary produce (the herb layer) through the intermediary of gregarious migratory herbivorous flocks or herds' can be conveniently arrived at (Lefebure 1977:2).[7] Both the truth and the inadequacy of such a definition is apparent. The cultural connotations that give meaning to, and represent, the essentials of pastoralism, are not reflected in this bare description. The complexities, therefore, of attempting to provide a widely-accepted definition of pastoralism are immense. For the present purpose it suits us to adopt the very general description of pastoralism as a

[6] The difference between 'tribe' and 'state' that Tapper notes might be useful to mention here: 'As bases of identity and political allegiances and behaviour, "tribe" gives primacy to ties of kinship and patrilineal descent, while "state" insists on the loyalty of all persons dwelling within a defined territory, what else their relation to each other. "Tribe" stresses personal, moral and ascriptive factors in status, while "state" is impersonal and recognises contract transaction and achievement. The division of labour in the "tribal" model is "natural"; in the "state" model it is complex. The "tribal" mode is socially homogeneous, egalitarian and segmentary, the state is heterogeneous, egalitarian and hierarchical. "Tribe" is within the individual, "state" external to him.'

[7] Lefebure also argues that 'Nomadic pastoral societies that have settled and become agro-pastoral have preserved their initial productive organisation'.

'cultural economy' which was 'dependent on extensive systems of livestock husbandry' (Rodgers 1991:201).[8] This allows for considerable space within which a large number of diverse societies might possibly be accommodated (Ratnagar 1991:187, 192).[9] Though a wide range of economic activities were often pursued by many such societies, an evaluation of 'the amount of time spent on such activities and the degree of dependence upon livestock' would also be important criteria (Salzman 1967:117).

The adoption of particular occupational practices by pastoral peoples can partly be explained by the nature of their interaction with sedentary society. Equally important has been the role of religious beliefs and customary practices as a means of retaining both an identity and an economic specialization that distinguished the pastoralists from the non-pastoralists. It is ecological factors, however, that seem to have normally been central to the emergence and sustenance of pastoralism and the multiple occupational strategies linked to it. A large number of studies of the phenomenon have, quite convincingly, argued it to be a response to the ecological conditions in which a society is situated (Brown 1987:125).[10] The role of ecology in the emergence of pastoralism is discussed by R. Champakalakshmi and Ajay Dandekar in their respective papers in this volume. That semi-arid conditions contribute towards making pastoralism a viable alternative to agriculture is one of the assumptions that my argument here shares in common with the two articles. I would agree with Kumkum Roy's suggestion during the workshop discussions that one has to keep in mind that subsistence strategies may have shaded into one another without being sharply juxtapositioned.

[8] Rodgers mentions several categories: nomadism, seasonal migrations, diurnal movement, stable pasture and also adds that 'a further set of agricultural activities could be superimposed on these simple categories.'

[9] Ratnagar has pointed out that the word *grama* included not only cultivated fields but also grazing grounds and that cultural values are another significant factor that needs to be seriously considered in studies of pastoralism.

[10] Typical of the ecology-centred approach to the study of Himalayan society is the statement of C.W. Brown that, '. . . the mountain ecology of the Himalaya confronts its inhabitants with special problems and each of its different ecological zones reflects a concomitant local adaptation in the integration of subsistence production and ecological finality'.

The Kinnaur pastoralists can be best understood from this perspective and, perhaps, be more accurately described as agro-pastoralists. In both capacities—tilling the soil and tending flocks—they were closely associated with the emergence and administration of the state.

KINNAUR

The area called Kinnaur (today a district) occupies the upper or north-eastern portion of what was formerly the princely state of Bashahr. It consists of the uppermost stretch of the Sutlej river trough which is bound by immense mountains, with peaks ranging from a height of 16,000 to a little over 21,000 feet above sea level. There are forests of pine, ilex oak, blue pine, fir, and the Himalayan cedar. Because of its location in the midst of the Great Himalayan range, Kinnaur is made up of an enormous mass of rocky spurs thrown out by the main range. These spurs create steep and narrow valleys through which mountain streams flow rapidly to join the Sutlej. So steep is the gradient that the Sutlej during a passage of 73 miles through the Bashahr territory, descends from 7,600 feet to 2,800 feet. Like the valleys of most of its tributaries, the Sutlej trough too is narrow and has hardly any open spaces suitable for agriculture flanking the river. Some open space is, however, available along the banks of the Baspa river, though most of the cultivable land and villages in Kinnaur are located much higher up along the slopes flanking the rivers. The state of Bashahr, according to tradition, was seen as consisting of broadly two territories: Kochi and Kinnaur. Kochi was the better cultivated and more open area lying southward in the Lesser Himalaya, while Kinnaur was, as we have seen, the extremely mountainous and sparsely cultivated territory in the Greater Himalaya and which was bordered at its north-eastern extremity by the Zaskar range.

In the whole of Kinnaur, the area suitable for agriculture is very limited. All cultivated land has been laboriously developed into terraces over a long period of time and is, therefore, permanently settled (Hamilton 1932:22).[11] Lt. W. Murray, Superintendent of the Simla Hill States in the 1820s, wrote in a communication to his

[11] Hamilton suggests that shifting cultivation, involving the cutting and burning of forests, was once a common practice. He argues that 'the large extent of abandoned cultivation, now naturally re-afforested' was caused by shifting cultivation. There is, however, little evidence to support the argument.

superior that Kinnaur '. . . does not exhibit a single level spot equal to the dimensions of a field of two acres, square measurement', and that 'The inhabited regions are confined to the dells and gorges which intersect them and drain off the streams, the cultivated parts forming so small a proportion as to appear as patches or steps of stairs up the slopes of the mountains' (*Records of the Delhi Agency* 1824: 32, 288).[12] As early as 1818, Gerard, a British official who toured the area, had noted that the grain produced in the villages of Kinnaur was 'insufficient for consumption' (Gerard 1993:294). Even today, the scope for the extension of agriculture remains almost as limited as before, though the encouragement of horticulture through the introduction of apple orchards has enabled the utilization of new and larger areas. Despite the emergence of many new economic options, however, pastoralism—the traditional supplementary activity of agriculture—has not yet been completely abandoned. Under the circumstances, it is extremely unlikely that there ever existed the possibility of a full-fledged agricultural economy emerging in the area either in pre-colonial or colonial times.

Neither could pastoralism, it must also be pointed out, have ever been a viable alternative by itself. Large-scale sheep rearing was impossible if the flocks were to remain within the territorial confines of Kinnaur throughout the year and depend entirely on the internal resources of the province. It was the adjoining lower areas to the south and south-west of Kinnaur that provided the necessary grain and summer pastures. Without access to these additional and external resources, life in the area would probably have been impossible (Molnar 1981:33).[13] The environmental factors and the combination

[12] This is noted in a letter from Lt. W. Murray to C.E. Elliot, dated July 1824. Later in 1932, Hamilton observed that 'Culturable ground is so limited and the forces of nature are so hostile that the country is not self-supporting.'

[13] See also Black-Michaud's study of Luristan in Iran (1986). The situation that the Selselah and Bairanwand pastoralists are placed in is because of the conjunction of certain circumstances. 'First, unlike any other Luri group, neither Selselah nor Bairanwand control territories in which they can keep sheep on a year round basis. Yet, secondly neither of them possess sufficient arable land anywhere to make sedentarization feasible for the entire population. Last, the upland territories of both peoples border in the south upon country in which sparse density of settlement affords long-range nomads the opportunity of reasonably good grazing at low and intermediate altitudes in precisely those seasons they require it.' See also Augusta Molnar (1981) for the Magar herders in Nepal.

of various occupations so essential for survival in Kinnaur were thus described by Murray in 1824:

> surrounded by rocks of difficult access, inimical to industry, offering little inducement to cultivation in a climate of protracted rigors, the inhabitants of Kunawar have followed the course which nature dictates, and we find them active, enterprising and industrious, occupied in extensive commercial intercourse and trade; rearing vast flocks which form their chief dependence and trafficking into remote countries under great hardship and privation to gain a comfortable subsistence for their families at home. (*Records of the Delhi Agency* 1824:278–9, 282)

An examination of the Forest Department report reveals that little seems to have changed more than a century later (Hamilton 1932: 32).[14] Whatever the mix of economic strategies adopted by the Kinnauras, it is evident that animal husbandry was central to agriculture and trade in the rugged and inhospitable area in which they lived. The pivotal position that the Kinnauras assigned to sheep and goat rearing in their lives is reflected by a detailed though unsympathetic report completed in 1959:

> The local people have come to believe that their economy is based on the rearing of sheep and goats. The tract is extremely cold. They need warm garments which are made of the wool from the sheep. The flesh of these animals is an integral part of food for them. The cultivated holdings are steep and so situated that carriage of farm-yard manure is inconvenient and uneconomical and their manuring is only possible by penning sheep and goats there. The terrain is so difficult that transport of foodstuffs and other necessities of life is not possible by other means of transport and that trade with Tibet is only possible with the sheep and goats. They, therefore, want that no limitations on their number and no restriction, whatsoever, of their grazing in the forests should be imposed. (Parmar 1959:58)

[14] Hamilton wrote '. . . the people make up for the shortage of food by importing grain from the low hills and plains and a large proportion of the community is engaged in this as well as in other trade with Thibet; for which purpose sheep and goats are the chief means of transport. Sheep are also kept for the production of wool both for trading purposes and for the local manufacture of clothing. There can, therefore, be no question of the great importance of sheep and goats for the very existence of the Kanawaris. . . .'

While reporting these arguments put forward by the Kinnauras, the official who conducted this study was far from persuaded by their point of view. From the very beginning, he was of the opinion that migratory flocks were 'an evil', a 'nuisance as they are allowed to enjoy unfettered freedom to graze' and that 'their number has got to be brought down with a heavy hand' (Parmar 1959:14). In conformity with the view that seems to have prevailed in bureaucratic thinking at that point of time, he felt that the Kinnauras by resorting to sheep farming had chosen an easier, unsustainable path which entailed the over-exploitation of forest resources. For purposes of 'development' this was considered a less desirable option than the terracing of more fields for cultivation and the adoption of modern agricultural techniques. The Kinnauras, it was felt, needed 'proper guidance' and in order to reduce their flocks which 'they are not going to do voluntarily . . . it is again necessary to achieve this by taxation' (Parmar 1959:59).

However, migratory shepherding in Kinnaur was not an isolated economic activity that could undergo changes or be deliberately modified without affecting other aspects of life in the area. Different sections of Kinnaura society, while engaging in specific, traditionally assigned occupations, were also participants—direct or indirect—in a network of production strategies. This makes it impossible to classify them into rigid categories. In fact, if we were to consider the most important economic activity of each section of the Kinnauras as the sole determinant, a large number of them would fail to qualify as pastoralists. On the other hand, because of the considerable income obtained from migratory flocks tended by some members of the family, many Kinnauras would not be considered as full-fledged agriculturists. An important portion of the population apart from being agro-pastoralists might even emerge as active traders! The complexity of the relationship between agriculture, pastoralism, and trade and their interdependence on each other makes it difficult to quantify their respective contributions to the total economy of Kinnaur.

The task of enumerating migratory flocks was inevitably difficult and prevented officials from arriving at accurate figures for the number of sheep/goats. The general impression until relatively recent times, however, has been that flocks in Kinnaur have been increasing rapidly (Chatur Bhuj 1928:20; Parmar 1959:57).[15] Flock owners and shepherds were also accused by officials of falsifying numbers in order to avoid taxes (Parmar 1959:57; Fraser 1982:212).[16] Even the deliberate reduction of the numbers of livestock by flock owners would make it clear that pastoralism constituted an essential part of Kinnaura life. Such as large parts of the economy revolved around sheep rearing that it was also the measure of a family's wealth and its capacity to pay taxes. Some rudimentary form of enumerating flocks must certainly have been followed in earlier periods by the pre-colonial state. This was essential for estimating the 'grazing tax' and other levies on wool and wool products which were an important source of state income (Singh 1998:28).[17]

In all Himalayan areas bordering the Tibetan plateau, castrated male sheep and goats have been used as pack animals for transporting essential goods and trade commodities (Furer-Haimendorf 1988:179;

[15] The *Tahsil Chini Settlement Report* of 1928 has given figures for the 1891 settlement also, and says that in the case of sheep and goats increase has been eightfold. It seems likely, however, that the figures for 1891 are wrong. The numbers for the earlier years are also mentioned by Parmar. The fluctuation in the recorded figures further confirms the difficulty of a census of migratory animals. The figures noted below are of Chini *tahsil* that coincided with the area of Kinnaur.

Year	Sheep and Goats	Year	Sheep and Goats
1884–9	38,305	1916	99,282
1904	1,02,968	1926	1,05,634
1910	76,707	1950–1	89,983
1913	55,556		

[16] In Pangi (Chini *tahsil*), a village of a hundred families, the sheep/goats were said to number ten thousand, though the revenue estimate was much lower. In the context of the area adjoining the south of Kinnaur, Fraser observed in 1815 that, 'The villagers always showed an unwillingness to disclose the amount and the sources of their property; and it may be presumed that their sheep, as one of those, were concealed from the view of strangers; a conduct that might arise from a fear of betraying grounds for tax or tribute to be imposed on them. . . .' Fraser's assessment may not have been entirely correct, because he visited the area at a time when the flocks were away in the summer pastures.

[17] In all the states of Himachal, and even in the British-administered districts, taxes on pastures and pastoral products were an important part of state revenue.

Fisher 1987: passim; Fraser 1982:263-4).[18] Similarly, the treacherous mountain paths of many parts of Kinnaur could only be negotiated by these sure-footed smaller animals. This is where trade and pastoralism overlapped, despite there being spheres in each of these occupations which were distinct and required some element of specialization. Goats and sheep can carry only small loads. In difficult terrain these loads became even smaller. Though many traders bought additional pack animals for transporting their goods, it was probably important for a successful Kinnaura entrepreneur to have a large flock of his own. But to maintain a large flock in arid, resource-starved Kinnaur a person required something more than merely a casual interest in shepherding. Only through skilful husbandry would the flocks increase sufficiently to yield an adequate number of pack animals. These pack animals, because they were a saleable asset, also represented what can be considered a purely pastoral form of income. Inevitably, the rearing of sheep and goats was thus the full-time occupation of a large section of the Kinnaur population.

It appears that despite this extensive involvement with the rearing of sheep and goats in Kinnaur, the requisite number of suitable pack animals was not always readily available. There was consequently a great demand for sheep of the adjacent Changthang area in Tibet, which were particularly appreciated both for their wool and their ability to carry large loads (Moorcroft and Trebeck 1970:207, 316). Few details regarding the number of sheep and goats imported into Kinnaur are available, but it could by no means have been negligible (Moorcroft and Trebeck 1970:316; Mitchell 1915:21; Furer-Haimendorf 1988:193).[19]

[18] These are among the more important of the numerous studies on this question that have been made, particularly in Nepal. Castrated male sheep and goats are normally used as pack animals. In the Kinnaur villages near Tibet, yaks were also bred and were especially useful for carrying the heavy loads of traders travelling to markets in the Tibetan plateau. Regarding the yak Fraser observed that in Kinnaur, 'They breed this animal in numbers, and account it their best riches next to corn.' It needs to be pointed out, however, that there were many trails too narrow even for the yak to traverse.

[19] Trebeck who travelled to Spiti (which adjoins Kinnaur) observed about that place that, 'The sheep are almost all imported from Chan-than, as well as the goats, the kids of which degenerate, both in size and quantity of wool.' The people of Spiti, it appears, depended on animals imported from Tibet. On the

The remarkable manner in which the transportation of goods and even survival in the cold desert depended upon sheep is described by Gerard. During the course of his journeys through the desolate countryside, Gerard often ran short of food. On those occasions when he successfully procured adequate amounts of grain, he would (as was natural in such a sparsely populated area) fail to muster the required number of porters to carry it. At one such time he expressed his concern to a resourceful Kinnaura who, he tells us:

> soon afterwards, returned with a large flock of sheep and said, 'I'll make you a real Tartar: you have grain for ten or twelve days, and now you have no use for porters; load the sheep with the grain, finish it first, and then kill and eat the sheep: this is the way we travel on the inhabitable tracts; we never think of grain as long as we have plenty of sheep. (Gerard 1993:149fn)

The flock for the Kinnaura was not simply the means of making a living; it was in times of desperation, the only means to preserve life itself.

Society and the Family

It is a reflection of the hegemonizing influence of Brahmanism that the rulers of Bashahr chose to trace their ancestry to one of the principal characters in Brahmanical mythology. Their right to rule was claimed from an ancestor who forcibly dislodged a powerful *asura* who had previously ruled the territory (*SHSG* 1910:5).[20] On

---

other hand, the administrative report of Bashahr State records that only about 1,000 sheep/goats were imported in 1914-15. This number might possibly be an underestimation, especially when compared with Haimendorf's assessment of the number of animals brought into Nepal from Tibet. He mentions that only through one of the routes (Thak Khola) between Nepal and Tibet were as many as 20,000 sheep and goats imported into Nepal. This number is exceptionally large and probably includes the pack animals of the Nepalese traders as well as flocks that had pastured in Tibet. In the absence of proper figures we can only conjecture that the number of sheep/goats entering Kinnaur from Tibet too must have been fairly large.

[20] The state gazetteer notes several local traditions. 'According to one story the ruling family is descended from the celebrated Sri Krishan of Hindu mythology through his grandson Parduman, who came to Sarahan in order to marry the daughter of Raja Basava Deo (or Banasar). We are not told whether the marriage

the other hand, it is equally indicative of the social proximity of Bashahr to non-Brahmanical Tibet that, according to local Buddhist belief, in Kinnaur 'each Raja of Bashahr is at his death reincarnated as the Guru Lama or Guru of the Lamas, who is understood to be the Dalai Lama of Tibet' (Rose 1970:I:98; *SHSG* 1910:5).[21] As was the case in the rest of Himachal during medieval times, the state of Bashahr probably originated with the rise to monarchical power of a chieftain after he had suppressed several other thakurs (feudal chiefs) of the area (Singh 1998:23, 25).[22] Kamru, a village in the Baspa valley of Kinnaur, was the original centre of the chiefship that seems to have expanded into the fairly extensive Bashahr state. However, the new state capital, Sarahan (*SHSG* 1910:6), with its temple of goddess Bhima Kali (the state deity), was situated in territory that lay outside and south of Kinnaur.[23] It was, perhaps, a recognition of the northern origins of the state that the Kinnauras continued to exercise considerable influence in the affairs of the Bhima Kali temple (Chatur Bhuj 1928:12).

Conforming to the general pattern of community or 'caste' distribution that prevailed in most princely states of Himachal, even in Kinnaur the Kanet agro-pastoralists constituted the largest and most powerful section of society. Below them were the artisan groups such as the Domangs (smiths), the Ores (carpenters), and the Chamangs (weavers) who made up the lower castes. The general term 'Koli' was also applied to these lower-caste groups whose members frequently worked as labourers in the fields of the richer Kanet landowners. Unlike more complex Brahmanized societies, in Kinnaur there were

---

took place, but Parduman is said to have killed his prospective father-in-law and usurped his power. His capital was at Kamru in Tukpa *pargana* of Kanawar.' Another myth, although less popular, traces the origins of the ruling family to two Brahman brothers from the south (*dakkan*). In both stories the Brahmanical (non-indigenous) roots of the rulers and the non-Brahmanical nature of the territory and the aboriginal population seems to be emphasized.

[21] The gazetteer also mentions that the raja was regarded as semi-divine and was worshipped by many of his subjects.

[22] Though specific information regarding Bashahr is lacking, the history of Chamba, Kulu, and Mandi provides examples of such a process of state formation.

[23] Much later, during the reign of Raja Ram Singh, a winter capital was established at Rampur, lower down on the left bank of the Satlej.

no intermediary castes. Not only was intermarriage between upper and lower castes socially prohibited, but considerations of untouchability also restricted common dining and the entry of the lower castes into the house of the Kanets (Rose 1970: II:446; Sanan and Swadi 1998:54).[24] Even between different clans of Kanets, however, there existed a differentiation based on a perceived hierarchical status. In a broad sense, as one progressed from the lower hills to the higher, more isolated mountains the position of the Kanet clans *within* the overall Kanet hierarchy declined. The notion of superior and inferior Kanets, nevertheless, did not seriously affect the status of a clan in the area in which it was located. This was because Kanet clans usually occupied distinct territories or different villages and were rarely ever hierarchically placed in the same area. As a result, not only did the Kanets of Kinnaur have a social grading of their own but the Kinnaura Kanet clans were also not to be found in other parts of Bashahr state. As might be expected, even within Kinnaur these clans dominated different *parganas* or different villages within *parganas* (Rose 1970:II:446-7). These territory-based divisions, nevertheless, did not rule out the consciousness of differential caste status or the possibility of upward mobility in a larger and shared caste-oriented social structure.

Towards the end of the nineteenth century it was observed that the Kanets of Kinnaur 'are called Jads or Zads and form a distinct sub-caste with which the Kanets of the lower ranges do not, as a rule, intermarry or eat, though they will smoke and drink with them' (Rose 1970:II:458). This statement may not, however, be entirely correct, because the term Jad was more appropriately applied to the Kanet population residing in the areas bordering Western Tibet (*SHSG* 1910:22).[25] The 'true' Kanets of the rest of Kinnaur considered themselves superior to the Jads. Though they were not subordinate to any substantial superior caste, the Kanets, it appears, were still not beyond the influence of a 'Sanskritizing' Brahmanism. While making a community-wise enumeration of the landowners in

[24] Rose mentions the system as it existed in the late nineteenth century.

[25] 'In Kanawar the *pargana* of Sialkar, seven villages in *pargana* Tukpa, and two or three villages in *pargana* Shua are inhabited by people of apparently pure Tibetan stock. These are called Nyams, or Jads or Zars, and are also alluded to as Kanets.'

Kinnaur for the 1928 settlement, Chatur Bhuj, the settlement officer, clarified that proprietors who had been classified as Kanets during the previous settlement were now—with the permission of the raja—entered under the caste name of 'Rajput'. In conformity with the hierarchy between clans, the Kanets of the border *parganas* of Sialkar and Pooh, however, continued to be mentioned under the head of 'Kanet' (Chatur Bhuj 1928:23).[26] Despite its considerable geographical isolation, Kinnaura society could escape neither the impact of an ever-expanding Brahmanical society nor the politics of upward caste mobility.

In terms of political and administrative power the three hereditary *wazirs* of the state—who were all Kanets—stood next only to the raja. A fourth, *sarhadi wazir*, was non-hereditary and was appointed from amongst the influential families of the border *parganas* adjoining Tibet (Chatur Bhuj 1928:23). This in effect meant that the Kanets in general, and the Kinnauras, in particular, occupied not only most of the administrative positions in the state but they also exerted considerable influence in the raja's court (Chatur Bhuj 1928:23).[27] Nandini Sinha has argued in her paper on the Bhils that interaction with, and participation in, the formal institutions of the state resulted in the emergence of a tribal elite. This appears to have occurred in Kinnaur too, particularly amongst the Kanets. With the establishment of British domination and their increasing intervention in the administrative affairs of Bashahr, it appears that the hereditary *wazirs* and other court functionaries were pushed into insignificance.

In the villages, however, Kanet social control was far more tenacious. Fluctuating political fortunes at the higher level seem to have had little effect on the control exercised by the hereditary village functionaries. Almost every large village in Kinnaur had its own local

[26] This change in the caste name from 'Kanet' to 'Rajput' was possibly prompted by the objective of making the caste status of the Kanets commensurate with their political influence. Prior to this, the term 'Rajput' was not applied to any social group of the area. There was no Brahman landowner in Kinnaur and of the others assessed for revenue in 1928 the numbers recorded are: Rajput (formerly Kanet) 4,608; Kanet (Jad) 728; Lohar 168; Koli 1,084; Baddi 157. The total population of *tahsil* Chini according to the 1921 census was 20,455.

[27] Chatur Bhuj notes that '. . . at the present moment most of the Raja's personal *entourage*, and the majority of the subordinate State officials are Kanawaris'.

deity and it was by virtue of being its representatives that these Kanet functionaries asserted themselves (Rose 1970:III:447).[28] Because of the absence of Brahmans in Kinnaur even the hereditary temple priests (*pujaris*) were Kanets (Rose 1970:II:470).[29]

This, then, was the broad socio-political system within which agro-pastoralism was practised in Kinnaur. We have seen that agro-pastoralism cannot be viewed as a straightforward economic response to a physical environment. As a strategy of survival that balances different economic activities it has been adopted by many societies. The relative share of agriculture and pastoralism in the total economy has always varied in each such society. Within these societies, furthermore, the dependence of separate social groups and families on these activities differed. There was also an array of corresponding cultural values and perspectives that contributed to, and sustained, the agro-pastoralist's world. In Iran, for example, the Luri tribesmen regarded the 'patrilineal extended family' as being endowed with 'almost infinite potential for economic expansion'. They believed that ideally around such a family an invincible 'agro-pastoral combine' could be most successfully organized (Black-Michaud 1986:57).[30] To be at the head of such a combine was the mark of a successful individual.

In most of Tibet, both agriculture and pastoralism contributed equally to the economy of its constituent sub-regions. Tibetan state

[28] Among the officials at the village level are mentioned the (1) *Chares*: the hereditary headman of each village; (2) *Grokch*: the hereditary *kardar* of the village deity, who speaks on his behalf; (3) *Mathas*: the hereditary *kardar* of the deity. His duty is to petition the deity on behalf of the public; (4) *Pujyares*: whose hereditary duty is to worship the deity.

[29] Even in other temples outside Kinnaur where the Kanets were dominant, we learn that 'The *pujaris* ordinarily belong to the first class of Kanets.'

[30] Black-Michaud argues, 'For an individual to achieve this ideal position three main conditions must be satisfied. The head of such a family must have several able-bodied sons or unmarried brothers to assist him, over 100 ewes and enough land to provide considerable grain surpluses, the cash profits from which may be reinvested in the purchase of male lambs and Kermanshah ewes. For it is reckoned that once a man controls sufficient land and unsalaried agnatic labour, beside enough ewes to keep a nomadic household and its sedentary dependants liberally supplied with milk products, his potential for pastoral expansion is limited only by his skill at combining the management of these various resources.'

and society, as a whole, too, seems to have been organized along lines that complemented such a combination. Muhammad Haidar Dughlat, who led a military expedition into western Tibet in the early sixteenth century, observed that 'the inhabitants of Tibet are divided into two sections. One is called the Yulpa—that is to say "dwellers in villages" and the other the Champa, meaning "dwellers in the desert" (Dughlat 1972:407). These were not two separate social formations of which Haidar Dughlat spoke of, and this is shown by his clarification that the pastoralists were 'always subject to one of the provinces of Tibet' (Dughlat 1972:407). Judging from his description, it seems that while the sedentary agriculturists dominated, the population of the nomads also was considerable, and a single flock of load-carrying sheep that was engaged in 'trade in Hindustan and in the mountains of Hindustan, could number ten thousand' (Dughlat 1972:408, 409-10).[31] Tibetan society, it appears, made the best use of the desolate landscape of the country by encouraging entire tribes to continue with pastoralism while simultaneously enabling the population of certain areas to engage in settled agriculture. While the overall economy was the result of a combination of agriculture and pastoralism, there may not perhaps have been any significant social section in Tibet that could be regarded as 'agro-pastoralist' by occupation.

The agro-pastoralism practised by the Kinnauras was, however, more akin to that followed by groups in western Persia and northern Africa. The unit of production was the family, which appears to have been particularly suited for this purpose. While inter-caste relations in Kinnaur exhibited in some small way the ideological impact of 'Sanskritization', family organization seems to have been influenced by economic compulsions rather than considerations of Brahmanical social propriety. Irrespective of the caste to which they belonged, most of the relatively prosperous, flock-owning families were usually divided into two: the *kim mee* and the *arung mee*. The *kim mee* members of a family resided permanently at their village home and tended the family's cultivated holding. On the other hand, the *arung*

[31] Muhammad Dughlat refers to the 'Dolpa' as a tribe of the Khampa. He might here mean the Dokpa. What is important for our purposes is that this tribe is believed to have numbered more than 50,000 families and was considered to be one among many more such tribes.

mee was the migratory, pastoral branch of the Kinnaura family and usually consisted of men and teenage boys who travelled virtually the year round with the flocks. The latter visited their homes only for short periods in the year as they migrated with the flocks from the winter to the summer pastures and vice versa.

When the adult sons of a family were considered mature enough to manage its affairs, one amongst them was chosen as the householder to look after the house and cultivated land. After retaining a small portion of the house for themselves, the parents retreated into a kind of semi-retirement. The new householder (*talang sa*) and his wife (*talang see*) now became the new heads of a joint family, while the other brothers (*zed sa*) were assigned the itinerant task of tending the family flocks. Appropriate maintenance of social relations and the fulfilment of family obligations *vis-á-vis* the village community were the specific responsibilities of the *talang sa*. Family status depended on how the *talang sa* was placed in the hierarchy of his own village. In this regard, much depended on the support he received from the *zed sa* and how successfully they managed the flocks and trading activities in order to obtain additional income for the family.[32] Despite the precise division of economic functions between individual members, the pastoral and agricultural possessions of the family were regarded as a joint holding and constituted a single economic unit. Because of the prevalent system of polyandry, the *talang see* was considered the wife of all the brothers (Rose 1970:III:448).[33] This is often seen by scholars as a method of population control in an area of extremely limited resources (Chandra 1981:210). True, polyandry led to a larger number of girls remaining unmarried and becoming *zomos* or Buddhist nuns. (The principal nunneries were at the villages of Kanam and Sonam [Rose 1970: III:453].) Further study, however, is needed to make this explanation more acceptable. According to the *Bashahr State Gazetteer*, 'Polyandry was in former times directly encouraged by the State through penalties exacted on partitions. When a set of brothers divided moveable

[32] For much of the information on family organization I am indebted to Vidya Sagar Negi—himself a Kinnaura—who allowed me to read the manuscript of the book on the Kinnaura pastoralists which he is jointly writing with R.S. Pirta.

[33] Rose notes that the 'marriage customs in Kinnaur resemble those of the Tibetans' with the '*lamas* solemnising the wedding. . . .'

property, one-half share of the whole was appropriated by the State, and divisions of immovable property were refused official recognition' (*SHSG* 1910:16). By the second decade of the nineteenth century, an increasing number of joint families based on polyandry were breaking up to build new houses and form separate units. The administrative report of 1911-15 sees this 'splitting up' as 'a sign of increased prosperity owing to the gradual opening up of the country and the influx of money spent on the roads, buildings and [forest] exploitation works' (Mitchell 1915:28). The amount of cash payments made by timber contractors to Bashahr State revenues and labourers during the late eighteenth and early nineteenth centuries was certainly much greater than ever before. Given the altered notions of propriety and progress that accompanied colonialism, the break-up of the joint family and the construction of separate houses might well have been considered a mark of 'increased prosperity'.

Pastoral Practices

Equally interesting is the fact that even the animals owned by the family were now divided into those kept permanently at the village (*kim zed*) and those that were seasonally shifted (*arung zed*) over long distances in order to exploit pastures situated at different elevations. Among the larger *kim zed* were cows and oxen necessary for cultivating the agricultural holding of the family. Usually a small number of sheep, rather than goats, were the other animals included amongst the *kim zed*. The number of the *kim zed* was maintained at a bare minimum because these animals had to be stall-fed through the long and harsh winter. During this period the surrounding countryside was under snow, or at any rate devoid of herbage suitable for them and the *kim zed* survived only on hay that had been cut and stored before the onset of winter. The *arung zed*, on the other hand, consisted of the greater part of the animals owned by the family and included both sheep and goats but never cows and oxen.

In order to meet the requirements of winter fodder for the animals kept permanently at the village, specified patches of land (*banjar ghasni*) in and around the village were set aside. It might be of interest to mention that in some areas even this land was irrigated (Chatur Bhuj 1928:23). Moreover, in some parts of Kinnaur grazing grounds called *panwis* were set aside for pasture. By established tradition, *panwis* were neither to be brought under cultivation nor allowed to become reforested (Hamilton 1932:11).[34] (Such pastures, it must be emphasized, were different from the vast stretches of grazing that sprout in the higher reaches above the treeline soon after the snow has melted. Few villages were located in the latter zone.) Grass in the *ghasnis* (hill slopes where animals were not permitted to graze) was allowed to dry naturally in autumn. It was then cut, further dried in the sun, and thereafter stored in the house for stall-feeding the animals during winter. *Panwis*, on the other hand, were opened in spring to all the animals of the village once the snow had melted. Despite this systematic procurement of adequate fodder for the *kim zed*, there was a limit to the amount of fodder that could be stored and hence always a shortage during winter. It was observed that the animals that stayed back in winter 'have to exist on a *seer* or half a *seer* (*pakka*) of food a day and are nearly dead by the end of winter. When the snow begins to clear away they are taken out to graze on these hills and in a week or two are in better condition than if they had been stall-fed on grain all winter' (*SHSG* 1910:53). It is hardly surprising, therefore, that because of this extreme shortage of fodder almost all the sheep and goats were taken to the lower hills during winter.

The migratory cycle of the Kinnaur flocks has been described as follows:

For grazing purposes the flocks belonging to the local people are sent to the Alpine pastures in Chini *tahsil* in the main Sutlej Valley, in Baspa Valley and Bhaba Valley during summer i.e. from about the middle of May to the end of October. The flocks start coming down in the end of October on their way to the lower hills in Mandi, Bilaspur, Kulu, Suket, Sirmur, Simla and Solan, when they graze from about the middle of December to the end of April. During April and May again the flocks remain in transit on their way to the Alpine pastures. All the flocks do not move to lower hills during winter. About a quarter of them remain in Upper Bashahr. Those that remain are pastured in the Valleys, low down on sunny slopes where the snow does not often come, or when it does, thaws quickly. In May these flocks are on their way up to the Alpine pastures; they linger, however, to graze the tender grass of the open slopes and then pass quickly through the forests to the higher

[34] According to Hamilton, '*Panwis* are burnt annually in the winter under the supervision of the local forest guard. . . . The burning of the coarse dry grass on the slopes below the forest belt, in addition to stimulating the growth of the new grass, serves as a useful means of fire protection.'

grounds where they remain till October. In parts of the valley they are brought down in September in certain places in the forests to be sheared, and are taken back again. Sheep are shorn twice a year, in spring and autumn. When the time for leaving the high ground is near, the goats being more delicate than the sheep, return first. Their stay in the forest is short, and is confined to open glades where the scant sweet herbage is supplemented by oak loppings and besides these places the only parts of the forests that are regularly grazed by both sheep and goats are those near villages, *dogris*, fields and along paths. (Parmar 1959:211)

Shepherds from different parts of Kinnaur took their flocks to specific pastures over which they had over the years probably acquired a strong customary claim. Each flock followed a migratory route that was established as a matter of tradition and which gave it access to different grazing grounds (Parmar 1959:54).[35] As they travelled to their winter pastures in lower areas, and even after reaching them, the Kinnauras engaged their flocks in transporting goods to, and out of, villages that were not easily accessible (Parmar 1959:51).

During the summer months, snows melt and extensive pastures spring to life above the treeline. Forest (mostly deodar) and meadow become available to pastoralists. Apart from ensuring the return of the Kinnaura flocks, this also encouraged shepherds of the lower hills to migrate northwards with their sheep and goats. Despite the sudden influx of animals that this entailed, it appears there was sufficient pasture available in Kinnaur, even though there arose occasional disputes for the best of them (Mitchell 1915:5; Chatur Bhuj 1928:2; Hamilton 1932:9; Parmar 1959:60). Shepherds raised temporary shelters (*dogris*) in the higher pastures where, Gerard observed, they resided with their flocks for four or five months in the year' (Gerard 1993:220).

It was this entwining of pastoralism, transportation, and trade that prompted and enabled the Khampa traders from Spiti and Tibet to

[35] Specific routes are followed even today by migrating flocks from different parts of Kinnaur. Peculiarly, Parmar in his study of 1959 says that there were no fixed routes. He does, nevertheless, mention several routes which were used by the shepherds. It is difficult to believe his statement that, 'Herds and flocks follow any route they like . . .', because the process of seasonal migration often involved the prior establishment of a working relationship with villages en route and the right to use pastures along the road that was followed.

bring their ponies and flocks to lower Bashahr in winter (Parmar 1959:51). Similarly, some of the Kinnaura shepherds moved with their flocks into Tibet in summer. It was not always easy to distinguish between traders and pastoralists in Kinnaur. Given the nature of the terrain, almost every trader was probably a pastoralist first and not simply—as one might be tempted to believe—an owner of pack animals. Either he, or the shepherds he employed, spent a considerable amount of time tending their sheep on a varied range of pastures. These sheep, whose milk was not a very important part of the diet, themselves were also partially the source of at least one very important item of trade: wool.

Migratory flocks (*arung zed*) further consisted of two categories of animals: the *laadi* (or *ladoo*) which were pack animals and the *shai zed* which were breeding animals, mainly female goats, ewes, lambs and kids (Parmar 1959:211).[36] The *laadi* were invariably the males of the species (usually castrated). Rams and male goats kept for stud purposes and the females of the species were never used as pack animals. While they were on their migratory route, the procedure for moving these two categories of animals between camps also differed. The *laadi* started at dawn and travelled rapidly with their loads straight to the next camp so as to reach by midday. They were thereafter unloaded and allowed to graze for the remainder of the day. The *shai zed*, on the other hand, moved at a more leisurely pace. They were allowed to browse as they went along—even making minor detours from the main route—and reached the camp only later in the evening. There were times, however, when during the course of the main summer or winter migration a flock of *laadi* (laden with merchandise) was taken on a trading detour which could be fairly long and time consuming.

TRADE

Apparently the particularly advantageous position of the western Himalaya, especially Kinnaur, in the Indo-Tibet trade was not initially appreciated by the British. Their attempts to capitalize on the existing trans-Himalayan trade through Nepal and other parts of the eastern Himalaya did not meet with success. British failure to link up in the

[36] This information was also personally communicated to me by Vidya Sagar Negi.

east with the Tibetan trade was largely due to the fact that the bulk of the trade within Tibet moved in an east-west direction. Only minor trade routes entered India over the eastern Himalaya (Pemble 1971:61). It has also been suggested that not only political power but also the internal trade of north India was centred in its north-western region, especially Panjab and Rajasthan; that as a result this area became the meeting place of merchants from Tibet, Kandahar, and the seaports of Gujarat (Pemble 1971:60). Tibet was one of the most important sources for wool and borax and these commodities were brought to India through the Satlej valley. Rampur, the capital of Bashahr, was the most important place in the valley to which merchandise from Tibet, Ladakh and the Panjab plains was brought (*Simla District Gazetteer* 1888-9:72-3).

In this network of trade the Kinnaura pastoralists played a significant part. They, with a smaller number of Tibetans, had a virtual monopoly of the trade from the Tibetan border to Rampur, the capital of Bashahr. (Below that level, other merchants carried the goods.) The pastoral Kinnauras not only handled the main strands of commerce that stretched from the Tibetan plateau to the north Indian plains, but they also created a fine web of exchange relationships throughout the mountainous region. The pastoralists migrated along with their flocks across a vast expanse of mountainous territory as they utilized the resources of even the remotest pastures. They were, therefore, best suited to connect the far-flung villages with the main trade routes. It was their ability to transport goods in fairly large quantities over treacherous, almost impassable paths that was crucial to the economy of the region. In 1888, it was noted that the 'hill paths by which the wool is brought down to Rampur are so precipitous that sheep, more sure-footed than larger beasts, are commonly used for the carriage of merchandise (*Simla District Gazetteer* 1888-9:72). Apart from wool and borax, salt too was an important commodity obtained from Tibet. Cotton piece goods, wheat, and rice were the main items of export that passed through Kinnaur to western Tibet (*Records of the Delhi Agency* 1824:289; Fraser 1982:275; *SHSG* 1910:61-2).[37]

[37] These were by no means the only articles of trade. *Pashm* was also brought in from Tibet along with *charas* and finished wool products such as *numdahs* and carpets. Other wool products manufactured locally and traded were *pattu* cloth

Almost all trade in Kinnaur eventually converged on the Satlej valley which acted as a natural channel for the flow of merchandise between western Tibet and Panjab. As it approached the Tibetan border, however, the main trade route split into three smaller ones which crossed into Tibet over different mountain passes. Each of these routes joined the road connecting Tibet with Ladakh and Central Asia at different points (Mitchell 1915:17, 21).[38] In western Tibet, the town of Gartok was the most important market (Sherring 1998:310).[39]

Gerard's description of Gartok (also known as Garoo and by several other names) illustrates the fascinating link between pastoralism and trade. He writes that Gartok

> is a collection of black tents inhabited by pastoral tribes for six months. In winter, the Tartars retire chiefly to Eegoong on the bank of the river, two stages down the stream, and the Chinese governors reside at the Fort of Tuzheegung, where they have houses. Garoo is the most famous mart for wool in Chinese Tartary, and there is a fair of 10,000 or 20,000 people in July, well attended by merchants from Yarkand. Wool, borax, and salt are the principal exports, and these articles are exchanged for the produce of the plains of India. (Gerard 1993:144-5)

Gartok, then, was evidently a summer market that attracted traders, pastoralists, and nomads in large numbers from Central Asia, Ladakh, Kinnaur, Lahaul, and the other parts of Tibet. It is neither possible, nor appropriate, to differentiate the people who came to Gartok on the basis of their occupation: trading, pastoralism, and some element of nomadism were for them inseparable and essential parts of life. The location of the market at Gartok in an open pasture and its

---

and woollen blankets. Among the exports to Tibet were raisins, *neozas* (edible pine nuts), tobacco, horseshoes, saddles, agricultural implements, firearms, etc. The commodities that were sent down the Satlej valley to Panjab were *neoza*, *zira* (cumin), honey, *ghee*, *karru*, violets, *dhup*, apricots, grapes, and yak's tails.

[38] The three routes were noted by Mitchell: (1) Sialkhar Chango; (2) Shipki; (3) Lingo Morang, and of these the first was the most frequently used.

[39] By the beginning of the twentieth century, the British had appointed one Jai Chand, a nephew of the Thakur of Lahaul, as their agent in Gartok 'to protect trade interests'.

temporary nature both underscore the importance of nomadic pastoralism as a facilitator of long-distance trade. Fraser, who travelled extensively through the western Himalaya around 1814, has provided an interesting—though probably exaggerated—account of the Kinnaura traders:

> The Kunawar merchants carry on a trade not only with the plains and the neighbouring Chinese provinces, but as above remarked, they are also the chief carriers between Gar,ha, Ludhak and Cashmere, and even push their commercial enterprises as far as La,hassa on the south-east, exchanging commodities between that place and Nepal, and between the latter and the Chinese towns in Little Thibet, and to the northward, trading between Cashmere, Yarkund, Kashgar, Gar,ha and the various cities and people of these quarters. (Fraser 1982:274)

Even if the Kinnauras did not trade directly with many of the places mentioned by Fraser, they were certainly part of a wide network.

Of the five Kinnaur *parganas*, it was the three border ones of Tukpa, Shua, and Sialkar which developed the closest links with the Tibetan-Central Asian trade routes. A combination of trade and pastoralism, rather than agriculture, was probably the primary source of livelihood here too. This seems to be reflected in the large size of the upper Kinnaur villages—so unlike the areas further south where tiny hamlets were scattered haphazardly near scarce cultivable land (*SHSG* 1910:48). When Gerard reached one such border village—Nisung in upper Kinnaur—he discovered that 'there were none but women and children in the village, all the grown up men having gone to Garoo [Gartok] for salt and wool' (Gerard 1993:102). This is perhaps the most telling evidence for the importance of the trade. The people of the village of Pilo in *pargana* Shua were known to be 'very rich, due to their trade with the Tibetans' (*SHSG* 1910: Appendix II:xx), but what precisely this means, we cannot tell. So also the references to successful traders in some villages of this *pargana* as '*lakhpati shahukars*' (*SHSG* 1910: Appendix II:xvii, xxiv).[40] About one such prosperous trader of Thangi village Gerard wrote, 'I reached the

[40] The appendix is based on a directory compiled by Pandit Tika Ram Joshi who was the private secretary to the Raja of Bashahr. Sonam Guru Shyaltu of Lippa is mentioned as being a '*Lakhpati Shahukar*' and so is Tapgya of village Pooh. The other 'rich men' of Lippa were Barji and Karam Ram.

village of Konoo without a single farthing, not even to pay the guides, owing to the money I expected having been sent up to the valley of the Satlej. An inhabitant of Thungee, whom I had only seen once, when he heard of this, advanced me twelve rupees, which he said I might repay when he visited Rampoor in November' (Gerard 1993: 76, 77, 102).[41] While the inhabitants of the villages near the border survived and at times even prospered on Tibetan trade, there were some traders further down the Satlej trade route, who also became 'men of considerable wealth' as a result of this trade (Mitchell 1915:18).

As a matter of tradition, traders from each of the border *parganas* were obliged to organize in separate groups. Each of these trader groups further had a Tibetan counterpart which also came to the Gartok trade fair in summer and with which all their commercial transactions were conducted (*SHSG* 1910:62). Any disputes that arose were settled by a committee that consisted of traders from different places, including Tibet (*SHSG* 1910:62).

Though money was certainly used, a substantial part of the commerce between Kinnaur and western Tibet was also in the nature of barter. This was more in the case of salt and rice. We learn that Kinnauras going to Tibet got 'two *seers* of salt for one *seer* of husked rice. When selling it again in Garhwal, Rohru or Rampur, they get two or two-and-a-half *seers* of husked rice for a *seer* of salt, thus making a handsome profit' (*SHSG* 1910:63). But this 'profit' may not really have been as large as it appeared. The shopkeepers at Rampur—the largest market in Bashahr—had evolved a devious method to skim off at least some of the gains that would otherwise have gone to peasants and small-time traders who came to sell their produce or merchandise. According to the *Rampur Assessment Report*: 'Every shopkeeper keeps two kinds of weights, one equal to 5 *seers* (*pukka*) and the other weighing 4 *seers*, which for the purpose of sale was considered a five-*seer* weight '*pachsera*'. Those articles which are given to the cultivators are weighed with the latter, while those things which are bought from them are weighed with the former. There is

[41] Elsewhere Gerard wrote, 'I was exactly in the same predicament when I left Soogum for Manes; and Putee Ram, the intelligent Koonawarée, mentioned by Mr. Fraser . . . gave me ten rupees, and told me I was welcome to a hundred if I required so much . . . .'

always a difference of 25 per cent, between both "weights"' (*SHSG* 1910:60).[42] Measures for purchasing and selling cloth at Rampur were similarly of two unequal kinds and used as unscrupulously by the shopkeepers for their own benefit.

Between Two Worlds

Geographically, it is obvious that Kinnaur either linked or separated—depending on one's perspective—the forested slopes and cultivated valleys of the great Himalaya and the barren, cold desert plateau of Tibet. It lay not only between strikingly different terrains, but also between very different societies. Yet its inhabitants had learnt to use the resources of these terrains and societies most effectively. They moved with adeptness between two physical and social worlds and successfully negotiated what appeared to be rather serious contradictions. In reality, however, their regular and periodic 'crossing-over', both literally and metaphorically, may not have been so difficult for them. It may, perhaps, never have been a 'crossing-over' at all. Kinnaur society seems to have reflected several of the characteristics associated with the two large ecological and social systems that flanked it. Kinnaur was not a place where 'The symbol systems of two different great traditions [Hinduism and Buddhism] compete for commitment . . .' (Fisher 1987:189). Fisher's study of Tarangpur (Nepal) has argued that Hinduism and Buddhism in the Great and Trans-Himalaya represented two poles that remained 'unaffected by each other'. He sees the traders of Tarangpur as '*brokers* of goods', on the one hand, but also as '*blockers* of ideas', on the other (emphasis mine). The integration they brought about, he argues, was 'distinctly economic' rather than ideological (Fisher 1987:96).[43]

Kinnauras, however, do not seem to have been unduly disturbed by their location on the fringes of two great traditions. Nor did they act as 'blockers of ideas' between Hinduism and Buddhism. In fact,

[42] All the business in Rampur *tahsil*, through which the trade of Kinnaur passed to north India, was controlled by outsiders. It is noted that, 'All the shopkeepers in the Rampur *tahsil* are natives of the Ambala, Hoshiarpur or Kangra districts, or of the Patiala State.'

[43] Fisher writes that 'Buddhists see and learn little of Hindus and Hindus see and learn little of Buddhists.'

the transition from one ideological world to the other seems to have taken place in Kinnaur itself. This is mirrored in the shades of belief prevailing in different parts of the region: the physical dimensions, as it were, of mental arenas. North-western Kinnaur and the upper Baspa valley were Buddhist, with most of the older Buddhist monasteries located there, and Brahmanical deities and even local *deotas* were almost entirely absent. In middle Kinnaur, Buddhist monasteries and temples of local folk *deotas* were given equal importance and the Kinnauras saw no contradiction in this (Chatur Bhuj 1928:3). Lower Kinnaur, further south, was the country of Brahmanical deities which held sway over the people through numerous local village *deotas* (Rose 1970:II:470 and II:454).[44] Though the state of Bashahr had originated in Kinnaur, when it expanded into a full-fledged kingdom, the centre of political authority shifted out and southwards to Sarahan and Rampur. With the institutionalization of monarchy, socio-political prescriptions of formal Brahmanism came to be followed by the raja and the ruling family in and around the capital towns. But as elsewhere Brahmanical injunctions did not destroy the legitimacy of folk tradition. They simply included it at a subordinate level. By this means a hierarchy amongst gods was created and maintained. For instance, the three sons and one daughter of the mythical Banasur (the deposed ruler of the region), who were believed to have been killed in battle with Krishna or one of his descendants, came to be accepted as important village gods of Kinnaur.[45] At the same time, like all other village gods, they occupied a place that was inferior to Lord Badrinath, the Brahmanical deity who 'ruled' the region from his temple at Kamru in Kinnaur.

[44] A hierarchical relationship existed between the two kinds of deities, with the Brahmanical gods dominating. As in the 'Hindu' area of the Simla Hill States, even in lower Kinnaur, 'The gods of the village-temples are subordinate to the god of a Deo *mandir* or "great temple", and they perform certain services for him, e.g. at a *yag* and at fairs, in *return* for the fiefs (*jagirs*) granted by him.'

[45] The three sons of Banasur came to be known as the three Maheshras and their temples were located at different villages. The local account attached as Appendix II to *SHSG* (*Bashahr*) 1910 gives a description of these Maheshras. See p. xii. 'It is said that Banasur who was a demon and who ruled in Sarahan, at a very remote period, was slain, and so the first son became the Maheshras of Shungra, the second of Kathgaon, the third of Chugaon, and Ukha, their sister, became the goddess of Nachar.'

The original home of the Bashahr rulers (notwithstanding their claim to be outsiders and the descendants of Sri Krishna), as already mentioned, was also Kamru.

No discernible boundary appears to have existed between Brahmanical convictions and folk tradition in lower Kinnaur. As one moved northwards and beyond, the influence of the Brahmanical 'great tradition' remained important, but in the context now of Buddhism as the institutionalized religion. They not only co-existed with Buddhism but also played a crucial role in the life of the Buddhist population. Flexibility in belief was possibly a necessity for Kinnaura society, in a situation where religious orthodoxy could jeopardize survival. Dr J.G. Gerard, who submitted a report to Captain C.P. Kennedy on the state of education in the Simla Hill States in 1824, remarked about Kinnaur that 'civilization, morality and knowledge have made the greatest progress in the remote and secluded regions of Koonawur'. He further wrote:

> Koonawur, in spite of the defects of the Bussahir government and its remoteness from the capital, ranks above every other State in point of intelligence, active industry and good feeling, but it is foreign to the purpose to detail the circumstances that have contributed to give it this superiority. I shall only remark that there are no Brahmins in that country and there is much less of blind devotion in religion, but more of superstition. Education is there less cultivated than the actual acquirement of knowledge, which their intercourse with Chinese, their commercial pursuits and habits of hardihood encourage and establish. (*Records of the Delhi Agency* 1824:315–16)

Trade with Tibet stopped abruptly in the early 1960s and has been restored only partially in recent years. The construction of roads, the advent of tourism, and the success of apple farming have opened Kinnaur both physically and economically to the rest of the country. Alternative sources of livelihood have emerged and few Kinnauras are now traders. Polyandry has virtually died out except amongst the poorest Kinnauras. The pastoralist of Kinnaur and his *arung zed* can still be found in the alpine pastures in summer, or in the shrub forests of the Shiwaliks in winter. The animals continue to provide for some meat and clothing for local consumption, but it is evident that both pastoralist and flock are, as it were, the remnants of an ancient but dying tradition.

REFERENCES

Asad, Talal, 'Equality in Nomadic Social Systems? Notes towards the Dissolution of an Anthropological Category', in *Pastoral Production and Society*, Cambridge: Cambridge University Press, 1977.

Black-Michaud, Jacob, *Sheep and Land: The Economies of Power in a Tribal Society*, Cambridge: Cambridge University Press, 1986.

Brown, C.W., 'Ecology, Trade and Former Bhotia Identity', in M.K. Raha, ed., *The Himalayan Heritage*, Delhi: Gian Publishing House, 1987.

Chandra, Ramesh, 'Sex Roles Arrangement to Achieve Economic Security in North Western Himalaya', in Christoph von Furer-Haimendorf, ed., *Asian Highland Societies: An Anthropological Perspective*, New Delhi, 1981.

Chatur Bhuj, *Report Tarmim Bandobast Tahsil Chini* (*Tahsil Chini Settlement Report*), 1928. I have used the Hindi translation made in 1970 of the original Urdu by Daulat Ram Tegta.

Dughlat, Mirza Muhammad Haidar, *Tarikh-i-Rashidi*: *A History of the Mughals of Central Asia*, tr. E. Denison Ross, ed. N. Elias, London, 1972.

Fisher, James F., *Trans-Himalayan Traders*: *Economy, Society and Culture in Northwest Nepal*, Delhi: Motilal Banarsidass, 1987.

Fraser, James Baillie, *The Himala Mountains*, Delhi: Neeraj Publishing House, 1982 (1st published 1820).

Furer-Haimendorf, Christoph von, *Himalayan Traders*: *Life in Highland Nepal*, Times Books International, 1988 (1st published 1975).

Gellner, Ernest, 'The Tribal Society and its Enemies', in Richard Tapper, ed., *The Conflict of Tribe and State in Iran and Afghanistan*, London: Croom Helm, 1983.

Gerard, Alexander, *Account of Koonawur in the Himalaya*, New Delhi: Indus Publishing Co., 1993 (1st published 1841).

Hamilton, A.F.P., *Revised Working Plan for the Kanawar Forests (Sutlej Valley) of the Upper Bashahr Division*, Lahore, 1932.

Lefebure, Claude, 'Introduction: The Specificity of Nomadic Pastoral Societies', in *Pastoral Production and Society*, Cambridge: Cambridge University Press, 1977.

Mitchell, Alan, *Report on the Administration of the Bashahr State, 1914-15*, Simla, 1915.

Molnar, Augusta, 'Economic Strategies and Ecological Constraints', in Christoph von Furer-Haimendorf, ed., *Asian Highland Societies: An Anthropological Perspective*, New Delhi, 1981.

Moorcroft, William, and George Trebeck, *Travels in the Himalayan Provinces of Hindustan and the Panjab; in Ladakh and Kashmir; in Peshawar, Kabul Kunduz, and Bokhara 1819-1825*, Patiala: Languages Department, 1970 (1st published 1837).

Parmar, B.S., *Report on the Grazing Problems and Policy of Himachal Pradesh*, Forest Department, Himachal Pradesh, 1959.

Pemble, John, *The Invasion of Nepal: John Company at War*, Oxford, 1971.

Raha, M.K. (ed.), *The Himalayan Heritage*,. Delhi: Gian Publishing House, 1987.

Ratnagar, Shereen, 'Pastoralism as an Issue in Historical Research', *Studies in History*, vol. 7, no. 2, 1991.

Records of the Delhi Agency, 1824. Chapter VIII. 'Report on Lapsed and Reserved Territory in the Protected Sikh and Hill States and on the Latter Generally, 1824.'

Rodgers, W.A., 'Environmental Change and the Evolution of Pastoralism in South Asia', *Studies in History*, vol. 7, no. 2, 1991.

Rose, H.A., *A Glossary of the Tribes and Castes of the Punjab and North-West Frontier Province*, Patiala: Languages Department, 3 vols., 1970 (1st published 1883).

Salzman, Philip S., 'Political Organization Among Nomadic Peoples', *Proceedings of the American Philosophical Society*, vol. 111, no. 2, 1967.

Sanan, Deepak, and Dhanu Swadi, *Exploring Kinnaur and Spiti in the Trans-Himalaya*, New Delhi: Indus Publishing Co., 1998.

Sherring, Charles A., *Western Tibet and the British Borderland: The Sacred Country of Hindus and Buddhists with an Account of the Religion and Customs of its Peoples*, Delhi: Asian Educational Services (1st published London, 1906), 1998.

SHSG, *Simla Hill States Gazetteer (Bashahr)*, Lahore: The 'Civil and Military Gazette' Press, 1910.

Simla District Gazetteer, 1888-9, Punjab Government, n.d.

Singh, Chetan, *Natural Premises: Ecology and Peasant Life in the Western Himalaya, 1800-1950*, Delhi: Oxford University Press, 1998.

Tapper, Richard, 'Anthropologists, Historians and Tribesmen', in Philip S. Khoury and Joseph Kostiner, eds., *Tribes and State Formation in the Middle East*, London: I.B. Tauris & Co., 1991.

Tapper, Richard (ed.), *The Conflict of Tribe and State in Iran and Afghanistan*, London: Croom Helm, 1983.

Vitali, Roberto (ed.), *The Kingdom of Gu.ge Pu.hrang. According to mNga'.ris rgyal.rabs by Gu.ge mkhan.chen Ngag.dbang graps.pa*, Dharamsala, 1996.

In the Name of Pastoralism: The Early Medieval Maharashtra

AJAY DANDEKAR

IN THE SOUTH ASIAN context, studies on pastoralism, or even its mention as a viable field of research in a historical context are few and even these are largely confined to protohistoric times. As we move from the protohistoric to the historical period, we find a remarkable paucity of studies on pastoralism per se. Even for the protohistoric period, the research that exists (Leshnik 1972; Murty and Sontheimer 1980; Ratnagar 1987; Dhavalikar 1988) is not, on the whole, concerned with the centrality of pastoralism. Leshnik and Sontheimer's work (1975) is largely introductory in nature. A more comprehensive treatment of the same subject in the early 1990s handles it with the sensitivity it deserves (Ratnagar, ed. 1991).

In this paper, we will pose the issue of centrality and pastoralism in the early medieval context for a region that falls between the upper reaches of the Bhima and the Krishna rivers. This area has not so far received adequate attention from the perspective of pastoralism. The need to rectify this very neglect shall be our concern here. The first section of this paper examines the dominant paradigm that situates pastoralism as a category on the margins of regions, states, or societies, as the case may be. The next section re-examines the region of the Deccan to demonstrate the ways in which the approach changes once the defining elements are changed. The subsequent sections examine the historical evidence (hero-stones and epigraphic data) to understand the region within the context of pastoralism.

I

Any discussion on the issue of the marginalizing of categories should emanate from the question about how we 'define' our regions. As Heredia repeatedly argued during the discussions in this workshop, the margin appears only when one sets up the page. It is this perspective that has played a key role in marginalizing the study of pastoralism.

Let us begin with the seminal work of Subbarao in delineating the natural and cultural regions of India. 'In a very broad sense, a region develops according to its agricultural potentialities considering the social and other consequences of food production' (Subbarao 1958: 12–15). Cohn thinks likewise insofar as historical regions are concerned; and for him the perennial or nuclear regions are the principal river basins that form the major agricultural areas; these include the Indus, the Ganga, the Godavari, the Krishna, and the Kaveri (Cohn 1967:12ff).

Stein expresses doubts whether 'historical regions' exist autonomously as givens, because there are other kinds of regions with other defining elements (Stein 1967:42–3). However, while rejecting the 'historical region', Stein nevertheless preserves the basic entity of the 'nuclear zone', the cradle of development, in identifying the prime mover in history. In fact, Stein then goes a few steps forward and makes the 'nuclear' or 'historical' region the bedrock on which the edifice of his 'segmentary state' is constructed (Stein 1980).

Schwarztsberg rejects empiricist definitions of the 'region' and states that it is a 'perceived segment of the time-space continuum differentiated from others on the basis of one or more defining characteristics' (1967:93). He classifies regions into three categories: the naively given, the instituted, and the denoted. A naively-given region is that entity which is recognized as a meaningful territory by its inhabitants. This conceptualization corresponds with Bhatt's 'folk' regions (1980). Instituted regions can be compared with administrative regions, for they are instituted by human agency as distinctive and discrete units limiting the areal extent of the operation of certain functions. Perhaps 'denoted regions' can also be considered under this category, as they are also 'conceived' to cater to a particular individual or group, and/or its administrative needs.

Within the realm of South Asian geography, the dominant trend is to classify space on the basis of its physical-biotic characteristics. The work of Spate and Learmonth (1967) and of Singh (1971) and innumerable state geographies produced by the National Book Trust of India illustrate this. Such studies have often become the bedrock on which the massive structures of socio-economic analyses are erected. Another emergent trend in this context is the growing emphasis on statistical techniques to determine the clustering of areal units with common quantifiable characteristics (Misra and Ramchandran 1972:458, 677).

The perennial nuclear region that has weighed heavily on the minds of scholars has, in fact, become a 'mindset'. Spate records that the dynamic forces of history, namely, the centres of power, were located in areas of intensive agriculture. This theory is followed by other geographers (Sopher 1980:292), who also identify as core areas those regions where settled agriculture was productive. Archaeologists and anthropologists are not far behind either. They wholeheartedly support the dominant sedentary bias and are quick to recognize dynamism in 'agricultural cores' (Malik 1968:77). A brief review of the work on economic history also confirms the same conclusion, viz., that the dominant bias has favoured agricultural systems. (For a survey of this kind, see Jha 1986:1-13). The entire debate on the nature of Indian feudalism also appears to be based on the premise that the economic base was always agriculture, and that the so-called agro-pastoral complex had given way to a dominant agrarian system by the beginning of the land-grant economy (Yadav 1973; Sharma 1965, 1987). This kind of theorization does not allow space for some grey areas of our past.

As no other alternative subsistence strategy has been studied on its own terms in Indian history, we constantly have to explain the grey areas of India's past in terms of the biased dominant paradigm. In this paper, however, it will be argued that pastoralism was a basic component of the economy and society of the early medieval Deccan, and that this cannot be wished away even if direct evidence regarding its existence is scarce.

II

Our area of study can be subdivided into its physiographic divisions as the first and primary step towards the construction of a region. These relief divisions are the west coast, the Western Ghats, and the plateau upland that contains three major river valleys.

The western coast of Maharashtra is a narrow strip of land not more than 50 miles at its widest. Bounded on the east by the massive scarp of the Ghats, its uneven topography primarily consists of uneven transverse ridges of the Ghats, isolated hills, low-lying plateaus, and narrow river valleys (Deshpande 1971:162). The rivers Ulhas, Vaiterna, Amba, Savitri, and Vasisthi cross the coastal plain. Navigation on these rivers, except at the river mouths, is impossible due to the sharp bends in their courses. The northern Konkan is characterized by sandy stretches close to the sea, and the coastal ranges alternating with longitudinal valleys further inland. These topographical features, apart from other factors, make the northern Konkan more agriculturally productive than its southern counterpart (Singh 1971:911). The southern Konkan has more rugged terrain, characterized by hills and elevated plateaus and is intersected by numerous creeks.

The Western Ghats form the western edge of the Deccan plateau. The Ghats, besides being the continental divide between the two water systems, one directed towards the Bay of Bengal and the other towards the Arabian Sea, are also a barrier between the coastal lowlands and the plateau uplands. The longitudinal range stretches from north to south, almost parallel to the coast, for more than 600 miles. The crestline is a succession of high plateaus and occasional rounded peaks connected by low saddles. Kalsubai, the mountain source of the river Pravara, is the highest point (1,646 m.) in the Western Ghat system. There are many lesser peaks, and saddles mark the eroded surfaces in the source regions of the rivers; passes that are locally called ghats connect the plateau to the west coast. Though structurally a part of the rest of the plateau, the Western Ghats present a distinctly different environment. Heavy rainfall, deeply dissected terrain, evergreen vegetation, and deep red lateritic soils are some of the important features of this environment.

The Maval is a narrow strip of land that runs almost parallel to the Western Ghats and forms a buffer, as it were, between the two environments to its east and west. Though more often than not the term Maval is applied to an area that falls in Pune district, it actually defines the transition zone in terms of climate, crop pattern, livestock, population density, and land use.

The Ajanta Hills, a lateral offshoot of the Western Ghats, divide the Tapi and the Godavari river systems. This range forms an effective barrier between Khandesh and the rest of the plateau.

The Godavari virtually bisects the plateau of Maharashtra. The river emerges on the eastern slopes of the Western Ghats near Trimbakesvar in Nasik district, and takes a south-easterly course. The Nasik district is the core of the upper Godavari river basin. Settlements in the valley have followed the watercourse and are located on the terraces at a safe distance from the floodwaters. Paithan, Ter, and Bhokardan, apart from Nasik, are some of the important nodes that have emerged along the river.

The Balaghat plateau forms the divide between the drainage systems of the Godavari and the Krishna. The height of this plateau ranges from 850 m. on the west to 600 m. in the east. The river Sina and the tributaries of the Godavari have divided the plateau into two distinct parts, the Ahmednagar plateau to the west and the upland basin of Manjra to the east. The Bhima and the Krishna rivers form the core of the Maharashtra region. Although the Bhima is a tributary of the river Krishna, it has certain unique features that allow us to teat it as a separate system in its own right. Starting at Bhimashankar on the crest of the Western Ghats, the Bhima collects water from the rivers Man, Nira, Ghod, and Sina from the north and the south, and develops into a wide, meandering river with flood plains and terraces.

The Mahadev range is the lateral eastern offshoot of the Western Ghats that divides the Bhima and the Krishna systems. The Saswad plateau is a topographic continuation of the range, but is separated by the Nira entrenchment.

The upper Krishna basin is the most fertile and well-watered tract of Maharashtra. The valley that is a broad trough at the source near Mahabaleshwar widens into a large flood plain near Satara, with fingers deep into the mountains along the tributaries. Intensively cultivated and densely populated, this valley supports the richer side of the landscape. Kolhapur, Sangli, Miraj, Ichalkaranji, Karhad, and Satara are some of the important towns of this valley. There is a tilt from west to east in the gradient of the plateau. The thickly wooded basins and the dissected highlands traversing the 'region' from west to east are the two contrasting features of the plateau.

Rainfall Patterns

We need to take into account the rainfall pattern to understand the region sketched above. Let us take Pune district as a case in point. The district of Pune may be divided into three rainfall zones. The western zone, the crest of the Ghats, receives the highest rainfall.

Here the average rainfall may even touch 4,500 mm. The amount of rainfall decreases significantly to the leeward side of the Ghats. In Maval, our second zone, the rainfall stabilizes around 800 mm. The eastern part of the district is zone three, where the annual precipitation is as low as 500 mm and sometimes even less. This area includes the Haveli, Sirur, Junnar, and Purandar talukas. A similar pattern is repeated in the areas south of Pune, in the districts of Satara, Sangli, and Kolhapur (Deshpande 1971). In each of these three districts that are immediately to the south of Pune, we can observe a similar pattern in the rainfall. In each district, the precipitation decreases noticeably towards the leeward side of the Western Ghats. Thus, in the Satara district the western part receives good rainfall but the eastern parts of the Man, Phaltan, and Khatav talukas receive scanty rainfall. In Sangli, the Khanapur and Jath talukas receive an average of around 500 mm.

To the south of this region lies the district of Belgaum, adjoining Kolhapur. Here the contrast is geological: archaic gneiss and granite as against the lava of the rest of Maharashtra. However, this geological difference does not translate into a different pattern of rainfall. From the confluence of the Bhima and the Krishna to the Tungabhadra, the decrease in rainfall is 500 to 620 mm. South of the Tungabhadra, the precipitation rises. Allchin refers to the neolithic pastoralists in this area, which had excellent pastures though scanty rainfall (Allchin 1963:6f).

To the east and north-east of the region lie the districts of Solapur, Usmanabad, and Ahmednagar. Here too the drift of the monsoon as determined by the rain shadow determines the quantum of annual rainfall. In Solapur district, the Karmala and Sangola talukas receive meagre rainfall. In Usmanabad district, the Parenda and Bhum *talukas* receive scanty rainfall as they lie towards the leeward side of the south-west monsoon, while the rest of the district gets its rain from the north-eastern monsoon. In Ahmednagar district, seven talukas (out of thirteen) face drought conditions, and the rainfall is as low as 550 mm. In the north-eastern area, we finally find the meagre rainfall giving way to a steady and regular rainfall. Thus, in Buldhana and Nagpur the situation in terms of the annual precipitation improves.

We can, therefore, broadly distinguish three agro-climatic zones for further investigation. Zone One encompasses the west coast and the crest line of the Western Ghats and is characterized by heavy rainfall, tropical evergreen vegetal cover, and rice cultivation. Zone Two is characterized by less heavy but stable rainfall, with tropical semi-evergreen and moist deciduous forest cover, and a system of intercropping. The Maval, the lower Krishna valley, the upper Godavari valley, and the north-eastern area would broadly fall under this zone. These are potential cultivating areas and are linked by communication networks with each other. Zone Three is a semi-arid area with uncertain and low rainfall, high rocky land, and rocky foothills. All the major avenues of communication that connect the agriculturally rich river valleys as well as the ports on the west coast have to pass through this vast terrain. This territory ranging from Khandesh to the Tungabhadra river, is an area characterized by the practise of pastoralism on a massive scale.

III

The observations of the British administrators are a good starting point for the discussion on pastoralism. T. Ogilvy in his memoir on the Satara territory remarks:

> The entire territory of Satara is divided into two distinct and very dissimilar parts by a chain of hills branching off from the Mahadeo range near Phaltan, and running from north to south for fifty to sixty miles nearly to the banks of Krishna near Malwa. This portion of territory is well peopled with industrious agriculturists, is well cultivated and productive and is rendered fertile and salubrious by reasonable showers. The division of the territory to the east of that chain of hills, though still intersected by spurs, is more flat and barren and it is ill cultivated by a thin unsettled, and in some degree, predatory population. The fall of rain is scanty and precarious and the climate is hot and insalubrious. These districts yield, however, excellent pastures which have encouraged the breeding of horses, celebrated among the Marathas and they maintain numerous flocks and herds. (Cited by Sontheimer, 1975:163)

'The general face of the country may be described as undulating. The uplands, with little depth of soil, afforded convenient pasturage, while the deeper soils of the two lands are capable under careful cultivation of yielding the richest returns' (Guha 1982:63).

In the eighteenth century, the Peshwas issued certain instructions that give us an insight into the organization of the pastoral system.

The orders refer to a tax on sheep, reserved pastures, and a system of permits. In one such instruction, Peshwa Madhavarao I states that some sheep flocks have 'entered and are grazing unauthorizedly in *prants* of Junnar, Parner, Sangamner, Nandur, Nevase, Akole and Shevagaon. The officers are instructed to collect a fine of Re. one per sheep from the owners of the flock' (Joshi 1911:96ff). Another instruction refers to the tax on sheep (Parasnis 1909:312), while one order specifically directs that the officers 'will not trouble three flocks of sheep and one flock of cattle' belonging to one Malhar who has been permitted to graze on government lands (Parasnis 1909:39).

This evidence on the land use pattern in the region is by now fairly well established for the earlier times as well, as Sontheimer (1975; 1977; 1985; 1987; 1989) argues. It appears from the evidence as well as from the nature of the semi-arid zone that sheep keeping was a major activity, but there are also references to cattle herds being maintained in the region. Let us now investigate the evidence available from early medieval period regarding the nature of pastoralism.

IV

In this section, we will mainly focus on data collected during field observations on hero-stones that depict cattle raids. Hero-stones form part of a matrix of what has been categorized as 'memorial' stones. The first comprehensive treatment of the subject came from work in the early 1980s (Thapar 1981; Settar and Sontheimer 1982). Memorial stones are spread across the subcontinent from the deep south to the arid reaches of the Rajasthan desert. Here we will confine ourselves to those found in Maharashtra. These date from about the eighth to the thirteenth centuries. There are sati-stones and stones set up in remembrance of dead men. The latter can be subdivided into those set up to commemmorate individuals who died a natural death, and those set up to honour 'heroes' who died in battle.

In our region the most frequent type of memorial that crops up is the hero-stone. Normally the hero-stone (locally known as *viragala*) has three panels. The lowest panel depicts the event such as a battle or skirmish in which the person had died. Sometimes this lowest panel was expanded or new ones were added according to the scale of the event in which the red death occur. The middle panel depicts the heavenly march of the dead, escorted by the *apsaras*. The topmost panel depicts the dead hero worshipping a deity, which in most cases is a *sivalinga*. In this stereotyped depiction there are variations to cater to the needs of different situations. In case more than one member of a family had died, two slabs were joined together or the slab may be vertically divided. We also come across quadrilaterally carved hero-stones, which depict three panels of identical size.

The hero-stones of Maharashtra carry no inscriptions, unlike those from Karnataka. Thus, we have to depend on the stylistic pattern as well as the context in which the stone is placed to derive any kind of general interpretation about their purpose or function.

Let us examine the Karnataka series to gain an insight into our region which adjoins it. In sheer numbers, the Karnataka series far outstrips the Maharashtra series. In addition, unlike in our region, the Karnataka series carries inscriptions. Thus, the historical context there is not lost. It also gives us some points of comparison with the Maharashtra series, enabling us to date the latter.

As in Maharashtra, we come across a variety in the Karnataka series. Apart from the stones erected for those who died defending their herds or a cattle raid, there are stones for those who died in battle or in the hunt, and also memorials for pets (*EC* V: 205; *EC* VII: 159,1219; Settar 1982:196).

It appears that a cattle raid was a major happening. There are references to an army laying siege to a village for cattle (*EC* II:785, 5), and to *nayakas* and *mahamandalesvaras* issuing orders to armies engaged in cattle raids. Thus, it appears that a great deal of importance was placed on cattle in the early medieval period in Karnataka. And so many points of comparison emerge between the Maharashtra and the Karnataka series. It appears that the composition of the lowermost panel in both the series was influenced by the immediate social context. In Karnataka, the inscriptions explain the last panel in terms of the event and the people associated with it. There is a great deal of similarity between the two series, particularly in relation to the number of panels (three to five), the symbols depicted (the sun and the moon), and the general style of carving.

We are now in a position to understand the cattle raid depicting hero-stones of our region. We can tentatively place the hero-stones of this genre in Maharashtra between the eighth and the thirteenth centuries. This chronology has been established on the basis of comparison with the Karnataka series.

Below is the list of places where hero-stones depicting cattle raids are located.[1]

TABLE 1: HERO-STONES IN THE SEMI-ARID BELT OF MAHARASHTRA

Sr. No.	District/*Taluka*	Find-spot	Climate	Rainfall Zone	Vegetation
1.	A'Nagar-Karjat	Shegud	Semi-arid	II	Dry Deciduous
2.	Barshi-Barshi	Malwandi	Semi-arid	II	Dry Deciduous
3.	Pune	Malsiras	Semi-arid	II	Dry Deciduous
4.	Pune-Purandar	Vir	Semi-arid	II	Dry Deciduous
5.	Satara-Wai	Sartale	Semi-arid	II	Dry Deciduous
6.	Solapur-Solapur	Solapur	Semi-arid	II	Dry Deciduous
7.	A'Nagar-Srigonda	Chandagaon	Semi-arid	II	Dry Deciduous
8.	A'Nagar-Parner	Ralegana	Semi-arid	II	Dry Deciduous
9.	A'Nagar-Karmala	Karmala	Semi-arid	II	Dry Deciduous
10.	A'Nagar-Pathardi	Pathardi	Transitional	IX	Dry Deciduous
11.	A'Nagar-Srigonda	Srigonda	Semi-arid	II	Dry Deciduous
12.	A'Nagar-Akole	Kalamb	Semi-arid	II	Dry Deciduous
13.	A'Nagar-Karjat	Rashin	Semi-arid	II	Dry Deciduous
14.	A'Nagar-Pathardi	Nandur	Semi-arid	II	Dry Deciduous
15.	A'Nagar-Pathardi	Tintarrana	Semi-arid	II	Dry Deciduous
16.	A'Nagar-Sangamner	Dolsane	Semi-arid	II	Dry Deciduous
17.	Pune	Koregaon	Semi-arid	II	Dry Deciduous
18.	Pune	Mhalunge	Semi-arid	II	Dry Deciduous
19.	Pune	Nayagaon	Semi-arid	II	Dry Deciduous
20.	Pune	Urali Devaci	Semi-arid	II	Dry Deciduous
21.	Pune	Limpangaon	Semi-arid	II	Dry Deciduous
22.	Pune	Varkute	Semi-arid	II	Dry Deciduous
23.	Pune	Varvand	Semi-arid	II	Dry Deciduous
24.	Pune	Makalwadi	Semi-arid	II	Dry Deciduous
25.	Pune	Koregaon	Semi-arid	II	Dry Deciduous
26.	Pune	Bhade	Transitional	XII	Moist Deciduous
27.	Pune	Aundh	Transitional	XII	Moist Deciduous
28.	Pune	Coraci Alandi	Transitional	XII	Moist Deciduous
29.	Pune-Purandar	Gulunce	Semi-arid	II	Dry Deciduous
30.	Pune-Purandar	Murti	Semi-arid	II	Dry Deciduous

(*contd.*)

[1] The data are based on investigations carried out by the author from 1986 to 2000. They are supplemented by the information already available through the studies of the late Prof. G.D. Sontheimer. I am grateful to the Indira Gandhi National Centre For the Arts for a fellowship which enabled me to undertake a study of hero-stones in 1994.

TABLE 1 (*contd.*)

Sr. No.	District/*Taluka*	Find-spot	Climate	Rainfall Zone	Vegetation
31.	Pune-Purandar	Kolhvihire	Semi-arid	II	Dry Deciduous
32.	Pune-Purandar	Jejuri	Transitional	IX	Moist Deciduous
33.	Pune-Purandar	Sakurde	Semiarid	II	Dry Deciduous
34.	Pune-Purandar	Yamai Shivre	Semi-arid	II	Dry Deciduous
35.	Pune-Purandar	Walhe	Semi-arid	II	Dry Deciduous
36.	Pune-Baramati	Supe	Semi-arid	II	Dry Deciduous
37.	Pune-Baramati	Nhavi-Rui	Semi-arid	II	Dry Deciduous
38.	Pune-Baramati	Sopeshvar-karande	Semi-arid	II	Dry Deciduous
39.	Pune-Daund	Sindavane	Semi-arid	II	Dry Deciduous
40.	Pune-Daund	Dalimba	Semi-arid	II	Dry Deciduous
41.	Pune-Daund	Varavanda	Semi-arid	II	Dry Deciduous
42.	Pune-Daund	Delavadi	Semi-arid	II	Dry Deciduous
43.	Pune-Haveli	Gavalyaci Undavali	Semi-arid	II	Dry Deciduous
44.	Pune-Haveli	Manjari	Semi-arid	II	Dry Deciduous
45.	Pune-Haveli	Vadaki	Semi-arid	II	Dry Deciduous
46.	Pune-Indapur	Nimgaon Ketaki	Semi-arid	II	Dry Deciduous
47.	Pune-Indapur	Bavda	Semi-arid	II	Dry Deciduous
48.	Pune-Indapur	Narsingpur	Semi-arid	II	Dry Deciduous
49.	Pune-Indapur	Bitarvangi	Semi-arid	II	Dry Deciduous
50.	Pune-Indapur	Ropale	Semi-arid	II	Dry Deciduous
51.	Pune-Indapur	Mirvangi	Semi-arid	II	Dry Deciduous
52.	Pune-Indapur	Vadapuri	Semi-arid	II	Dry Deciduous
53.	Pune-Junnar	Vadada	Semi-arid	II	Dry Deciduous
54.	Pune-Maval	Chandkhed	Semi-arid	II	Dry Deciduous
55.	Pune-Maval	Vadgaon	Semi-arid	II	Dry Deciduous
56.	Pune-Maval	Kamshet	Semi-arid	II	Dry Deciduous
57.	Pune-Purandar	Morgaon	Semi-arid	II	Dry Deciduous
58.	Pune-Purandar	Harni	Semi-arid	II	Dry Deciduous
59.	Pune-Purandar	Mandki	Semi-arid	II	Dry Deciduous
60.	Pune-Purandar	Saswad	Semi-arid	II	Dry Deciduous
61.	Pune-Purandar	Dhalewadi	Semi-arid	II	Dry Deciduous
62.	Pune-Purandar	Kumbhalaga	Semi-arid	II	Dry Deciduous
63.	Pune-Purandar	Naigaon Sid	Semi-arid	II	Dry Deciduous
64.	Pune-Purandar	Mavadi	Semi-arid	II	Dry Deciduous
65.	Pune-Purandar	Mavadika-depathar	Semi-arid	II	Dry Deciduous
66.	Pune-Purandar	Pandeshvar	Semi-arid	II	Dry Deciduous
67.	Pune-Purandar	Pangare	Semi-arid	II	Dry Deciduous
68.	Pune-Purandar	Hivre	Semi-arid	II	Dry Deciduous
69.	Pune-Purandar	Parince	Semi-arid	II	Dry Deciduous

(*contd.*)

TABLE 1 (*contd.*)

Sr. No.	District/*Taluka*	Find-spot	Climate	Rainfall Zone	Vegetation
70.	Pune-Purandar	Rakh	Semi-arid	II	Dry Deciduous
71.	Pune-Purandar	Modhave	Semi-arid	II	Dry Deciduous
72.	Pune-Purandar	Waghapur	Semi-arid	II	Dry Deciduous
73.	Pune-Shirur	Karegaon	Semi-arid	II	Dry Deciduous
74.	Pune-Shirur	Hangevadi	Semi-arid	II	Dry Deciduous
75.	Pune-Shirur	Hingani	Semi-arid	II	Dry Deciduous
76.	Satara-Satara	Mahuli	Semi-arid	II	Dry Deciduous
77.	Satara-Man	Dahivadi	Semi-arid	II	Dry Deciduous
78.	Satara-Wai	Kudal	Semi-arid	II	Dry Deciduous
79.	Satara-Bhuinj	Kikli	Semi-arid	II	Dry Deciduous
80.	Satara-Man	Mhasvad	Semi-arid	II	Dry Deciduous
81.	Satara-Phaltan	Adarki	Semi-arid	II	Dry Deciduous
82.	Satara-Phaltan	Javali	Semi-arid	II	Dry Deciduous
83.	Satara-Phaltan	Vedhani	Semi-arid	II	Dry Deciduous
84.	Solapur-Madha	Manegaon	Semi-arid	II	Dry Deciduous
85.	Solapur-Madha	Papari	Transitional	IX	Moist Deciduous
86.	Solapur-Malsiras	Purandavade	Transitional	IX	Moist Deciduous
87.	Solapur-Malsiras	Natepute	Transitional	IX	Moist Deciduous
88.	Solapur-Malsiras	Dighanci	Semi-arid	II	Dry Deciduous
89.	Solapur-Malsiras	Moronci	Semi-arid	II	Dry Deciduous
90.	Solapur-Malsiras	Piraci Kuroli	Semi-arid	II	Dry Deciduous
91.	Solapur-Malsiras	Akluj	Semi-arid	II	Dry Deciduous
92.	Solapur-Malsiras	Rede	Semi-arid	II	Dry Deciduous
93.	Solapur-Malsiras	Khudus	Semi-arid	II	Dry Deciduous
94.	Solapur-Malsiras	Mire	Semi-arid	II	Dry Deciduous
95.	Solapur-Malsiras	Velapur	Semi-arid	II	Dry Deciduous
96.	Solapur-Malsiras	Mhalunge	Semi-arid	II	Dry Deciduous
97.	Solapur-Malsiras	Malsiras	Semi-arid	II	Dry Deciduous
98.	Solapur-Mohol	Mohol	Semi-arid	II	Dry Deciduous
99.	Solapur-Pandharpur	Pandharpur	Semi-arid	II	Dry Deciduous
100.	Solapur-Pandharpur	Tondale	Semi-arid	II	Dry Deciduous
101.	Solapur-Pandharpur	Bondale	Transitional	IX	Moist Deciduous

What emerges from this tabulation are the following observations:

1. We have so far identified 101 sites that contain cattle raids depicting hero-stones. Out of these 92 sites are located in the semi-arid zone. The remaining 9 sites are located in the transitional zone, of which 6 are on the edge of the semi-arid zone, and the remaining 3 lie in the transition zone proper. In other words, it can be surmised that nearly 90 per cent of the cattle raids depicting hero-stones lie in what has been designated as the semi-arid zone. The remaining 10 per cent have been discovered in the

transitional strip that acts as a buffer between the semi-arid zone and the massif of the Western Ghats.

2. All the sites are located at a convenient distance from a seasonal water source. Therefore, it may be suggested that the cattle raids took place either while the cattle were being watered, or at the homestead. We will, return to this point in a different context. For the moment, we surmise that there was confrontation amongst the people associated with cattle in the semi-arid zone.
3. We do not come across a single cattle raid depicting hero-stone in the agriculturally rich, fertile areas of the Godavari and Krishna valleys (Sontheimer 1982, 1989). Neither have I found any hero-stones that depict a cattle raid on the west coast. We do, however, come across hero-stones that depict sea battles on the west coast. It may be suggested that cattle-raid stones are not to be found in the so-called perennially nuclear regions. Thus, the cattle-raid stones reflect the ecology of the regions in which they are found. They are markers of an economy characteristic of the semi-arid region.

As against the geographic distribution of cattle-raid memorials, we also need to understand the distribution of land grants in Seuna *desa*, Kuntala *desa*, and in Maval, areas that flank the semi-arid zone to its north, south, and west respectively. This information is shown in Table 2.

From the eighth century AD onwards, there appears to have been a sustained emphasis on land grants in the Seuna *desa*. The momentum, which began in the seventh century AD, was sustained by the Rastrakutas and then by the Yadavas.

Within the Seuna *desa*, the largest number of grants were given in the Godavari river basin, followed by the Pravara basin. We do not find any break in the practice of opening of the agrarian areas or the enlarging of the existing ones within the Seuna *desa*.

In one of the earliest records of the Yadavas, the *mahasamanta* Bhillama II granted land to twenty-one *brahmanas* who lived at Sindinagara, identified with Sinnar (*EI* XI:213ff). This record is dated AD 1000.

The Asvi plates of Airamadeva dated AD 1108 record a grant of a village situated in the Seuna *desa* (*EI* XXXVI:254). This record further states that King Seunacandra I build the city of Seunapura in Simhinera division, now identified with Sinnar in the Sangamner

TABLE 2: LAND GRANTS, SEUNA *DESA*

	Kalacuri	Calukya	Sendrak	Rastrakuta	Yadava
Godavari Basin					
Nasik			4	6	2
Chandwad				3	3
Dindori		1	2	1	2
Sinnar					
Paithan			2		
Waijapur			4		
Gangapur					
Girna Basin					
Malegav				5	
Nandgav			2	1	
Pravara Basin					
Newase					10
Sangamner					8
Rahuri					2
Sahayadri Hills					
Igatpuri		1			
Anjeneri		1			
Satmala Hills					
Baglan		1	7		
Aurangabad				1	7
Ellora				1	
Ahmednagar					3

Sources: *EI*, vols. VIII, XI, XII, XV, XXII, XXV, XXIX, XXXII, XXXVII, *IA*, vols. IX, XI, XII; *SMHD*, vols. 1, 2: PMKL.

taluka of Ahmednagar district. The inscription refers to Candradityapur (Chandor, Nasik district), Dududera (Dudeirar temple: Sangamner), Konachigrama (near the temple, Maniyaraligrama in a Monoti, Sumiyararegrama (Soorve on the Pravara), Vadagavagrama (Wadgaon), and Kapathukugrama (Kavathe Kamlesvare).

All the places lie in the Sangamner taluka of Ahmednagar district. The Seuna *desa* is also referred to by Yadava Mahadev in the Kalegaon grant. The inscription mentions that the king gave a grant of a village, Kalugrama, from his camp on the left bank of the river Godavari flowing in the Seuna *desa* (*EI* XXXII:42).

The Seuna *desa* also figures in the inscriptions issued by Ramacandradeva Yadava. The Paithan plates state that villages Vadathanagrama, Vaidyaghograragrama, and Patulapimapalagram in the Seuna *desa* were donated to 57 brahmanas (*IA* XIV:317).

TABLE 3: KUNTALA *DESA*

	Rastrakuta	Calukya	Silahara	Yadava
Krishna Basin				
Sirol	3		1	
Hathkanangale	4	1	1	
Krishna-Yerala Basin				
Miraj	3	1	2	1
Walve				
Khanapur-Jath Plateau				
Jath				
Kanpur			1	2
			1	
Kolhapur Plateau				
Kagal	1			
Kolhapur	3	3	7	1
Karvir			1	
Gadhinglaj Plateau				
Gadhinglaj	1			
Sangli		3		2

Sources: *EI*, vols. III, IV, XII, XV, XXII, XXIII, XXV, XXVII, XXXIV, XXXVII; *IA*, vol. XVI; *JBBRAS*, vol. III.

Another sustained process of agrarian consolidation occurs in what has been designated as the Kuntala *desa*. The administrative unit of the Kuntala *desa* comprised the area around Kolhapur, Sangli, Miraj, and some area to the south of Karhad *taluka*. It contained the Krishna basin, the Krishna-Yerala basin, the Khanapur Jath plateau, and the Gadhinglaj plateau.

Table 3 lists the distribution of and reference to, the settlements in the Kuntala *desa*.

Out of 48 references to grants in the Kuntala *desa*, it appears that the majority occurred in the period between the ninth to the thirteenth centuries, but again there appears to be no discontinuity in the practice of donating land grants. The Rastrakutas account for almost 38 per cent of the total; the rest are shared largely between the Silaharas and the Yadavas. The settlements seem to be equally divided between the Krishna, the Krishna-Yerala basin, the Khanapur-Joth Plateau, and the Kolhapur plateau. The township of Kolhapur emerges as important urban centre, as referred to in the epigraphic data.

Table 4 refers to the grants given in the transitional strip.

The Maval, the transitional strip that runs between the wetter west

TABLE 4: LAND GRANTS: THE TRANSITIONAL STRIP AND THE EDGE OF THE SEMI-ARID ZONE

	Calukyas	Rastrakuta	Calukya (Kalyani)	Silaharas	Yadavas
Nira Basin					
Sirwal		2	1		
Mula Valley					
Haveli	3	6		1	
Pune	1	1		1	
Krishna Catchment Area					
Wai					
Koregaon		3			
Satara		1			

Sources: *EI*, vols. XIII, XXII, XXV; *IA*, vol. 25.

and the drier east, was also crucial thanks to its strategic location. The important trading centres of Karhad and Junnar flanked Maval in the south and the north. It appears that from the sixth to almost the twelfth century, land grants were given in this geographically transitional strip.

Apart from these three units, a brief consideration of the northern and north-eastern side, comprising the Ambe *desa* and their subunits, is required. As Table 5 indicates, the Rastrakutas and especially the Yadavas were keen to explore the possibilities of expansion and consolidation on the eastern side. We will deal with this point more substantially when we take up the Yadava pattern of expansion.

On the basis of the analysis of the epigraphic data presented in Table 5, I suggest the following points for consideration:

1. There appears to have been a steady expansion of settlements in the Seuna, Kuntala, and Ambe regions (especially after the ninth and the tenth centuries). This can be ascertained from the clusters of settlements that emerged in these areas.
2. This phase of steady pressure was by and large applied by the Rastrakutas and later, and more vigorously, by the Yadavas. The Silahara dynasty of Kolhapur also maintained the pressure.
3. It appears that there were geographic shifts in terms of dynastic preferences for certain areas, which is clearly visible in the area of the Seuna *desa*. The Yadavas opened up a completely new area in Ahmednagar, and, as we will later see, in the semi-arid zone. Could

TABLE 5: LAND GRANTS: EASTERN AREA

	Vakataka	Rastrakuta	Calukya	Yadava
Manjra Basin and Usmanabad Plateau				
Nilanga			3	
Usmanabad				3
Manjra Basin				
Latur			1	1
Umbarage Plateau				
Umbarage			1	
Ahmadapur Plateau				
Udgir				5
Godavari Basin				
Nanded	2	2	1	3
Akola-Amaravati				
Purna Basin				
Achalpur	2			
Amravati	2			
Akola Plain				
Akola	2			
Chandur Plateau				
Chandur		1		
Penganga Valley				
Washim	1	7		2
Purna Valley				
Bhir		8		
Sindphana Basin				
Bir		5	3	2
Manjra Basin				
Ambe				2
Kuntala				2

Sources: *EI*, vols. XV, XXVII, XXXVII; *SMHD*, vols. 1, 2 3; *PMKL*, vols. 20; *Karnataka Ins.*, vol. 2.

it be that fresh areas were brought under cultivation to increase revenue earnings?

Against this background, let us now consider how land grants were made within the semi-arid zone itself. We do not find significant numbers of land grants within it. In fact, they appear to have come to a halt in the eighth century (Table 4). Between the eighth and the thirteenth centuries, we do not find a single major land grant in the semi-arid zone. There are, however, two minor and one major sacred complexes at Pulunj Velapur, and Pandharpur.

As the pattern reveals, the semi-arid zone emerges, despite its lack of significant land grants, as an important unit. We need to understand the pattern of Yadava expansion to comprehend the constellation of settlements in the various administrative zones.

The early history of the Yadavas suggests that the family secured a toehold in the Nasik district or what has been termed as the Seuna *desa*. The Bassein grant describes Dridhaprahara as being so powerful that he broke the heads of the foot soldiers and the elephants of his enemies (*IA* XI:121). Seunacandra, the local Yadava chieftain, founded a city after his name, now identified with Sinnar in the Nasik district (*IA* XII: 1212). The next significant development in the fortunes of the local chieftain's family occurred when it transferred its loyalty to the Calukyas of Kalyani. The district of Ahmednagar came under the influence of the Yadavas and their control over the Seuna *desa* was now consolidated. In the Sangamner copper plates, Bhillama II is referred to as *mahasamanta*, which indicates that the Yadavas had not yet attained the status of royalty, but had gone up a few notches in the social and political hierarchy.

The next phase of expansion came in the eleventh century, when Seunacandra II, taking advantage of an uncertain political situation, brought Khandesh under his influence (*EI* XI:221-8). Seunacandra is referred to as *mahamandalesvara* in the Bassein grant (*IA* XII:124), indicating that the feudatory status of the Yadavas remained unchanged. The Bassein grant also refers to several high-ranking officers of the Yadavas. The grant indicates that the Yadavas were very well entrenched in the Nasik, Khandesh, and Ahmednagar regions.

There followed a succession of kings in the period after Seunacandra's death and the reign of Bhillama V without any significant change in the area governed (*EI* XXXVI:126-9). It appears that Seunacandra III belonged to the collateral branch of the Yadavas because Hemadri, the Yadava minister and scholar, does not mention him.

At the time of the accession of Bhillama V, there was a political vacuum in the Deccan and this vacuum was fully exploited by the Yadavas. Bhillama first acquired for himself a footing in the Konkan. Hemadri mentions that Bhillama captured Srivardhan, Torana, and Bhor and then moved south-east to capture Mangalwedha. The

Muttage inscription gives a fair account of the areas conquered by Bhillama: 'He was a severe pain in the head of Malvas, a thunderbolt to the mountain, a lion to those elephants, the Kalingas, the dread roar of a cloud to the flocks of those swans, the Gurjaras, Colas, and Pancalas; a Kala to the brilliant kings of Anga, Vanga and Nepala' (*EI* XV:37). In spite of the great exaggeration, especially the mention of Anga, Vanga, and Nepala, the reference to the Gurajaras and to Malwa in this record is significant. It does appear that the Yadavas raided to the west and the north of their territory.

Jaitugi consolidated the Yadava hold over the Bijapur area and also 'put an end to the pleasure of the beloved ones of the distressed ladies of Andhra' (*EI* XXXII:33). Jaitugi also claimed to have conquered the Gurjaras, the Pandyas, the Colas, and the country of Lata and Gouda (*EI* V:28-31). However, those conquests were no more than raids on the provinces of the Gurjaras, the Latas and the Malwas. Singhana conquered Banavasi in 1200 from the Hoysalas, and thus finally consolidated Yadava hold on the south (*IA* II:297). The Silahara principality of Kolhapur was finally annexed to the Yadava domain (*PSOCI* II:112; *Karnataka Ins.* II:416) by Singhana. Singhana also launched campaigns in Gujarat, and against the Kakatiyas. The find-spots of Singhana's inscriptions are spread over the Lata, Konkan, Vidharbha, Mysore, and the Andhra *desa*. Singhana thus effectively transferred the domain into an empire, the core of which lay in the Godavari valley. We may note the following points based on the Yadava pattern of expansion of their kingdom.

1. The Yadava state first gained a foothold in the region around Sinnar, as the Bassein grant indicates.
2. The expansion then moved towards the semi-arid zone, with Ahmednagar district coming under Yadava influence in the next phase.
3. They next touched the 'Gavli country', as Khandesh is known to have been dominated by the Abhirs. In fact, we find that as late as the thirteenth century the Yadava state engaged in a deadly duel with the 'Gaula Kings' of Khandesh. The Purshottampuri plates of Ramacandra Deva Yadava issued in the year AD 1310 mentions that his army almost exterminated the Abhira *desa* (*EI* XXV:202). The same inscription states that Ramacandra Yadava defeated with 'ease the mighty lord of the extensive Dahala country, subjugated

the ruler of Bhandgavi, dethroned the king Vajrakara and defeated in battles the prince of Cowherds' (ibid.:206).

In the next phase of expansion the Yadava state took control of the access to the west coast and tried to secure a toehold in the strategic Banavasi country in order to profit from the trade network. In its last phase of expansion, the Yadav state made forays into Gujarat and Malwa, both again with a view to influencing important trade routes. The expansion pattern of the Yadavas is revealing. It appears as if the Yadavas were securing the flanks of the semi-arid zone and were thus insulating the latter from all sides. Against this background of the expansionist pattern, we are now in a better position to contextualize the cattle-raid hero-stone *vis-à-vis* the epigraphic evidence available.

1. As has been noted elsewhere, in the semi-arid zone the majority of the grants were assigned to temples, mainly at Pandharpur, but also at Pulunj and at Velapur in the Solapur district, in the heart of the semi-arid zone. The grants were made in the late twelfth and the early thirteenth centuries AD at all the three places. The Yadava phase of expansion, interestingly, comes to an end at about the same time (late twelfth century).
2. Almost all the hero-stones that depict cattle raids are found in the semi-arid zone and precisely in that area which is largely untouched by land grants. The question thus is: what is the meaning of the cattle-raid hero-stones for this area? In other words, is the Yadava kingdom, whose rulers probably came from the semi-arid zone, giving a kind of special status to that area and making temple grants there in a quest for legitimacy (especially at Pandharpur).[2]
3. Lastly, the nature of the hero-stones itself is problematic. While found in econiches conducive to *sheep* rearing, the evidence of the stones points to a valorization of *cattle* as the prized animals. Can we assume that cattle rearing gave way to sheep herding in the late medieval period? One could be audacious and suggest that multiple

[2] This was then emulated, between AD 1270 and 1304, by other chiefs and notables of the surrounding area. All known ruling lineages that called themselves 'Yadava' seem to have made donations at Pandharpur.

cattle-raid memorials reflect a period when cattle pastoralism was under threat, and, that perhaps because of the disappearance of the gallery forests (Malhotra and Gadgil 1984:441-58). But we need to look for better answers to these questions.

There is yet another point relevant to this epigraphic evidence that we need to consider. A large number of sites in the Deccan have been explored and excavated. In our region, the sites that have been explored and excavated belong to western Maharashtra, Vidharbha, and Marathawada. In an incisive study Mate pointed out a strange feature. 'All the sites that have been explored and excavated reveal a significant gap in occupation. Many of the sites go back to the chalcolithic phase assigned to the 15th-14th centuries AD and have debris coming down to the 18th century AD—but with a wide gap of seven to eight centuries between the 5th and the 13th centuries AD' (Mate 1990:247). It is this period that saw the flourishing of the famous dynasties of the Deccan: The Calukyas, the Rastrakutas, and the Yadavas of Devagiri. Varma too (this volume) has cited a similar lacuna in Kathiawar, where she reports a hiatus in occupation of 600 years between the chalcolithic and the early historical periods. She attributes this hiatus to the process of the formation of a mound. She primarily discusses this 'absence' of the mound in terms of the land use strategy and against the backdrop of the larger social and political context. It is clear that we cannot even begin to understand the so-called gap before we contextualize it within a larger framework of analysis. The issue then before us is more complicated. Did the Rastrakutas and the Yadavas exist as actual 'states' or were they the kingdoms of warring pastoral chiefs? What kind of resource mobilization strategy did they adopt? What role did cattle pastoralism and cattle raids play in resource mobilization and in the state formation processes? We are reminded of the thesis of Gurukkal (1998:252-6) concerning the 'redistributive' role of raiding chiefs in early Tamil society. Skaria (1998:201) too, though for a different society, finds that among the Bhils of the early nineteenth century, 'Being a raja . . . involved raiding in order to create the resources to distribute amongst followers.'

In the first section I have argued for the centrality of pastoral systems in the region under discussion. I now contend that to understand the contrast provided by the archaeological and epigraphic evidence we will have to break the shackles of the dominant paradigm that assigns a prominent place to the 'nuclear region'. One of the major reasons why the archaeological debris of towns and villages is almost non-existent might be the dominance of a pastoral system (see Varma, this volume). This is not to deny a role to agrarian structures, but rather to argue for a more balanced approach and offset it with other rural processes. We can then modify the centre-periphery argument in favour of pastoralism. Such a reversal is supported by the evidence cited above. Such a reversal also questions the primacy assigned to the dominant paradigm of state formation. That paradigm, one may recall, assigns state origins to the so-called nuclear, rich, and flourishing agricultural river valley and its 'surplus' production.

This paper raises more questions than it answers. However, it does make a plea for a change in the perspective for the region under discussion.

REFERENCES

Allchin, F.R., *Neolithic Cattle-keepers of South India: A Study of the Deccan Ashmounds*, Cambridge: Cambridge University Press, 1963.

Bhan, K.K., 'Late Harappan Settlements in Western India', in J.M. Kenoyer, ed., *Old Problems and New Perspectives in the Archaeology of South Asia*, Madison: Wisconsin Archaeology Reports, vol. 2, 1989.

Bhatt, B.L., 'India and Indian Regions: A Critical Overview', in David Sopher, ed., *An Exploration of India*, Ithaca: Cornell University Press, 1980, pp. 35-64.

Cohn, B. S., 'Regions, Subjective and Objective: Their Relations to the Study of Modern Indian History and Society', in R.I. Crane, ed., *Regions and Regionalism in South Asian Studies*, Durham: Duke University Monograph No. 5, 1967, pp. 5-37.

Deshpande, C.D., *Geography of Maharashtra*, New Delhi: National Book Trust, 1971.

Dhavalikar, M.K., *First Farmers of Deccan*, Pune: Ravish, 1988.

Fleet, J.F., 'Sanskrit and Old Canarese Inscriptions', *Indian Antiquary*, vol. 14, 1885, pp. 315-19.

Gai, G. S., 'Asvi Plates of Yadava Arramadeva', *Epigraphica Indica*, vol. 26, 1936, pp. 249-56.

Guha, Sumit, 'Some Aspects of Agricultural Growth in Nineteenth Century India', *Studies in History*, vol. 4, no. 1, 1982, pp. 58-86.

Gurukkal, R., 'The Beginnings of the Historic Period: The Tamil South', in

Romila Thapar, ed., *Recent Perspectives of Earth, Indian History*, Bombay, 1st Paperback ed., 1998, pp. 237-65.

Indian Archaeology—A Review (*IAR*)

Indraji, B.L., 'A New Yadava Dynasty', *Indian Antiquary*, vol. 12, 1883, pp. 117-26.

Jha, D.N., 'The Economic History of India upto AD 1200: Trends and Prospects', in R.S. Sharma, ed., *Survey of Research in Economic and Social History of India*, New Delhi, 1986. pp. 1-40.

Joshi, Bapu P. (ed.), *Selections from the Satara Raja and the Peshwa Diaries, Peshwa Madhavarao I*, Pune: Deccan Vernacular Press, 1911.

Leshnik, L.S., 'Pastoral Nomadism in the Archaeology of India and Pakistan', *World Archaeology*, vol. 4, 1972, pp. 150-66.

Leshnik, L.S. and G.D. Sontheimer (eds.), *Nomads and Pastoralists in South Asia*, Wiesbaden: Otto Harrassowitz, 1975.

Malhotra, Kailash and Madhav Gadgil, 'The Ecological Basis of the Geographical Distribution', in J. R. Lukacs, ed., *The People of South Asia*, New York: Plenum Press, 1984, pp. 295-324.

Malik, S.C., *Indian Civilisation: The Formative Period*, Simla: Indian Institute of Advanced Studies, 1968.

Mate, M.S. 'The Clay Feet?', *Bulletin of the Deccan College Post-Graduate and Research Institute*, vol. 49, 1990, pp. 243-9.

Misra, R. and Ramchandran, 'Quantitative Methods in Indian Geography', *Survey of Research in Geography*, Bombay: ICSSR, 1972, pp. 313-23.

Murty, M.L.K. and G.D. Sontheimer, 'Prehistoric Background to Pastoralism in the Southern Deccan in the Light of Oral Traditions and Cults of Some Pastoral Communities', *Anthropos*, vol. 73, 1980, pp. 163-83.

Parasnis, D.B., *Selections from the Satara Raja's and Peshwai's Diaries*, Deccan Vernacular Press, vol. I, 1907.

Ratnagar, S.F., 'Pastoralists in the Prehistory of Baluchistan', *Studies in History*, vol. 3, 1987, pp. 135-54.

_____, 'Pastoralism as an Issue in Historical Research', *Studies in History* (n.s.), vol. 7, no. 2, 1991, pp. 181-93.

Schwartzsberg, J.E., 'Prolegomena to the study of South Asian Regions and Regionalism', in R.I. Crane, ed., *Regions and Regionalism in South Asian Studies*, Duke University monograph, 1967, pp. 89-111.

Settar, S., 'Memorial Stones in South India', in S. Settar and G.D. Sontheimer, eds., *Memorial Stones*, Dharwar: South Asia Institute, 1982, pp. 183-97.

Settar, S. and Sontheimer, G.D., *Memorial Stones*, Heidelberg: South Asia Institute, 1982.

Sharma, R.S., *Indian Feudalism, c. 300-1200*, Calcutta, University of Calcutta, 1965.

_____, *Urban Decay in India 300-1000*, New Delhi, Munshiram Manoharlal, 1987.

Singh, R.L., *India: A Regional Geography*, Varanasi: National Geographical Society of India, 1971.

Skaria, Ajay, 'Being Jungli: The Politics of Wildness', *Studies in History*,14 vols., no. 2, 1998, pp. 193-215.

Sontheimer, G.D., 'The Dhangars', in L.S. Leshnik and G.D. Sontheimer, eds., *Nomads and Pastoralists in South Asia*, Wiesbaden: Otto Harrassowitz, 1975, pp. 139-170.

_____, 'King Vikram and Kamlu Sinde: The Shepherd Bhakti Episodes from an Oral Epic of the Dhangars of Maharashtra',. *South Asian Digest of Regional Writing*, vol. 6, 1977, pp. 97-128.

_____, 'Hero and Sati Stones of Maharashtra', in S. Settar and G.D. Sontheimer, eds., *Memorial Stones*, Dharwar: South Asia Institute, 1982, pp. 261-81.

_____, 'Folk Deities in the Vijayanagara Empire: Narsimha and Mallanna/Mailar', in A. Dallapiccola, ed., in collaboration with S. Zingel - Ave Lallemant, *Vijayanagar—City and Empire, New Currents of Research*, Wiesbaden: South Asia Institute, 1985, pp. 145-58.

_____, 'Rudra and Khandoba: Continuity in Folk Religion', in Milton Israel and N.K. Wagle, eds., *Religion and Society* in *Maharashtra*, Toronto: University of Toronto, 1987, pp. 1-31.

_____, *Pastoral Deities of Western India*, tr. Anne Feldhaus, New York: Oxford University Press, 1989.

Sopher, David, 'The Geographic Patterning of Culture in India', in David Sopher, ed., *An Exploration of India*, New York: Ithaca, 1980, pp. 289-327.

Spate, O.H.K and A.T.A. Learmonth, *India and Pakistan: A General and Regional Geography* (3rd revd. edn.), London: Methuen, 1967.

Stein, Burton, 'Comments on Bernard Cohn's Paper', in R.I. Crane, ed., *Regions and Regionalism*, Durham: Duke University Monograph No. 5, 1967, pp. 41-70.

_____, 'The Segmentary State in South Indian History', in R.G. Fox, ed., *Realm and Region in Traditional India*, Durham: Duke University Monograph, No. 14, 1977, pp. 3-51.

_____, *Peasant State and Society in Medieval South India*, Oxford University Press, Delhi: 1980.

Subbarao, B., 'Regions and Regionalism in India', *Economic Weekly*, vol. 10, 1958, pp. 1215-20.

Thapar, Romila, 'Death and the Hero', in R. Thapar, *Cultural Pasts*, Delhi: Oxford University Press, 2000, pp. 680-95.

_____, 'Death and the Hero', in S.C. Humphrys and H. King, ed., *Mortality and Immortality: Anthropology and Archaeology of Delhi*, London, 1981, pp. 291-313.

Tulpule, S.G., *Pracin Marathi Koriv Lekh*, Pune: Pune University, 1963.

Yadav, B.N.S., *Society and Culture in North India in the Twelfth Century*, Allahabad, 1973.

Mobility and Craft Production

JAYA MENON

> Despite their repeated efforts and the diversity of methods adopted to do this, nomads never managed to organize handicraft production in a proper quantity and of a proper quality in their own society.
>
> KHAZANOV 1983:202–3

> The chance to develop more elaborate and specialized technologies, which may be prohibitively expensive for a mobile group because of transportation difficulties, may also provide a marked selective advantage to sedentary groups. RAFFERTY 1984:118

> Handicrafts and the beginnings of industry, as well as internal exchange of commodities, were much more weakly developed in the steppe than in China. The Mongol smith, for instance, could move easily to the supply of ore and easily carry away with him enough to keep him employed on a very small scale. He could not, however, settle down at the source of supply of his raw material to develop his craft on a larger scale without detaching himself from his society. Nor could he without settling near the supply of raw materials, employ apprentices or workmen for production on a larger scale. He never even became an itinerant professional artisan but remained an owner of livestock and a normal member of a pastoral society. LATTIMORE 1988:69–70

> Also associated with permanent settlement were a series of new crafts involving important technological discoveries. Among these were the manufacture and use of pottery . . . and the discovery of the smelting of copper and its alloys. ALLCHIN AND ALLCHIN 1981:99

The epigraphs above express the common understanding that full-fledged craft production can only be practised by sedentary populations. The reasons are various: the immovable nature of facilities

* I would like to thank Rudolf Heredia and Ajay Dandekar for inviting me for the workshop. I am indebted to Shereen Ratnagar for the extensive discussions centred on the paper. Many thanks to the participants of the workshop, particularly to Supriya Varma and R. Champakalakshmi.

such as pottery kilns, dye vats, and furnaces; the time required for technological processes to develop and evolve; and necessary interaction with the clientele. Moreover, increasing specialization and the ensuing separation of craft processes (such as the dyeing, weaving, and printing of cloth) require interaction with other craftsmen. The question then arises: has craft production in history been limited to sedentary peoples?

The answer is in the negative. In fact, there is in the modern context a definite 'peripatetic niche' which revolves around craft production. This niche has been observed in Africa, South Asia, and Europe. Bollig (1987:209), in the context of Africa, notes that 'this niche exists due to the interaction between a whole lot of service jobs determined by the dominant mode of production, the complex social environment and the techniques the strangers, to whom these odd and despised jobs are left, employ'. Yet, the peripatetic niche in question is part of a market system, in which mobile people seek out customers with purchasing power (Rao 1987:2).[1] Braudel (1982: 307-8), in fact, had noted that rural and urban artisans in France were, before the industrial age, 'the most mobile sector of the population', a situation necessitated by the spasmodic and episodic character of production, demand, and wages. Thus, while it may be advantageous for craftsmen to be sedentary, there may be other compulsions that require mobility.

Today we have numerous examples of artisans who frequently move, and it appears that the absence of sustained demand in one place is the main reason. Moreover, the modern context is also one of extreme specialization, where different occupations find their separate niches. But to what extent can we expect the situation to have been different in the past? And if, in the past, craftsmen did move, what were the conditions under which they did so?

The attempt in this paper is to understand the connections between mobility and craft production, writing from the perspective of one who has specialized in archaeology, specifically the rich and varied craft production of an early civilization. Obviously this is not a theme that can be explored with archaeological data alone.

[1] Such modern-day peripatetic groups are largely non-food producing, traditionally itinerant, usually endogamous, and dependent on the host population (Rao 1982:124-5).

Archaeologists cannot escape taking recourse to historical information and ethnographic data. Moreover, the latter are so sparse, and, where India is concerned, so rooted in 'the Indian tradition' paradigm that the social and economic variables become hard to isolate. In this paper, I shall take into account factors such as the role and status of craftsmen, the social contexts within which they worked, and the degree and range of their movements in order to throw light on equipment, techniques, the quality of output, and the range of crafts observed among craft producers who are mobile. Thus, in order to explicate the patterns we need to undertake a cross-cultural survey.

In our analysis, we distinguish between groups which are mobile as hunter-gatherers or pastoralists from those whose mobility is primarily for the purposes of production and the exchange of their crafts (see Figure 1).

Occasional or Episodic Movements

One part of Figure 1 deals with episodic or occasional movements of craftsmen, which we shall consider briefly as it does not form the centre of our discussion. Craftsmen's movements could take place for various reasons such as the dictates of a state or other authority. Zaccagnini (1983:253) opines for Bronze Age western Asia that 'gifts and artisans are on the same level: specialists are considered gifts and

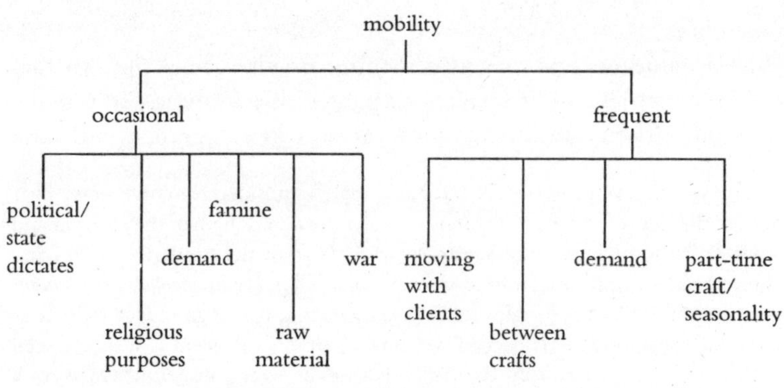

FIGURE 1: THE RELATIONSHIP BETWEEN MOBILITY AND CRAFT PRODUCTION.

are requested, refused and despatched like gifts. In addition to their actual professional function, they are an important means for maintaining peaceful international relations between foreign courts.' Similarly, in the Inka empire, specialist smiths were shifted to separate administrative settlements, to work for the rulers. Their output was utilized by the state for its own purposes (Earle 1987:74). In the same way, weavers were recruited from local communities to form specialist villages (Earle 1987:72). These are cases of 'attached specialization' where goods and techniques were developed for elite consumption. The context was newly emerged states with relatively large palace or temple or elite sectors of production and wealth distribution.

This pattern did not die out altogether after the period of the earliest states. There is a historical tradition that in the second century, Vima Kadphises, the Kushana ruler, brought craftsmen from Ujjayini to Bactria (Harmatta 1994:425-7). Russell and Hiralal (1916 [1975]: 359) record a Telugu caste of weavers who were brought from Orissa by the Raja of Sonpur to make clothes for the images of deities. Similarly, the movement of *patola* weavers has been seen in the light of royal diktats.[2] Bühler and Fischer (1979:326) note that 'if one considers how often small and large dynasties changed in India, how often rulers' courts were consequently given up and new ones founded, how new commercial centres were also called into being, then it seems reasonable to conclude that the spread and migrations of silk weavers were very largely due to such eventful political occurrences'.

In the same context, we may mention medieval inscriptions that refer to the settlement of weavers, carpenters, blacksmiths, and potters, along with their families, in new areas often together with the

[2] The weaving of *patola* in Gujarat has initiated considerable controversy over whether the weavers were indigenous to the area or whether they originated elsewhere. To some extent, the controversy arises from the similarity in weaving techniques. Thus, according to traditions maintained in Patan, *patola* weavers were brought from the Marwar region of Rajasthan during the reign of Kumarapala in the twelfth century. The transfer of weaving traditions to Orissa is similarly seen as a dispersal of weavers from the Delhi-Rajasthan area, a dispersal which took place probably because of the movement of the patrons themselves (Mehta 1961). Jain sources refer to silk weavers at Patan as having come from the regions of Deogiri and Paithan (Bühler and Fischer 1979:329).

establishment of new villages (Ramaswamy 1985:34, 36, 40; Sharma 1965:135). These have to be seen as shifts of population rather than as periodic movements. Also they took place at the behest of the state or the temple.

Persecution too resulted in the resettling of population. Craftsmen's origin myths often maintain records of movement from one area to another (sometimes over great distances and over a long period) due to military raids or depredations. Examples in the medieval period are of the cotton printers of Sanganer near Jaipur (Irwin and Hall 1971:111) and of the 'Saurashtras' or Pattavayaka or Pattunulkarar in Tamil Nadu (Dave 1976: 18; Ramaswamy 1985:151).

Inscriptions record the flight of craftsmen when oppressed, their action seen as a form of protest. There are references to a reduction of taxes to lure back craftsmen who had fled in protest.[3] Ahuja (1998: 403) notes for the early colonial period that flight or 'collective withdrawal' served to express social contradictions as long as patron-client relationships held, but increasing commercialization brought forth a more disintegrative aspect to movement. Obviously, oppression could have both a temporary and a permanent impact on the movements of craftsmen. It is also possible that such shifts occurred for more than one reason: there was war, for instance. Timur uprooted from Damascus weavers of silk and makers of bows, glass, and earthenware; from Turkey, he took away archers, masons, silversmiths, and men who knew how to make war machines (Markham 1859: 171). Similarly, the Chin Tartars could demand specialized craftsmen such as goldsmiths, silversmiths, blacksmiths, weavers, and tailors from the Sung capital at Khaifeng on besieging it (Needham 1965:20).

There are also references to the movement of craftsmen where no reasons are given for their mobility. An oft-quoted example is of the Mandasore Stone Inscription of Kumaragupta and Bandhuvarman (Fleet 1887 [1970]:79-81). The inscription refers to a guild of silk weavers having built and later contributed to the repair of a temple at a place called Dasapura (modern Mandasore) in western Malwa. The history of the community is recorded as that of a group which

[3] Ramaswamy notes that during the period of the Hoysala Ramanathadeva in 1277, the Dandanayaka Ravideva made a report that the weavers of Kandaradittam in Tiruchirapalli had emigrated owing to high taxation; on the basis of the report, the king reduced the taxes.

had migrated from the Lata *vishaya*, central and south Gujarat. This was clearly a permanent shift.

Occasional movements are also known to take place for purposes of obtaining raw materials, or to exploit seasonally available resources. While it is generally accepted that attached specialists can rely on raw materials procured by elites from great distances, it is expected that independent specialists work on raw materials available in their vicinity. Yet this simplistic assumption may not always hold, as, for example, where Rye and Evans (1976:127) found that a potter in the Chitral Valley, Pakistan, who used a distant clay source, and travelled a full day to get it. The Inadan of Niger annually trek in small groups to soapstone mines where they make objects such as arm rings out of soapstone (Kirtley and Kirtley 1979:293). Their reluctance to allow others to participate in their craft skills may be one of the reasons why they collect the required raw material themselves.

Natural calamities such as famine or drought may also result in the emigration of craftsmen. They may or may not come back to their original home. Bühler and Fischer (1979:326) refer to migration as a result of catastrophic famines such as the one in Gujarat in 1630-2. Weavers of Salem, Coimbatore, and Madurai moved into Tiruchirappali and Thanjavur to escape famine (Arnold 1984:100). Migration as a reaction to natural disasters, a reaction involving not only artisans but also agriculturists, probably did not result in itinerancy.

Early historic inscriptions illustrate the movement of craftsmen for other reasons. At Karle in Maharashtra, an inscription (Burgess and Indraji 1881 [1976]:30; Lüders 1912:117) refers to a carpenter from Dhenukakata (now Dharanikota, near Amaravati) who made the doorway. Misra (1975:16) makes note of inscriptions at Sanchi (in Madhya Pradesh) which record the work of artisans from Ujjayini (modern Ujjain), Varanasi, and from the Maharashtra region. Yet, even if we acknowledge the initiative of contemporary rulers in attracting craftsmen to work on large monuments, the language of the inscriptions seems to indicate otherwise. It appears that the craftsmen in question themselves wanted to be recognized for their work. Such feelings may have arisen from the piety that was associated with such work. In that case, it is surely significant that craftsmen had the social ability to choose to move, and to work wherever they wished.

Historical Patterns in the Migration of Craft Producers

A few historical patterns are discernible in the type of movements that we have discussed. Craftsmen in the Bronze Age moved according to the instructions and needs of ruling elites. The production of luxuries for a small ruling class and the need for imported copper or bronze for craft tools made for elite control over the procurement and distribution of raw materials, the production of tools, and the dispersal of produce. So too the movements of craft producers would have been controlled by ruling elites. As we shall see below, powerful nomad chiefs had specialist craftsmen attached to them.

The early historic period saw the introduction of coinage which presumably resulted in the spread of retailing as an exchange mechanism amongst strangers. There were expanding networks of trade. In such conditions, along with the exchange of luxuries and utilitarian goods, we could tentatively also envisage the movement of craftsmen. Inscriptions mentioning craftsmen who worked at the sites of religious monuments (as for example Sanchi) may indicate that these craftsmen were invited or that they came of their own accord. In the early medieval period, a number of inscriptions refer to grants of land being made to craftsmen. This has been taken by Sharma (1987: 166) to indicate spatial and occupational immobility, with the tying down of artisans to the land and the cementing of *jajmani* relations. In this period, the resettling of craftsmen took place mostly with state/temple patronage as a corollary to the establishment of new villages.

Some of the medieval period movements were at the behest of the state; Mughal *karkhanas* (especially during Akbar's reign) testify to the settling of skilful master craftsmen and workmen from outside the subcontinent (Blochmann 1977). Imperial workshops or *karkhanas* were replicated at local levels by nobles (Swaroop 1996:12). In the same period, local or rural manufacturing saw the juxtaposition of *jajmani* relations and production for the market, where one of the major reasons for the continuance of the system was the safety net it provided. (It was noted that those weavers who had moved into production for the market were totally devastated by the 1630s famine in the Surat area [Raychaudhuri 1982:179-80].)

In the eighteenth century, 'the development of new kinds of regional kingdoms, the strengthening of mercantile capitalism, the growing significance of external commerce and the rise of the East India Company may have stimulated an acceleration of movement by weavers' (Haynes and Roy 1999:66). This is symptomatic as by now we find many references to the mobility of textile producers; the Coromandel weaver was particularly mobile, needing, it was claimed, little more than a shady tree under which to work (Irwin and Schwartz 1966:31-2; Ludden 1988:106; Ramaswamy 1985: 120-1). Thurston (1909 [1975]:96) similarly refers to the Devanga weaver in the Nilgiris who came with his portable hand loom and sufficient thread for weaving cloth and turbans. State patronage continued with the Marathas such as Rani Ahilyabai Holkar who encouraged the establishment of new trading centres to which weavers were brought (M.W. Burway cf. Gordon 1994:179; Jaitly 1990:57). The Maratha rulers often preferred living in camps and tents which were veritable cities on the move; craftsmen such as goldsmiths, carpenters, tailors, farriers, silversmiths, ironsmiths, and coppersmiths and their families formed an integral part of these settlements (J. Forbes cf. Gillion 1968:33). We may also note that in this period, artisan mobility primarily refers to the movement of weavers. Rarely do we hear of other craftsmen in the same context.

Craft Production by Mobile Groups

In Figure 1, we have distinguished a level of mobility as repetitive or rhythmic. From the point of view of this paper, this is more significant than episodic mobility. We have noted that mobility may impose certain constraints on craft production. Yet, craft work can be done while on the move.

I find that only certain kinds of crafts are practised by groups whose mobility is integral to their subsistence pursuits. These crafts tend to revolve around raw materials to which nomadic peoples have ready access, as, for example, animal skin for leather and, wool for carpet weaving and cloth. Many pastoralists use the skins of slaughtered animals turned inside out as storage bags for water, sour milk, and buttermilk. Goatskins are used as small containers for butter. Tanning is a pastoralist craft.[4] Camel pastoralists are known to make

[4] See also Beck's (1991) interesting description of the treatment of animal skins for making containers and water bags.

vessels from camel hides. Some amount of woodworking also seems to have been done by nomads. Simple utilitarian objects of wood, such as tent poles and pegs, wooden hooks and loops (Barth 1964:9), or stone mills for grinding flour (Musil 1928:91) were produced by nomads for their own use. Wool is made by the Basseri into felt, while sheep's wool and camel hair are also sold or spun and woven. Goat hair is used in a similar fashion (ibid:8). Spinning of camel or goat hair is commonly practised among pastoralists on the move, by both men and women (Musil 1928:67; Beck 1991:65; Rangnekar 1993:31). Embroidery too is a craft 'rooted in the pastoral and herding traditions' (Jaitly 1990:69).

One of the assumptions made about pastoralists is that such groups would necessarily have to limit the quantity of their material possessions, which would be a burden on their movement. Thus, it is understood that crafts which need heavy or bulky implements are not practised. We know, however, that pastoralists do carry certain heavy implements with them. The best instance is provided by the weaving of carpets and cloth among pastoralist nomads across western Asia. This is a craft judged to probably have nomadic origins. Of utilitarian value in the tent, the carpet also came to be a work of art, to have high market value, and also to have symbolic association with the tribe in question who manufactured it.

Ethnographies indicate that the typical loom used by nomads is a horizontal one which can be staked to the ground or be supported by side pieces on the ground (Crowfoot 1954:425; Musil 1928: Figure 10; Wulff 1966:199-201). Its advantage lies in that it can be easily assembled and dismantled while on the move (Siudmak 1977:12; Wulff 1966: 199). It appears that sedentary weavers in contrast tend to use the vertical loom as it is more comfortable to operate (Siudmak 1977), but it is not portable.[5] The horizontal loom was also well suited to work in the open air (Hodges 1970:151-2), though weaving was also done within the tent (Masson 1843:440). Coon (1951:214) notes

[5] The vertical loom also took less space in a weaver's house. However, one must keep in mind the fact that in the Indian subcontinent, apart from the north-east, hand-loom weavers have traditionally preferred to use horizontal looms. A survey of weaving (Sruti 1995:36) has shown that often weaver families had no course but to sleep under the looms. But the carpet loom used by the sedentary weaver is inevitably a vertical one.

that nomadic tribes in the Atlas Mountains used horizontal looms that were built into the framework of the supporting poles of their tents. Moreover, Cribb (1991) also found that Yoruk pastoralists used a loom consisting of three heavy wooden beams. Similarly, the Alikanli in Nemrut Dag in Eastern Anatolia (ibid.:70) used a wooden comb for wool, and a loom and spindle. Here, Cribb (1991:210) also noted piles of unprocessed wool outside nomad tents; many women were involved in beating, spinning, and dyeing woollen yarn inside the tents. In Baluchistan, Masson (1843:440) found that the colouring of yarn with madder, indigo, turmeric, and other materials was done in the tents of pastoralists.

Many of the craft products made by pastoralists appear to have been made for their own use. Barth (1964:9) emphasizes that none of the articles made by the Basseri (leather bags, woollen cloth, goat- and camel-hair rope, woven saddlebags, packbags, sacks, carpets, and wooden articles) were produced for sale. Yet, we know that weavings by semi-nomadic Turkoman tribes near large cities such as Merv, Pendeh, and Khiva were produced for barter (Bennett 1977:158). Perhaps, originally such objects were manufactured for the nomads' own use, but gradually incorporation into a wider economy would have seen their products used also for exchange.

So far, we have considered the crafts of mobile animal herders. These groups do not move for craft purposes. Whatever crafts they practise are incidental to their primary activities and are designed for home consumption. It also appears that when craft production is undertaken, such groups practise all stages of the craft process.

The needed craft items are not all made by pastoralists themselves. An important analytic division in Figure 1 relates to the mobility of craftsmen who accompany pastoralist clients. Specialized craftsmen groups such as blacksmiths with the Rwala Bedouin (Musil 1928: 281-2) or the Inadan who accompany the Tuareg in Niger in Africa (Casajus 1987; Kirtley and Kirtley 1979) are peripatetic because their pastoral clients are. Among the Sunnas (smiths), a family would attach itself to each noble tribe and act as farriers, swordsmiths, and gunsmiths (Coon 1951:200). We could give many more such examples, but the important point is that the craft makers mentioned above do not independently have a mobile existence. William and Fidelity Lancaster (1987:314) mention smiths in precisely this context. They were peripatetic only insofar as 'they lived, worked and migrated with their Bedu protector'. The multi-animal pastoralists of Central Asia are an extreme example of this.

Khazanov (1983:225-6) found that the pastoralists of Central Asia (they moved in large groups and with several species of animals, were formidable military forces, and had powerful chiefs) preferred to create handicraft and agricultural sectors in their economy. They did so by moving craftsmen and agriculturists from their settlements into nomad territories or by using captured slaves in such a capacity. Writing about the steppes of Mongolia in the seventeenth and eighteenth centuries, Lattimore (1988:92-3) argues the nomad economy ceased to be self-sufficient when:

> Chinese itinerant smiths did metal work for the Mongols, driving out of business the herd-owning Mongol smiths who could not work continuously at their craft. Other smiths and artisans of all kinds worked permanently in the few towns. . . . Chinese carpenters made carts and water butts and even parts of the wooden framework of Mongol tents. Chinese wool clippers and felt makers travelling with the buyers who collected wool from the Mongols . . . made for the Mongols the felts with which they covered their tents.

In a third kind of situation, mobile groups are dependent for material on the outside world. The Veddas of Sri Lanka, who were hunter-gatherers, when they needed arrows, would hang up a load of meat outside a smith's shop, along with the pattern required in the form of a leaf. There would be no direct transactions, the completed arrows being 'paid' for by meat (Seligmann and Seligmann 1911:6-8). It is well known that a substantial part of the food consumed by nomads is procured from sedentary communities. Significantly, however, there were also craft items, plus materials relating to ideology or identity. For example, Rabari pastoralists in Kutch and Kathiawar are dependent on urban goldsmiths to produce their traditional jewellery which, in many cases, is a specific marker of community identity (Frater 1995). Similarly, Marx (1992:257) noted that objects such as sets of coffee-pots that are specifically designed for nomadic customers in the Arab world are typically urban manufactures.

The notion of the peripatetic niche is used by Rao (1987) and Bollig (1987) and implies craftsman mobility in response to inadequate demand. In fact, Rao (1987:16) aptly noted that 'the lower the frequency of demand the greater the mobility of the peripatetic community must be, since a larger potential customer population must be reached by wider ranging migration circuits'. Mobility, in turn, would depend not only on the frequency of demand, but also on its predictability (Rao 1987:17). Bollig (1987) prefers to see this peripatetic niche as being occupied by those who straddle the divide between the extremes of agriculturist or pastoralist or craftsman. Mobility is a strategy which ensures livelihood for small communities. 'The economy of these groups is an "opportunistic" and highly flexible adaptation to the social environment. This adaptation requires spatial mobility in order to reach a large number of potential customers. . . . Typically they migrate in small bands, or even individually to rejoin the main group after visiting a certain customer. The carrying capacity of the peripatetic niche is low and highly dependent on factors beyond the control of the exploiter, and optimal exploitation of this niche requires a highly flexible group organization' (Bollig 1987:210). This form of craftsman mobility must be clearly differentiated from that practised by groups such as the Inadan which accompany nomadic patrons.

Smithing has long been acknowledged in many cases to have been peripatetic in nature, and groups which practise it are referred to as gypsies or tinkers. In fact, Childe (1942:85-6) considered the earliest specialists (apart from those dealing with ritual) to have been smiths who very often led a peripatetic existence. In Africa, smiths 'bring with them a small stock of iron and copper and travel about from village to village, making knives, arrowheads, beads and rings for which they receive sheep and goats . . .' (McKiernan cf. Bollig 1987: 199). The Persian Kouli are itinerant smiths who buy scrap iron which is forged into various implements (Wulff 1966:49). A very similar situation prevails in India among the Gaduliya Lohars in Rajasthan (Ruhela 1968; Mishra 1977) or the Ghisadis or Bailne Kumbhars of the Deccan, Konkan, and Karnataka (Enthoven 1922 [1997]:3, 5).

The Gaduliya Lohars practise no smelting, work on purchased iron or scavenged scraps, and move according to the dictates of the agricultural cycle and the needs of farmers for tools and their repair. Thus, we find that the numbers of such groups are few in the more unproductive and desert areas of Rajasthan and greater in the fertile and populated areas. The distances travelled by the Lohars depend on the spatial patterning of villages; fewer villages would mean movement over greater distances, while a more clustered pattern would imply shorter distances. Routes thus range from about 80-130 km. at one end to 190-400 km. at the other. There is also considerable organization among the Gaduliya Lohars, with routes and regions strictly demarcated among sub-groups (Ruhela 1968: 142-4). Entire families travel with their belongings on two-wheeled bullock carts. Apart from the rainy season, when groups settled at encampments called *thiyas*, movement is frequent, with camps being made for two to four days at a time (Ruhela 1968:64-5). Thus, the Gaduliya Lohars provide an example of the classic peripatetic group whose mobility is strategic and is designed to reach a large number of potential customers (Bollig 1987:210; Gmelch 1986:310).

This kind of mobility is obviously not restricted to smithing. Childe (1942:93), in fact, refers to modern potters in the Aegean and Crete who travel from village to village along with their wheel. In the Kabyle country of Algeria, expert saddlemakers and wooden bowl carvers were known to make the rounds of villages (Coon 1951: 305). They used wood provided by their customers. Similarly, the LawBe woodcarvers of West Africa need to migrate in order to find customers. They make saddlebags, stools, and other domestic items which rarely need to be repaired, hence requiring a search for new customers (Dupire 1985:88). The source of raw material would vary with different groups as the Gaduliya Lohars ask villagers only for coal or dry wood for fuel (Ruhela 1968:149).

Mobility in Terms other than Spatial

Another part of Figure 1 deals with mobility in non-spatial terms. Inadequate demand for craft objects is handled in another way: mobility between occupations or part-time craftwork. The concepts of seasonality and of part-time/full-time production are much interlinked. Though the archaeological correlates of these concepts are yet to be refined, we have a clear notion of such a scale of production through historical and ethnographic evidence. Seasonality of craft production may be due to climatic factors where certain raw materials are only seasonally available, or where certain techniques can only be practised at certain times of the year. Alternately there is a periodic shift between craft and subsistence production, with craft work as a subsidiary activity. Crafts requiring heating facilities or dry weather are very often necessarily abandoned during the monsoon.

We can cite textile printing, and industries requiring large inputs of charcoal, such as metallurgy and pottery production. A craft such as shell working would also require artisans to work on the available stocks or else abandon work during the monsoon (Kenoyer 1984: 102).

Apart from mobility between occupations as a response to seasonality, we may find mobility between crafts and agriculture. Inscriptions of early medieval India illustrate the relationship between craft working and agriculture. A number of inscriptions refer to land being granted to craftsmen for cultivation by themselves (Sircar 1949-50a:189; Sircar 1953-4: 18-19; Sircar 1968:295; Sircar 1983:576; Rangacharya 1919: 275, 320, 388, 601, 626, 634, 653, 723, 947, 1204, 1206, 1339, 1655-6, 1664). Tchitcherov (1998:28) noted that in Tamil Nadu, craftsmen were given hereditary rights to a small plot of land by the community. Heitzman (1997:87) mentions lands granted to village service personnel, such as carpenters and goldsmiths. Moreover, we find that some medieval inscriptions refer to grants of land to highly skilled craftsmen who had produced religious icons. For example, an early seventeenth-century inscription in Cuddapah district refers to the grant of land to a craftsman for casting an image of Chennakesava or to two sculptors in the sixteenth century for carving a Hanumantha image (Rangacharya 1919:601, 634).

There is yet another feature, the ability of craftsmen to move between crafts. The well-known Sanchi Inscription records a stone carving as the work of the ivory carvers of Vidisa (Bühler 1894: 378). And numerous early medieval inscriptions indirectly show the shift between crafts. Gai (1961-2) records an eleventh-century reference to a *svarna-loha-cari*, one who perhaps worked with both gold and iron. Many inscriptions give concrete evidence that often inscriptions were engraved by craftsmen who are not termed workers in stone or copper, but are described as *lohars* or blacksmiths (Kielhorn 1896-7a:124-6); brassworkers or *pitalhara* (Cartellieri 1896-7:156; Hiralal 1921-2:9-10; Sircar 1957-8:124); braziers or *kamsaṛa* (Bhattacharyya 1935-6:79, 290-2; Chakravarti 1935-6:266; Kielhorn 1896-7b:198-201; Rath 1927-8:135), and goldsmiths or *suvarnakara* (Chhabra 1935-6:141; Hultsch 1925-6:312; Mirashi 1935-6:82; Mirashi 1963:58, 62; Mirashi 1977:253; Sircar 1949-50b:274; Sircar 1951-2:40; Sircar and Subrahmanyam 1962-3:58).

In the pre-industrial period, shifts between carpentry and blacksmithing appear to have been common and there were *sutar-lohars* in the Deccan (Fukazawa 1991:212-15). The Jingars of the Deccan and the Konkan are a good example of the same type of flexibility: they were weavers, blacksmiths, metal casters, goldsmiths, wire-makers, and painters (Enthoven 1922 [1997]:99-103). *Lohars* or blacksmiths in Belgaum district can do skilled work in brass, silver and gold (ibid.:384). The well-known group of artisans in the Karnataka and Madras regions, the Panchals, are a guild working in five materials: gold, iron, brass, wood, and stone (ibid.: 156-8; Krishna Rao 1955-6:4; Sircar 1962-3:292). The Meghvals of Kutch are not only tanners and shoemakers but also weavers (Enthoven 1922 [1997]:44, 51). Similarly, the Gudigars of South Canara are expert ivory carvers, as also workers in sandalwood (ibid.:20-1; Thurston 1909 [1975]:302-3).

This flexibility can be thought of as a diversification strategy, especially in the case of crafts such as carpentry and blacksmithing. Fischer and Shah (1970:67) note that a carpenter must know how to handle metal, as a number of their wooden manufactures incorporate metal parts. Thus, small-scale repairs and the joining of the two materials are skills available to carpenters. Interestingly, Fischer and Shah (ibid.) also note that a forge with bellows and a small anvil are to be found in nearly every carpenter's workshop. Perhaps this flexibility was another means of dealing with the limited demand for certain crafts or with a situation where artisans were scarce. But scholars (see Moorey 1994:15; Burford 1972:86, 96) have noted that in the early periods this was a strategy which was practised largely among master craftsmen, those who produced luxuries, or those who had exceptional skills, but not the practitioners of utilitarian craft production. It was probably the limited demand for luxuries that necessitated the knowledge of other skills.

Implications of Mobility

Generally speaking, it was the specialist craftsman who would move according to his own wishes or to the dictates of the state or other political entity. Haynes and Roy (1999:38) found that 'mobility' was not noted among low-caste agricultural labourers who did part-time weaving, but among those who regarded weaving as a hereditary profession and, more important, those who possessed the specialized skills and knowledge and who were really in demand. Most often, we find large-scale movements among those weavers who produced higher quality or luxury cloth of silk or cotton such as *ikat* or *patola*. Those possessing special skills, such as jewellers, or boat builders, or metal craftsmen, were likely to move further than potters and leather workers. In the context of weaving, Haynes and Roy (1999:52) found that movements of craftsmen took place from the peripheral areas to the core regions: craftsmen appeared to move from areas experiencing regional decline to those where there was vitality. They also cite the pre-colonial movement of the silk weavers of Lata to Mandasore, as perhaps due to the decline of the former region. Craftsmen producing utilitarian objects or those who gave equal importance to agriculture were less likely to move, and if they moved, it would be over short distances. Brumfiel (1987:106) notes that in the event of part-time specialization, ties to agricultural land would impose residential immobility on craft workers.

Among truly peripatetic craftsmen the best known are smiths. Perhaps the iron-smelting Agaria became specialists centuries ago. Russell and Hiralal (1916 [1975]:7-8) note that they 'move about from village to village with an anvil, a hammer and tongs, and building a small furnace under a tree, make and repair iron implements for the villagers'. Unlike the Gaduliya Lohars who do no smelting, the Agaria smelt ore (which also necessitated movement over distances) and forge implements.

What then are the implications of mobility for craft production? (From the viewpoint of this paper, we are more interested in the 'true itinerants' than in those craftsmen who may move once in their lifetime due to some impetus.) Let us roughly categorize economic and social implications of the following discussion.

One dimension to the discussion would be the access to raw materials. Mobile pastoralists, as noted in the above survey, mostly worked with materials that were directly accessible to them (wool or animal skin). Honey, tans, and such materials would have found their way via the market—as in the case of the Baigas, as shown by Archana Prasad in her paper. But what about raw materials such as metal ores? These were rarely exploited by mobile groups, such as the Agaria, except in cases where large quantities of fuel are regularly used and trees must be felled in different areas each year.

Peripatetic craftsmen carried their own raw materials, and we assume that there would have been a limit to the stocks they carried. The other option was to obtain raw materials locally. In the case of peripatetic smiths such as the Gaduliya Lohars who practised no smelting, raw materials were procured through purchase and scavenging. Yet there would have been groups which smelted, like the Agaria—hence their movements, on whatever scale, would have depended on the availability of trees for charcoal production. Similarly, Dupire (1985:88) noted that the LawBe artisans of West Africa 'migrate because they need to find quality trees' for their woodworking activities.

Mobility may also impose limitations on output. Weaving by pastoral nomads is usually in a small format, due to the limitations on the size of the portable loom. But in urban workshops, loom frames are made of beams as long as trees (Milhofer 1971:18, 100). Beck (1991:143) notes the case of a newly settled Qashqa'i woman who was able to weave larger carpets than if she were nomadic (and hence was able to increase her income). Not only that, there is also a quantitative and qualitative difference in the output of nomad and settled weavers. In Turkmenistan and Baluchistan, nomad weavings were often recognized (apart from the design) by the predominant use of wool and sometimes goat hair for the warp (Milhofer 1971: 100). The Baluchi rarely use silk (which they would have to obtain from the market) and when they do, for miniscule areas ranging from a single knot to a cluster of half a dozen or so (Bennett 1977:177). Colours used are combinations of the natural wool colours and sometimes white. Typologically, artefacts manufactured by mobile peoples would centre on their household requirements such as tools, containers or coverings, or otherwise for dowry purposes, which we shall deal with further below.

We must also emphasize that craft work may be intensive in the brief periods of sedentariness in a nomad's routine. Qashqa'i women undertook their major weaving projects in the winter and summer at their campsites. These relatively stationary periods at their campsites were precious (Beck 1991). During the migration periods, in contrast, only small pieces such as bags could be woven. The major problem with weaving during the migration was that dismantling the loom with an unfinished textile inevitably meant problems with tightening of the warp and weft threads on assembling and a reduction in the quality and shape of the final product (Beck 1991:119, 179). Such problems would not have existed with crafts such as embroidery. So too, processing activities such as the collection of dyeing materials, spinning of wool, and dyeing could be practised during migration.

The practice of crafts during migrations brings home the fact that these activities were part of the routine of the nomad's life. 'Despite a busy day of breaking and making camp and collecting firewood and water, Katayun still found time to set up her loom and weave for an hour or so in the hope of completing a water-bag carrier. . .' (Beck 1991:178). Beck (1991:124) also recorded that, at the winter campsite of the Qashqa'i group with whom she travelled, the job of setting up the loom took all morning. This was in the case of more complicated weaving. Ruhela (1968:66) also shows that in a normal day for a Gaduliya Lohar family with breaking camp, moving to another place, and making a fresh camp, only three to four hours were available for metallurgy. Thus, we can infer that constant movements were definitely a drawback to craftwork.

We have found in our cross-cultural survey that a number of crafts are theoretically feasible during a mobile existence, as the tools required are relatively simple. But where a technology required high temperature facilities and specially built kilns, sedentism would be necessary for the artisan. From the archaeologist's point of view, thus, it may be confidently said that certain crafts could have developed only in a sedentary, if not urban, milieu: faience production of the Harappans, stoneware bangles presumably worn by the elite in Harappan cities, ceramics such as the Painted Grey Ware and the Northern Black Polished Ware of the Iron Age, glass, the Red Polished Ware of Gujarat between first and 6th centuries AD and the mould-made terracotta artwork of the early historic towns of northern India.

This brings us to the question: would periodic movement have any repercussions on the tool kit of craftsmen? Obviously, a hand spindle is preferred by nomads and shepherds, while settled peoples may prefer spinning on the wheel (Wulff 1966:185). We have noted that pastoralists used the horizontal loom which was easy to move and could be assembled outdoors, as opposed to the vertical loom of sedentary weavers. (This contrast is not so clearly evident among settled weavers of cotton, as it is among carpet weavers.) Moreover, the simplest loom used by nomads was one without heddles, though simple heddle-rod looms were also used (Wulff 1966:199-202). But nomad weavers were unlikely to use the multi-heddled loom, a feature of sedentary weaving. Another example is that of the metal craftsmen of Iran (Wulff 1966:36-7), who use a variety of embossing chisels—such a variety would be absent among peripatetic metal workers. The simplification of nomadic tools and techniques is noted in other crafts too. The itinerant *dhokra* casters in eastern India adapted their technology to suit their movement, by using a mould-cum-crucible (Horne 1994:271, 273). Similarly, the peripatetic Inadan of Niger used to cast jewellery in ingot moulds, while settled craftsmen use the more complicated lost-wax process (Casajus 1987:299). We are thus fairly certain that elaborations in tool kits and methods tend to be adopted only by sedentary craftsmen, and particularly those in urban areas.

One of the basic social implications of mobility is the scope it affords for interpersonal interaction. Elwin (1942:14) had noted that the Agaria, because of their craft, have always had more to do with outsiders than have other groups. The world required Agaria produce. Thus their proverb: 'If you think iron is nothing, look out of your house and see it wandering all over the three worlds.' The Gaduliya Lohars, pastoralists, and the Persian *kouli* smith all have daily encounters with outsiders. Yet we also need to give attention to the fact that, in most situations, the mobile group/individual is the outsider and is the one at a disadvantage. Bollig (1987:210) notes that 'the moral code of the host society negatively evaluates the strategies left to the peripatetics'.

To a large extent, the marginalization of such groups is because of their mobility: the traditional antagonism between the settled and the nomad.[6] Agrawal (1999:16) records a pastoralist as saying, 'we are strangers . . . in these lands . . . through which we travel. We don't belong, so everybody mistreats us. Why else do you think that for the manure of the same sheep penned in a field we get such a low price

[6] The advantage may not always have rested with the settled—examples are cases of pastoralism as the predominant subsistence mode, as in Central Asia. Dandekar in this volume argues for a similar situation in the Deccan. Haaland (1969) has also shown that economic advantages may rest in some cases with the nomad, so much so that wealthy farmers may intentionally become marginal nomads.

here and a higher price at home?' The Qashaq'I, out with their flocks on the roads of Iran, have been jeered at by passing car drivers. Worse, migrations which take place when the fields are not yet harvested are often plagued by conflict, justifying the nomads' tendency to travel in groups for protection. This is nothing new, as in most parts of South Asia and West Asia, nomads are increasingly being pushed into narrowing niches with the expansion of cultivation. Irrigated agriculture has meant the takeover of common lands, hence decreasing pastures. Attempts by the state to settle nomads in most areas are symptomatic of the prevailing attitudes to mobility.

A common feature of peripatetic groups is their despised status. Apart from mobility, Dupire (1985:90) also sees attitudes of contempt practised by non-artisans towards artisans. Attitudes are reflected in avoidance behaviour, notable in the case of the Gaduliya Lohars; their position was degraded when they began to castrate bullocks secretly at night (Ruhela 1968:25). Archana Prasad (this volume) points out that the Agarias are considered outcastes by the Baigas.

One aspect left relatively unexplored in the literature is that of relations between peripatetic and caste artisans. Ruhela (1968:91) notes that the Malaviya and the Maru Lohar castes have no jealousy or enmity with the Gaduliya Lohars. They appear to despise them because they have to move. But it would be interesting to see how craft adjustments, if any, are made.

At the same time, we must note that there are mechanisms to offset marginalization. Many of the despised peripatetic groups perform other functions which are significant. In Africa, these could be ritual services such as circumcision, grave digging, healing, or acting as mediators or messengers (see Archana Prasad for the Agaria role as messengers because of their mobility), or as beggars or collectors of religiously prescribed alms (Bollig 1987:209). Not only this, but peripatetic groups also fill a particular niche. Their movements are never random but are specific, and they may have long-lasting relationships with particular individuals. In any case, the marginality of any group is from the viewpoint of the dominant section: no group will consider itself as inherently inferior. As consumers, however, nomads are not marginalized. Their custom may be valued. Certain goldsmiths such as the Budhbhattis in Bhuj specialize in making Rabari jewellery (Frater 1995:50); so too does Choksi Kantilal Jaychand Soni in Ahmedabad (Sruti 1995:113). The

Choksis fulfil all the Rabari orders themselves, while urban demand is met by hired goldsmiths. It appears that Rabari customers are not only bound to the jewellers by tradition, but are also valued.

The greater interactions which mobility would entail may have some implications for the transfer of styles, design, or technology over distances (Childe 1942:86). Though there are numerous ways in which designs can be transmitted spatially, as through travellers or merchants, we cannot rule out artisans themselves as the medium. The introduction of floral designs in carpet weaving in the Timurid period was perhaps due to the influence on Persian art of Chinese motifs (Bennett 1977:41), just as carpet weaving in Akbar's *karkhanas* was heavily influenced by Persian aesthetics and motifs because of the Persian craftsmen working there.

An important element in artefact style is the symbolism which may be attached to particular designs. Spooner (1986:208) has pointed out that carpets served an intensely symbolic purpose. Although the symbols used did depend on the individual weaver—as a household task, carpet weaving was the work of women who wove 'intricate pattern(s) from memory'. That designs were at the same time also part of a common tradition is seen from the fact that closely related weavers worked with closely related designs and characteristics that could be recognized. On Turkoman carpet weavings, design motifs such as '*guls* were once symbols of autonomy and possession, they were battle standards and heraldic emblems' (Bennett 1977:190).

It needs to be said that much may have depended on technical factors such as the way the warp and weft were combined and the type of knot used, or the treatment of the selvedge (Siudmak 1977:18). Also, in some cases Spooner (1986:210) found that symbolism in carpets was confusing as similar designs could be produced by isolated nomadic communities and in royal workshops where motifs would obviously have had different meanings in different social situations. Similarly, while stitches and motifs contribute to distinctive embroidery styles among communities such as the Rabaris, Bharwads, the Ahirs, the Jats, and the Sodhas in Gujarat (Jaitly 1990:69), it appears that some motifs were adopted from other communities. The parrot and circle motif derived from Mochi embroidery (Frater 1995:71) is a case in point. Community identity as portrayed through the style of artefacts is thus difficult though not impossible to comprehend. The difficulty primarily arises in that traditional motifs may not remain within the purview of a community; artisan mobility may spur the adoption of motifs and styles of one group by another.

The emerging implication of the above observations is that crafted items often had an overriding symbolic function. Ostensibly for home consumption, articles such as carpets, garments, containers or bags, or adornments for animals were vested with symbolic value. The gradual incorporation of nomadic groups/individuals into market situations as well as the pushing of such groups into disappearing ecological niches meant the increasing marginalization of people and their products. The results were very often symbolic losses such as the sale of precious weavings or embroideries. Frater has documented the reluctance of Rabari women to show their embroideries, many of which were produced for dowries, and hence imbued with symbolic meaning. Significantly, more settled Rabari groups (such as the Patanwadis who have been farming for over a hundred years) were more forthcoming about showing their embroideries; here clearly the cultural values of such artefacts were already diminished (Frater 1995:121). The Qashqa'i, in the 1970s, were in many cases already crafting objects for the market, but at the same time, more elaborate weavings were for personal dowries. Beck (1991:189) relates an incident, full of pathos, of a laboured-over weaving being sold due to the need for cash.[7]

It can be hypothesized that the settling of nomads has resulted in a greater willingness to sell, perhaps due to more regular interactions with outsiders and changing values. The issue of marginalization is clearly complex. Let us take the specific case of carpet weaving among the Turkmen of south-western Central Asia, that is, Afghanistan, Iran, and Soviet Turkmenistan (Spooner 1986). Spooner has investigated the role of carpets as commodities. These are objects manufactured in a variety of contexts, ranging from isolated nomadic camps to small villages to urban centres. Carpets for the producer fulfilled certain utilitarian and symbolic purposes. The commoditization of carpets changed not so much their function (they could still be used as floor coverings) but instilled new meaning into them.

[7] The sale of valued objects was often due to distress conditions. Spooner (1988:131) found many heirlooms on the market in Afghanistan due to such compulsions. In India too, the recent sale of Rabari embroideries has been due to distress. Many thanks to Prof. Anil Gupta for discussions on this point.

Carpets were able to command high prices and became collectors' items in the West, valued particularly for their authenticity. Spooner (1986:221-2) points out that it was not age or the number of knots per inch that affected the quality or authenticity of carpets nor the use of vegetable dyes, but rather their fulfilling a role as exotic textiles valued more for their design than for their function, and for the fact that they were hand-made. '. . . (T)he rug was an exotic product made in its own exotic production process for its own exotic purpose.' The extent of commoditization is clear from the fact that certain carpets, hardly noticed twenty years earlier, such as the Baluchis or the south Persian tribal rugs, also start being valued by Western collectors. A similar case can be made for the silver jewellery manufactured by the Inadan or for Rabari embroidery. Thus, while we are dealing with the products of nomadic peoples, the value and function of their products have in certain contexts been vastly changed. This is not the case with all nomadic craft, but the value of some craft styles clearly derives from their nomadic background. This may imply that nomadism need not in all cases be synonymous with marginalization.

The changing of focus by the producer of crafted objects is explicated by Roy (1999:201-2): crafting for the market means production for unknown consumers. An item that traditionally has one purpose often gets to be used in a totally different way by the purchaser. This has long-term implications for the quality, with the relaxation of standards. Consider, for example, the fact that during the colonial trade, Persian carpets had to be 'tested for dead wool, fleeting dyes, short pile . . . abuses unthinkable in dowry, prayer or court carpets'. Roy (1999:203-4) also found that production for different consumers often meant a clash of aesthetics—designs had to be altered, dimensions had to be reduced (carpets, for example, had to share space with furniture), details cut out or simplified—which could only result in 'de-skilling' and the loss of content. In the long term, this would result in the devaluation of a tradition of craftsmanship.

Emerging Ideas

We may attempt to tie up the threads of the discussion so far. This paper has attempted to point out that there is no necessary correlation between sedentism and craft production. There are, however, certain points which emerge from our analysis. For one, numerous crafted objects were made by the nomads for their own use, whether utilitarian or symbolic. These were clearly important for the nomad but the more special among these only entered the market under duress.

The assumptions often made that the system of the division of labour could only develop in a sedentary situation have been sought to be refined in this paper. Second, while sedentism implies greater craft specialization, in many cases, it was the specialist who was also more likely to travel greater distances. These are, however, instances of infrequent or episodic movements of craftsmen due to various reasons or pressures.

Our real interest lies with itinerant craftsmen. Their mobility primarily ensued from a dispersed consumer base, or was dictated by their patrons, themselves nomads or else settled people. Let us point out here that mobile people, in general, and mobile craft workers, in particular, would have needed to make more intricate social and economic adjustments as compared to their sedentary counterparts. Adjustments in their work include arrangements to obtain raw materials or to ensure the portability of their tools, or in the size or quantity of their output. Adjustments were also required at social levels in their dealings with customers, or sedentary craftsmen, and, in general, with strangers. Bilingualism or multilingualism, and the building up of trust with exchange partners, are just a few of the social skills which such a peripatetic life would have required. While we have seen that mobile groups practise crafts, it is also clear that elaborations of crafts in techniques, tools, and organization occurred only when craftsmen were sedentary.[8]

Further, we need to reiterate that the mobility of artisans must be seen in ways that are not only spatial. In fact, we may begin to question whether the strict categories which are so familiar to us from the modern context can really be accepted for the past. Not only does there appear to be a fluidity between different subsistence strategies as between agriculture and craft production, but also between different crafts. Thus, the Gaduliya Lohars are metal workers

[8] Archaeologically, too, one does note a similar trend. In the Cholistan Desert of Pakistan, the settling of people in the fourth millennium BC seems to have had an impact on the increase in craft or industrial activities (Mughal 1982:91).

and also cattle traders. And the Maa-speaking pastoralists practise a mixture of pastoralism, foraging, as well as iron smelting (Larick 1986). Flexibility of strategies has also been explored by Chetan Singh and Supriya Varma in this volume. Singh has tried to show that the economy of Kinnaur necessarily involved a combination of agriculture, pastoralism, and trade, while Varma focuses on the frequency of village desertions which, in turn, may have reflected the use of multiple subsistence strategies.

Structural changes have occurred in the twentieth century. Crafts are now practised by entirely separate groups, which may not have been the case in the past. We can take the example of the Kurubas in Karnataka, shepherds as well as farmers and weavers. The Hande Kurubas are a group who used to be sheep breeders; they are now weavers of woollen blankets (Sontheimer 1993:9). The Rabaris, a specialist pastoral group of Kutch and Kathiawar, used to formerly spin wool and weave blankets (Jain 1980: 51). In the present, Jain says, Rabari men carry spindles with which they prepare camel wool yarn. This they take to a weaver for weaving blankets, veilcloths, or skirts. After collecting the output from the weaver, they take it to dyers for the application of the required colours and designs. The Rabaris and the Kuruba pastoralists appear to have been practising a traditional craft that, with increasing specialization, has become differentiated so that textile production and animal husbandry are now practised by different sub-groups. Bollig (1987:181-3) finds that in the context of African peripatetics, 'one must be cautious not to think of the pairs non-food producing versus food producing, spatial mobility versus sedentism . . . as antagonistic'. Bollig notes quite correctly that these pairs should not be treated as dialectical, but rather as 'broad continua on which "social entrepreneurs" merge according to individual strategies to gain access to resources under the strains of a given environment'. Here, very often one tends to think of agriculture as the major or alternate means of subsistence, but it really appears that the shifts can be between a far greater range of subsistence and livelihood strategies. At the same time, we may also note the negative angle: that flexibility of strategies can also lead to social marginalization. Marginality is not due only to mobility but also due to the inevitable incorporation of such groups into the modern market. Yet we must also take note of a more recent trend, of tribal craft elevated by non-nomadic consumers to a different position, but one devoid of its original content and meaning. Those patterns of flexibility which are visible to us historically and ethnographically illustrate that past strategies cannot be analysed in a unidimensional way.

REFERENCES

Agrawal, A., *Greener pastures: Politics, markets and community among a migrant pastoral people*, Delhi: Oxford University Press, 1999.

Ahuja, Ravi, 'Labour unsettled: mobility and protest in the Madras region, 1750-1800', *Indian Economic and Social History Review*, vol. 35, no. 4, 1998, pp. 381-404.

Allchin, F.R. and B. Allchin, *The rise of civilization in India and Pakistan*, New Delhi: Selectbook Service Syndicate, rpt., 1981.

Arnold, David, 'Famine in peasant consciousness and peasant action: Madras, 1876-8', in R. Guha, ed., *Subaltern Studies III*, Delhi: Oxford University Press, 1984, pp. 62-115.

Barth, F., *Nomads of south Persia*, Oslo: Universitetsforlaget, 1964.

Beck, L., *Nomad: A year in the life of a Qashqa'i tribesman in Iran*, Berkeley and Los Angeles: University of California Press, 1991.

Bennett, I., 'Oriental and African rugs and carpets', in I. Bennett, ed., *Rugs and carpets of the world*, London: Grange Books, 1977, pp. 23-257.

Bhattacharyya, P.N., 'Badakhimedi copper-plates of Indravarman', *Epigraphia Indica*, vol. XXIII, 1935-6, pp. 78-80.

Blochmann, H., tr., *The Ain-i Akbari by Abu'l Fazl Allami*, Delhi: Oriental Books Reprint, 1977.

Bollig, Michael, 'Ethnic relations and spatial mobility in Africa: a review of the peripatetic niche', in A. Rao, ed., *The other nomads*, Koln, Wien: Bohlau Verlag, 1987, pp. 179-228.

Braudel, F., *Civilization and capitalism 15th-18th century*, vol. II. *The Wheels of Commerce* (S. Reynolds), London: Fontana Press, 1982.

Brumfiel, E.M., 'Elite and utilitarian crafts in the Aztec state', in E.M. Brumfiel and T.K. Earle, eds., *Specialization, exchange and complex societies*, Cambridge: Cambridge University Press, 1987, pp. 102-18.

Brumfiel, E.M. and T.K. Earle, 'Specialization, exchange and complex societies: an introduction', in E.M. Brumfiel and T.K. Earle, eds., *Specialization, exchange and complex societies*, Cambridge: Cambridge University Press, 1987, pp. 1-9.

Bühler, A. and E. Fischer, *The patola of Gujarat*, 2 vols., Basle: Krebs AG, 1979.

Bühler, G., 'Further inscriptions from Sanchi', *Epigraphia Indica*, vol. II, 1894, pp. 366-408.

Burford, A., *Craftsmen in Greek and Roman society*, London: Thames and Hudson, 1972.

Burgess, J.A.S. and B. Indraji, *Inscriptions from the cave-temples of western India with descriptive notes*, Delhi: Indian India, rpt., 1881 (1976).

Cartellieri, W., 'Semra plates of Paramardideva [Vikrama-] Samvat 1223', *Epigraphia Indica*, vol. IV, 1896-7, pp. 153-74.

Casajus, D., 'Crafts and ceremonies: the Inadan in Tuareg society', in A. Rao, ed., *The other nomads*, Koln, Wien: Bohlau Verlag, 1987, pp. 291-310.

Chakravarti, S.N., 'Plates of Bhupendravarmadeva', *Epigraphia Indica*, vol. XXIII 1935-6, pp. 261-9.

Chhabra, B.C., 'Upalada plates of Ranaka Ramadeva', *Epigraphia Indica*, vol. XXIII 1935-6, pp. 141-3.

Childe, V.G., *What happened in history*, Middlesex: Penguin, rpt., 1942 (1982).

Cline, E.H., 'Tinker, tailor, soldier, sailor: Minoans and Myceneans abroad', in R. Laffineur and W.D. Diemeier, eds., *Politeia: society and state in the Aegean bronze age*, Liege and Austin: Universities of Liege and Austin, 1995, pp. 265-83.

Cohen, R., *The Kanuri of Bornu*, New York: Holt, Rinehart & Winston, 1967.

Coomaraswamy, A.K., *The Indian Craftsman*, New Delhi: Munshiram Manoharlal, rpt., 1909 (1989).

Coon, C.S., *Caravan: the story of the Middle East*, London: Jonathan Cape, 1951.

Cribb, Roger, *Nomads in archaeology*, Cambridge: Cambridge University Press, 1991.

Crowfoot, Grace M., 'Textiles, basketry and mats', in C. Singer, E.J. Holmyard and A.R. Hall, eds., *A history of technology*, Oxford: Clarendon Press, 1954, pp. 413-47.

Dave, I.R., *The Saurashtrians in south India*, Rajkot: Saurashtra University Press, 1976.

Dupire, M. A, 'Nomadic Caste: The Fulani Woodcarvers. Historical background and evolution', *Anthropos* 80, 1985: 85-100.

Earle, T.K., 'Specialization and the production of wealth: Hawaiian chiefdoms and the Inka empire', in E.M. Brumfiel and T.K. Earle, eds., *Specialization, exchange, and complex societies*, Cambridge: Cambridge University Press, 1987, pp. 64-75.

Elwin, V., *The Agaria*, Oxford: Oxford University Press, 1942.

Enthoven, R.E., *The tribes and castes of Bombay*, 3 vols., Delhi: Low Price Publications, rpt., 1922 (1997).

Fleet, J.F., 'Inscriptions of the early Gupta kings and their successors', *Corpus Inscriptionum Indicarum*, vol. III, rpt., 1887 (1970).

Fischer, E. and H. Shah, *Rural craftsmen and their work*, Ahmedabad: NID, 1970.

Frater, J., *Threads of identity*, Ahmedabad: Mapin, 1995.

Fukazawa, H., *The medieval Deccan peasants, social systems and states. Sixteenth to eighteenth centuries*, New Delhi: Oxford University Press, rpt., 1991 (1998).

Gai, G.S., 'Boddapadu plates of Vajrahasta (III), Saka 982', *Epigraphia Indica*, vol. XXXIV, 1961-2, pp. 42-4.

Gillion, K.L., *Ahmedabad: A study in urban history*, Berkeley and Los Angeles: The University of California Press, 1968.

Gmelch, S.B., 'Groups that don't want in: gypsies and other artisan, trader, and entertainer minorities', *Annual Review of Anthropology*, vol. 15, 1986, pp. 307-30.

Gordon, S., *Marathas, marauders, and state formation in eighteenth century India*, Delhi: Oxford University Press, rpt, 1994 [1998].

Goswamy, K., 'Itinerant Kashmiri artists: notes on the spread of a style', in M.W. Meister, ed., *Making things in south Asia: the role of artist and craftsman*, Philadelphia: Department of South Asian Regional Studies, 1988, pp. 86-95.

Haaland, G., 'Economic determinants in ethnic processes', in F. Barth, ed., *Ethnic groups and boundaries: The social organization of culture difference*, Bergen-Oslo and London: Universitetsverlaget and George Allen Unwin, 1969, pp. 58-73.

Harmatta, J., 'Languages and literature in the Kushan empire', in J. Harmatta, B.N. Puri and G.F. Etemadi, eds., *History of civilizations of central Asia*, vol. II, Paris: UNESCO Publishing, 1994, pp. 417-40.

Haynes, D.E. and T. Roy, 'Conceiving mobility: weavers' migrations in pre-colonial and colonial India', *Indian Economic and Social History Review*, vol. 36, no. 1, 1996, pp. 35-67.

Heitzman, J., *Gifts of power. Lordship in an early Indian state*, Delhi: Oxford University Press, 1997.

Herskovits, M.J., *Dahomey: an ancient west African kingdom*, vol. I., Evanston: Northwestern University Press, 1967.

Hiralal, Rai Bahadur, 'Mahoba plates of Paramardideva [Vikrama] Samvat 1230', *Epigraphia Indica*, vol. XVI, 1921-2, pp. 9-15.

Hodges, H., *Technology in the ancient world*, New York: Barnes & Noble, rpt., 1970 (1992).

Horne, Lee, 'Itinerant brasscasters of eastern India', in B. Allchin, ed., *Living traditions: Studies in the ethnoarchaeology of south Asia*, New Delhi: Oxford & IBH, 1994, pp. 265-80.

Hultsch, E., 'Tekkali plates of Rajendravarman's son Devendravarman', *Epigraphia Indica*, vol. XVIII, 1925-6, pp. 311-13.

Irons, W., 'Variation in economic organization: a comparison of the pastoral Yomut and the Basseri', in W. Irons and N. Dyson-Hudson, eds., *Perspectives on nomadism*, Leiden: E.J. Brill, 1972, pp. 88-104.

Irwin, J. and M. Hall, *Indian painted and printed fabrics*, vol. I, Ahmedabad: Calico Museum of Textiles, 1971.

Irwin, J. and P.R. Schwartz, *Studies in Indo-European textile history*, Ahmedabad: Calico Museum of Textiles, 1966.

Jacobsen, T.W., 'Seasonal pastoralism in southern Greece: a consideration of the ecology of neolithic Urfirnis pottery', in P.M. Rice, ed., *Pots and potters.*

Current approaches to ceramic archaeology, Berkeley and Los Angeles: University of California Press, 1987, pp. 27-43.

Jain, J., *Folk art and culture of Gujarat*, Ahmedabad: Shreyas Institute, 1980.

Jaitly, Jaya, *The craft traditions of India*, New Delhi: Lustre Press, 1990.

Kenoyer, J.M., 'Shell industries at Mohenjodaro, Pakistan', in M. Jansen and G. Urban, eds., *Reports on field work at Mohenjodaro: interim reports*, vol. I, Aachen & Rome: RWTH and Istituto Italiano per il Medio ed Estremo Oriente, 1984, pp. 99-115.

Khazanov, A.M., *Nomads and the outside world*, Cambridge: Cambridge University Press, 1983.

Kielhorn, F., 'Plate of Jayachandra of [Vikrama-] Samvat 1231', *Epigraphia Indica*, vol. IV, 1896-7a, pp. 124-6.

———, 'Ganjam plates of Prithvivarmadeva', *Epigraphia Indica*, vol. IV, 1896-7b, pp. 198-201.

Kirtley, M. and A. Kirtley, 'The Inadan Artists of the Sahara', *National Geographic*, vol. 156, no. 2, 1979, pp. 282-98.

Krishna Rao, B.V., 'Two Sailodbhava charters from Kanukollu', *Epigraphia Indica*, vol. XXXI, 1955-6, pp. 1-10.

Lancaster, W. and F. Lancaster, 'The function of peripatetics in Rwala Bedouin society', in A. Rao, ed., *The other nomads*, Koln, Wien: Bohlau Verlag, 1987, pp. 311-21.

———, 'Limitations on sheep and goat herding in the eastern Badia of Jordan: an ethnoarchaeological enquiry', *Levant*, vol. XXIII, 1991a, pp.125-38.

———, 'Tribe, community and the concept of access to resources: territorial behavior in south-east Ja'alan', in M.J. Casimir and A. Rao, eds., *Mobility and territoriality. Social and spatial boundaries among foragers, fishers, pastoralists and peripatetics*, New York: Berg, 1991b, pp. 343-63.

Larick, Roy, 'Iron smelting and interethnic conflict among precolonial Maa-speaking pastoralists of north-central Kenya', *African Archaeological Review*, vol. 4, 1986, pp. 165-76.

Lattimore, O., *Inner Asian Frontiers of China*, Hong Kong: Oxford University Press, 1988.

Lloyd, P.C., 'Craft organisation in Yoruba towns', *Africa*, vol. XXIII, 1953, pp. 30-44.

Ludden, David, 'Craft production in an agrarian economy', in M.W. Meister, ed., *Making things in south Asia: the role of artist and craftsman*, Philadelphia: Department of South Asian Regional Studies, 1988, pp. 103-13.

Lüders, H., 'A list of Brahmi inscriptions from the earliest times to about A.D. 400 with the exception of those of Asoka', Appendix to *Epigraphia Indica and Record of the Archaeological Survey of India*, vol. X, 1912, pp. 1-226.

Markham, C.R., tr., *Narrative of the embassy of Ruy Gonzalez de Clavijo to the court of Timur at Samarcand A.D. 1403-6*, London: Hakluyt Society, 1859.

Marx, E., 'Are there pastoral nomads in the Middle East?' in O. Bar-Yosef and

A. Khazanov, eds., *Pastoralism in the Levant*, Madison: Prehistory Press, 1992, pp. 255-60.

Masson, Charles, *Narrative of a journey to Kalat including an account of the insurrection at that place in 1840; and a memoir on eastern Baluchistan*, London: Richard Bentley, 1843.

Mehta, R.N., 'Bandhas of Orissa', *Journal of Textile History*, vol. VI, 1961, pp. 62-74.

Milhofer, S.A., '*The color treasury of oriental rugs*', New York: Thomas Y. Crowell Co., 1971.

Mirashi, V.V., 'Pattan plates of Pravarasena II', *Epigraphia Indica*, vol. XXIII, 1935-6, pp. 81-8.

Mirashi, V.V., ed., 'Inscriptions of the Vakatakas', *Corpus Inscriptionum Indicarum*, vol. V, 1963.

———, ed., 'Inscriptions of the Silaharas', *Corpus Inscriptionum Indicarum*, vol. VI, 1977.

Mishra, P.K., *The nomadic Gaduliya Lohars of eastern Rajasthan*, Calcutta: Anthropological Survey of India, 1977.

Misra, R.N., *Ancient artists and art activity*, Simla: Indian Institute of Advanced Study, 1975.

Moorey, P.R.S., *Ancient Mesopotamian materials and industries: The archaeological evidence*, Oxford: Clarendon Press, 1994.

Mughal, M.R., 'Recent archaeological research in the Cholistan desert', in G.L. Possehl, ed., *Harappan Civilization: A Contemporary perspective*, New Delhi: Oxford IBH, 1982, pp. 85-95.

Musil, Alois, *The manners and customs of the Rwala Bedouins*, New York: American Geographical Society, 1928.

Needham, Joseph, *Science and civilization in China*, vol. 4, pt. II, Cambridge: Cambridge University Press, 1965.

Parasher-Sen, A., 'Of tribes, hunters and barbarians: forest dwellers in the Mauryan period', *Studies in History*, vol. 14, no. 2, 1998, pp. 173-91.

Rafferty, J.E., 'The archaeological record on sedentariness: recognition, development and implications', in M.B. Schiffer, ed., *Advances in archaeological method and theory*, vol. 8, Orlando: Academic Press, 1984, pp. 113-56.

Ramaswamy, Vijaya, *Textiles and weavers in medieval south India*, Delhi: Oxford University Press, 1985.

Rangacharya, V., *A topographical list of the inscriptions of the Madras Presidency*, Madras: Government Press, 1919.

Rangnekar, S., 'Studies of indigenous knowledge, work-sharing and perceptions of livestock production by women from pastoralist families', in *Proceedings of the Workshop on Transhumant Pastoralism in Gujarat*, Ahmedabad: IRMA, 1993, pp. 27-34.

Rao, A., 'Non-food-producing nomads and the problem of their classification: the case of the Ghorbat of Afghanistan', *Eastern Anthropologist*, vol. 35, no. 2, 1982, pp. 115-34.

———, 'The concept of peripatetics: an introduction', in A. Rao, ed., *The other nomads*, Koln, Wien: Bohlau Verlag, 1987, pp. 1-32.

Rath, T.C., 'Vishamagiri plates of Indravarmadeva', *Epigraphia Indica*, vol. XIX, 1927-8, pp. 134-7.

Ratnagar, S., 'Hunter-gatherer and early agriculturist: archaeological evidence for contact', in D. Nathan, ed., *From tribe to caste*, Shimla: Indian Institute of Advanced Study, 1997, pp. 117-35.

Raychaudhuri, T., 'Non-agricultural production', in T. Raychaudhuri and I. Habib, eds., *The Cambridge economic history of India*, vol. I, New Delhi: Orient Longman and Cambridge University Press, 1982, pp. 261-307.

Roy, T., *Traditional industry in the economy of colonial India*, Cambridge: Cambridge University Press, 1999.

Ruhela, S.P., *The Gaduliya Lohars of Rajasthan—a study in the sociology of nomadism*, New Delhi: Impax India, 1968.

Russell, R.V. and Hiralal, *The tribes and castes of Central Provinces of India*, Delhi: Cosmo Publications, rpt., 1916 (1975).

Rye, O.S. and C. Evans, *Traditional pottery techniques of Pakistan*, Washington: Smithsonian Institution Press, 1976.

Seligmann, C.G. and B.Z. Seligmann, *The Veddas*, Cambridge: Cambridge University Press, 1911.

Sharma, R.S., *Indian feudalism c. AD 300-1200*, New Delhi: Macmillan, rpt., 1965 (1985).

———, *Urban decay in India (c. 300-c. 1000)*, New Delhi: Munshiram Manoharlal, 1987.

Sircar, D.C., 'Kendupatna lates of Narashimha II; sets II and III, *Epigraphia Indica*, vol. XXVIII, 1949-50a, pp. 185-95.

———, 'Nagari plates of Anangabhima III; Saka 1151 and 1152', *Epigraphia Indica*, vol. XXVIII, 1949-50b, pp. 235-58.

———, 'Two Sailodbhava grants from Banpur', *Epigraphia Indica*, vol. XXIX, 1951-2, pp. 32-43.

———, 'Bhubaneshwar inscription of Anagabhima III; Anka year 34', *Epigraphia Indica*, vol. XXX, 1953-4, pp. 17-23.

———, 'Three Chandella charters', *Epigraphia Indica*, vol. XXXII, 1957-8, pp. 118-28.

———, 'Epigraphia notes', *Epigraphia Indica*, vol. XXXV, 1962-3, pp. 287-92.

———, 'Paschimbhag plate of Srichandra, year 5', *Epigraphia Indica*, vol. XXXVII, 1968, pp. 289-304.

———, '*Select inscriptions bearing on Indian history and civilisation*, vol. II, Delhi: Motilal Banarsidass, 1983.

Sircar, D.C. and V.S. Subrahmanyam, 'Two inscriptions from Kalyanpur', *Epigraphia Indica*, vol. XXXV, 1962-3, pp. 55-9.

Siudmak, J., 'Techniques and materials of oriental carpet weaving', in I. Bennett, ed., *Rugs and carpets of the world*, London: Grange Books, 1977, pp. 9-21.

Smith, M.G., 'A study of Hausa domestic economy in nothern Zaria , *Africa*, vol. XXII, 1952, pp. 333-47.

Sontheimer, Gunther-Dietz, *Pastoral deities in western India*, Delhi: Oxford University Press, 1993.

Spooner, B., 'Weavers and dealers: the authenticity of an oriental carpet', in A. Appadurai, ed., *The social life of things: Commodities in cultural perspective*, Cambridge: Cambridge University Press, 1986, pp. 195-235.

———, 'The craft and commerce of oriental carpets: cultural implications of economic success and failure', in M.W. Meister, ed., *Making things in south Asia: The role of artist and craftsman*, Philadelphia: Department of South Asian Regional Studies, 1988, pp. 127-33.

Sruti, *India's artisans: A status report*, New Delhi: Sruti, 1995.

Swaroop, S., *Mughal art: A study in handicrafts*, Delhi: Agam Kala Prakashan, 1996.

Tchitcherov, A., *India: changing economic structures in the 16th-18th centuries: Outline history of crafts and trade*, New Delhi: Manohar, 1998.

Thurston, E., *Castes and tribes of south India*, New Delhi: Low Price Publications, rpt., 1909 (1975).

Wulff, H.E., *The traditional crafts of Persia*, Cambridge: M.I.T. Press, 1966.

Zaccagnini, C., 'Patterns of mobility among ancient near eastern craftsmen', *Journal of Near Eastern Studies*, vol. 42, no.3, 1983, pp. 245-64.

In the Absence of Mounds: Shifting Villages, Pastoralism, and Depopulation

SUPRIYA VARMA

THERE APPEARS to be a hiatus spanning about six hundred years, perhaps longer, between the chalcolithic and the early historic periods of occupation in Kathiawad. The first of these periods was marked by small villages of average size 3 to 4.5 hectares spread across the peninsula that grew *jowar*, *ragi*, *bajri*, barley, gram, lentils, hyacinth beans, peas, mustard, and linseed, and that kept cattle, sheep, and goats. The period ended some time between 1400 and 1000 BC. The early historic period was characterized by larger villages (about 7 hectares on average) that domesticated the some animals, cultivated the same crops (with the addition of *math*), produced iron and glass, and had a few houses built around open courtyards and utilizing baked clay tiles for roofing. This period is conventionally dated from the second half of the first millennium BC onwards.

Why is it that there is a gap in the archaeological record of our region? Are we to infer that Kathiawad was devoid of settlements and/or people between 1000 and 400 BC?[1] Or could it be that the

* I thank Rudi Heredia and Ajay Dandekar for inviting me to the workshop on pastoralism held in December 1998. I will remain indebted to Shereen Ratnagar for drawing my attention to this problem. For the errors in the argument I alone am responsible. The discussions that took place during the workshop were also immensely helpful and I am grateful to all the participants.

[1] We need to spell out the problems of chronology in some detail. It is now evident that in the protohistoric period in Kathiawad there are two distinct types/categories of archaeological sites. In the first category are sites such as Lothal, Nageshwar, and Kuntasi and in the second category are Rangpur, Rojdi, and Kanewal. While the sites in the former category are termed 'Mature

population of this period is not archaeologically visible? In this paper we shall survey such historical evidence as is available on the abandonments of villages in different periods and places in order to gain insights into the circumstances that may lie behind the absence of protohistoric village sites.

The abandonment of ancient habitations is now identified as a key process in the formation of the archaeological record (Cameron 1993:3). Site abandonment may be a single event, but there could also be a continuous process of abandonment and reoccupation (Schlanger and Wilshusen 1993:85; Tomka and Stevenson 1993:192). Thus, abandonment is in some cases 'part of settlement systems that involve seasonal or periodic abandonments' rather than the depopulation of a region (Cameron 1993:4), and village abandonment is inextricably linked with land-use patterns of many subsistence systems, including those of hunter-gatherers, pastoralists, and agriculturists (ibid.:5). Depending

---

Harappan' or 'Sindhi Harappan', numerous labels such as 'Rangpur II B-C', 'Sorath Harappan', 'Local Harappan', 'Late Mature Harappan', 'Sub-Indus', and 'Saurashtrian Indus' have been used for the latter. The dates for the Mature Harappan period in Kathiawad (between 2550 and 2160 BC) are fairly well established (Possehl 1980: 41). What remains controversial is the chronology of the Rangpur II B-C sites.

While the dates (ranging between 2600 and 1800 BC) seem to indicate that the Rangpur II B-C sites may have been contemporary to the Mature Harappan, the stratigraphic evidence from at least two sites, Lothal and Kuntasi, suggests otherwise. At both these sites, the Rangpur II B-C occupation clearly succeeded the Mature Harappan (Rao 1979: Plate XIV; Dhavalikar, Raval and Chitalwala 1996: Figs. 4.2-4.4).

Possehl (1993: 242-4) has however cautioned us about using dates based on charcoal samples. Among the several methodological and theoretical problems associated with radiocarbon dating is the issue of: 'the precise relationship between the charcoal samples used for dating and their association with the history we are attempting to date. There are also unresolved problems related to the burning of wood from very old trees which is then incorporated into the archaeological matrix, as well as the reuse of wood over several centuries.'

In Kathiawad there are several species that are over 400 years old. Among these are the *ardusi* or *marook* (*Ailanthus excelsa*), *amli* (tamarind), *udumber* (*Ficus glomerata*), and neem (*Azadirachta indica*) (personal communication, S.D. Sabnis, April 2000). Hence, we cannot rule out the possibility that the radiocarbon dates may be skewed, especially when viewed in the context of the stratigraphic evidence.

on the form of subsistence, a group could use several residences/sites in sequence. We will return to this point later.

The scale of abandonment can vary from the intra-site level to large geographical areas. During abandonment certain activities (commonly referred to as abandonment processes) occur, such as the curation (taking away) or the caching of tools, and the occasional dismantling of structures. Factors that can influence abandonment processes are the extent of planning, the speed of vacating a settlement, distance to the next or new settlement, whether a return is anticipated, and if so the period of abandonment. Apart from these, another factor that can also affect abandonment processes is a change in land use. For instance, we could guess that in the case of a shift in subsistence strategies from agro-pastoralism to specialized agriculture, the archaeological assemblage at one of the several residences may be discarded without substantial curation. The abandonment processes in this situation would be identical to a situation of catastrophic abandonment. Yet another scenario is equally possible: that the assemblage is curated (Tomka 1993:23).

We find that abandonment of settlements has been mainly related to land-use strategies involving a certain amount of mobility. However, the issue concerns not only mobility but also flexibility and the tapping of multiple resources. Flexibility in subsistence strategies and its implications for the formation of the archaeological record will now be investigated.

In the light of this discussion, it is best to leave open the chronology of the Rangpur II B-C sites. If we accept the stratigraphic evidence, then the Rangpur II B-C sites can be dated between 2160 and 1700 BC (Possehl 1980:44). Several scholars (Dhavalikar and Possehl 1992:72-3; Pandya 1980-1:59-60; Rao 1973: 43; Shinde and Thomas 1993: 145; Sonawane and Ajithprasad 1994:133) have suggested that chalcolithic villages in Kathiawad may have existed prior to the Rangpur II B-C period, but in view of the known evidence, it becomes difficult to support the hypothesis (Varma 1997:82-4).

The Rangpur II B-C sites are followed by the Rangpur III sites. Perhaps we can infer that the Rangpur III occupation began around 1700 BC for it succeeds the earlier sub-period at Rangpur and Prabhas Patan. While at this stage we cannot suggest firm dates for the end of the chalcolithic period in our region, it is possible that it ended sometime between 1400 and 1000 BC (ibid.:105, 107).

The early historic period in Kathiawad can be roughly dated between the fourth century BC and the sixth century AD.

Land-use Strategies

It has now been recognized that divisions between economies based on herding, hunting, gathering, and agriculture may not have been as sharp as has been projected. Concerning western Asia, Lancaster and Lancaster (1991a:136) have suggested that 'individuals or groups could and did move across the conventional divides between agriculture, pastoralism and hunting/gathering for longer or shorter periods and in every possible direction. All the groups would have been doing everything some of the time though the emphasis would vary.'

In south-east Oman, where neither herding nor fishing in itself can sustain the population over an annual cycle, Lancaster and Lancaster (1991b) observe that while families may identify themselves either as fishermen or herders, in practice most of them were engaged in both activities. For instance, within fishing families, older men, women, and young boys and girls were often involved with herding and, in a reverse situation, sometimes herding groups had households participating in fishing as well. Apart from fishing and herding, other activities include trade, transporting of dried fish and dates, as well as making charcoal.

Chetan Singh in his paper drew our attention to the agro-pastoralists of Kinnaur. He does not regard the prevalence of agro-pastoralism in this region as merely an adaptive response to the physical environment; rather, he suggests that cultural factors also played a role. Kinnaur society may have held the head of an 'agro-pastoral combine' as a symbol of success. The transportation and trading of goods were also integral to the survival strategies in this region.

Prasad (1995) has argued that the topography, soil conditions, and natural vegetation in the Maikal Range (the area inhabited by the Baigas) required long fallow cycles, the maintenance of which necessitated multiple subsistence strategies that alternated between hunting, gathering, and cultivation. The causal factor behind the flexibility in subsistence strategies, however, is not just ecological, according to Prasad. In her paper in this volume she points out that the survival strategies of the Baiga should be seen as reflecting the ways in which these tribal groups were integrated in the local and regional political economy. And Menon in this volume finds that the strategies of craftsmen too can be flexible, depending on economic circumstances.

In a study of the settlement history of a people known as the Il Chamus in northern Kenya, Anderson (1988) found that between 1840 and 1880, the land use was mainly agriculture, with some herding, hunting, and fishing. During this period, the Il Chamus absorbed large number of pastoralists who had become destitute due to warfare, drought, and cattle plague. When destitute, pastoralists began to cultivate the soil, but once they had built up their herds they reverted to pastoralism. Some families may have cultivated for a relatively short period, while others may have taken two or three generations.

The reason for the large number of pastoralists seeking refuge with the Il Chamus and the quick rebuilding of herds was the opportunity provided by the caravan trade up to about 1880. Not only was grain exchanged but elephants were also often hunted by the Il Chamus and ivory supplied to traders. After 1880, the Il Chamus themselves started to change over to herding, and by the mid-1920s almost all their villages were deserted. Between 1920 and 1980, instances of shifts between herding and cultivation have been noted but there is no longer a 'permanent base of a reservoir of *cultivating pastoralists*' (ibid.:255). In this phase too, herders shifted to cultivation during periods of environmental stress.

There are also instances of pastoralists turning to hunting-gathering during periods of crises brought on by warfare, drought, or disease (Hodder 1982:87, 97–8), until they could build up their herds again. Conversely, hunters have been known to have made a shift to herding within a few decades in the early part of the twentieth century when several displaced pastoralist groups moved into their habitat. In order to claim residence in that area, these herding groups started intermarrying with the hunters. As a result, the latter received livestock as bride wealth. Hence, within a few decades hunters became primarily herders (Cronk 1989).

Thus, the flexibility that we encounter in land-use strategies can be attributed to multiple and often interrelated factors. 'There is perhaps a dialectical relationship between the "social", "cultural" and the "ecological" realm of pre-capitalist subsistence systems: the boundaries between the "ecological" and the "cultural" becoming quite obscure in some instances' (Prasad 1995:228). At the same time, we also have to bear in mind that flexibility may be related to modern-day pressures when increasingly groups are being pushed out of their habitats. Hence, flexibility is the key to the survival of many disadvantaged groups. Yet, Bird-David (1992:39-40), writing about the Nayakas (of the Nilgiri-Wynaad highlands), reminds us that 'while to us it seems that they shift between subsistence activities, from their perspective [the Nayakas] simply obtain their resources afforded by the environment through whatever means happens to be suitable'.

We thus expect flexibility in the past as well. Human populations have always had to deal with uncertainty. Multi-pronged subsistence strategies are mechanisms for dealing with uncertainty of rainfall, political insecurities, and oscillations in birth and death rates. Such flexibility is not revealed by the archaeological record.

Moreover, and more specifically, what kinds of sites does an archaeologist look for? Perhaps attempts to identify 'sedentary villages' as a category distinct from 'seasonal pastoral camps' or 'farmsteads' may be futile. It is possible that during the history of settlement at a 'site', its functions changed. For the archaeologist, the problem is that if such changes occur within a span of, say, two or three decades, they are unlikely to be discernible in the archaeological record. Equally important is the issue of the duration of the occupation of the sites, a major factor in the formation of mounds.

'Instability' and 'Stability' of Settlements: Implications for the Archaeological Record

Let us first consider how archaeologists view the permanence/impermanence of settlement. Some residents of permanently-settled villages may be absent periodically or seasonally (as in transhumant patterns) (Rafferty 1985:115-16), and the seasonally-occupied sites of the mobile families are considered to be a part of the sedentary settlement system. The problem with this definition is that all settlements are called sedentary, despite the varying degree of permanence ranging from a year (of continuous occupation) to several thousand years. It also implies that the sedentary settlement system would be inherently stable.

It is known that societies cannot be neatly slotted into two categories, mobile versus sedentary. Rather, mobility is an inextricable feature of most early subsistence and social systems. Even so, it continues to be assumed that sites are 'sedentary' or 'stable', although function/s may vary from time to time.

This kind of understanding of sedentary settlements can lead us to a problem. There are, for instance, shifting agriculturalists who have no villages. They are highly mobile, shifting residence every few years. Such shifts are often made by single households without consulting other families (Hodder 1978:226). In this situation, individual settlement sites are occupied all the year around; hence they could be termed sedentary. Would it not be better to speak of settlements in terms of permanence and short-term residence? Moreover, if a residence were to be abandoned every few years, there would be little mound formation.

There is some historical information on mobile groups. For instance, during the Mughal period, the gross cultivated area did not exceed 55 per cent of the gross cultivated in 1909-10. Singh (1988) points out that large portions of the empire were uncultivated, and were probably utilized by mobile groups such as the Jats and the Lohanis. The former were pastoralists who were gradually becoming 'settled peasants', while the latter were involved in herding and trading. Jat 'sedentarization' is attributed to the growing requirements of agricultural labour in the Mughal agrarian system. Yet in a period of economic crisis/recession, the recently 'sedentarized' Jats may have had to shift back to herding. Consequently, many of the newly-settled areas may have been deserted in the eighteenth century.

We need also to examine the historical evidence on the lifespan of villages. What proportion of villages are occupied for long periods? Sunder (1997:44-5) reports that families in Bastar 'routinely uprooted themselves and moved on'. She attributes this phenomenon to a low population, the absence of a strong central authority, and a production system involving hunting-gathering and shifting cultivation. For us the pertinent point is whether this kind of mobility concerns individual families or involves entire villages. Moreover, we also need to examine the reasons for the desertion. So too a distinction has to be made between village abandonments in tribal and state societies. Hence, we now turn to scattered ethnographic, archaeological, and historical sources to put together a patchwork model of rural settlement desertions.

The Desertion of Villages

Agricultural systems that do little to restore soil fertility see declining levels of output, and once the land becomes exhausted, villages are moved and new land is cleared for cultivation. A factor in the inability to maintain soils, particularly among agro-pastoral societies, could be that animals graze at a distance. In such a scenario, there may not have been enough manure for the fields (Ratnagar 1989:293-4). The frequency of ploughing has also to be considered. For instance, in Kathiawad for *kharif* crops ploughing is done twice, thrice, or even more often to improve the soil structure, in particular to encourage aeration and porosity (*Census of India, Gujarat*, V.6.1, 1961:31). And for the *rabi* crops fields were ploughed at least six times (Watson 1884:186-7).

Perhaps labour too was a constraining factor in the maintenance of soils in the protohistoric past. If people choose to practice intensive cultivation of fields (see O'Shea 1989:63), preferring to maintain a small number of large fields rather than a series of small dispersed fields, villages have to be relocated every ten to twenty years in order to maintain soil fertility.

Another response to environmental degradation can be a change in subsistence strategy. In south-western Iran at the end of the fifth millennium BC, archaeologists have inferred, land ceased to be agriculturally viable due to over-exploitation (Sumner-Columbus 1986:199-209) and a large majority of the sites were deserted. Initially, it had been thought that fewer sites implied a population decline. However, it is now being suggested that although villages had been abandoned, 'the region was neither desolate nor deserted' (ibid.:207). Instead of sedentary farmers, it was then inhabited predominantly by nomadic pastoralists who leave few archaeological traces. Farming was not entirely given up, which would explain the existence of some 'agriculture villages'. Sumner-Columbus' hypothesis is that this period was characterized by a 'tribal polity, sometimes fragmented and sometimes united'. Perhaps in tribal conditions there is greater flexibility and mobility in land use than is possible in state societies.

The collapse of the Classic Maya civilization began in the ninth century AD and in just over a hundred years, large sections of the southern sector of the lowlands had been abandoned, never to be re-occupied (Culbert 1988:69). The collapse of the Chacoan state too was followed by widespread abandonment of the San Juan basin in north-western New Mexico, after 1300 AD (Tainter 1988:183).

A similar scenario followed the civilizational collapse in the Harappan case. Ratnagar (2000:29) reports that out of 132 Harappan settlements taken into account because of the reliability of information, 101 were abandoned. It has been suggested that at least at three sites, Mohenjo-daro, Harappa, and Dholavira, there is evidence for hurried departure due to violence (ibid.:31, 35-48). The desertions have been attributed to group migrations and relocations (ibid.: 58-9). The relocated groups may have been initially small and hence remain invisible in the archaeological record. One factor that could have enabled village desertions was the absence of the institution of the temple. Further:

> in the absence of private ownership of land and registration of plots, of agricultural marketing, or expensive inputs such as insecticides and fertilizers, and given that in protohistoric times there would have been few people in proportion to the land available, and also that protohistoric subsistence never relied solely on agriculture but also involved the gathering of food, fishing, pastoral production, and hunting, we can assume that people were not irrevocably bound to particular villages. (ibid.:78)

It is also likely that in the Harappan period people were more dependent on the state than on each other, and hence with the collapse of the Bronze Age state, village economies may have required reorganization along new or different lines (ibid.:80-1).

In medieval France, the desertion of villages was fairly common.

> The disappearance of villages did not particularly disturb either the sovereign power or the preacher or the philosopher. The first thing to be stressed is the silence of the texts on this point. If the documents hardly ever mentioned these facts, the reason was no doubt that the desertion of villages was considered a normal event by contemporaries, precisely because it was so frequent. (Pesez and Le Roy Ladurie 1977:72)

A study of villages situated north-west of Paris reveal that longevity was related to size. For instance, only 3 per cent of the larger villages disappeared between the fourteenth century and the present, while the figures for smaller villages and hamlets are much higher: 15 per cent for small villages (21 to 49 households) and 30 per cent for hamlets (5 to 20 households). Studies in other regions of France confirm these findings. Marthelot (cf. Pesez and Le Roy Ladurie 1977:77) has remarked that the smaller settlements were more 'vulnerable to every crisis that arose such as war and economic and especially demographic, crises'.[2] Apart from war, epidemics, floods, silting, and fire, taxes and indebtedness also contributed to desertions. But Pesez and Le Roy Ladurie tell us that the desertion of villages cannot entirely be attributed to these factors. Instead, 'the lost villages appear to be no more than the fallout of a complex evolution that favoured some population centres at the expense of others, leading to a progressive concentration in some places and accentuated dispersal in others'. In Alsace, for instance, villages were forsaken for towns. Given this scenario, we could conclude that a quest for security prompted villages to be abandoned; yet often even after the restoration of security, the peasants did not return to the deserted villages (ibid.:85-7).

A similar scenario has been sketched by Gordon (1975, 1979 [rpt. 1994]) and Guha (1985, 1996, 1999) for the Deccan in the period between the seventeenth and the nineteenth centuries. Asir fort, located 16 km. from Burhanpur, often served as a place of refuge for the residents of Burhanpur in times of war. A seventeenth-century Portuguese account mentions that when Akbar reached the city in 1600, he found it completely deserted. Similarly, in 1775, Colonel Upton and his troops found only one man at the village of 'Tarlah Gon' (about 25 km. east of Burhanpur).

Gordon [1979 (rpt. 1994)] has examined the impact of adversity on villages in Malwa and Khandesh. Adversity for a village is defined 'as either a rapid decline in the supply of food (or money to buy it) or a rapid increase in demand for food or money by some agent outside the village' (ibid.:101). The decline in the supply of food could be a result of drought, floods, plant and animal disease, or human epidemics; external causes include increased revenue demand, exploitative local elites, passing armies, and marauders. During short-term adversity resulting from levies or exactions from passing armies, villagers often disappeared into the surrounding countryside till such time as the army moved on. For instance, Charles Malet while

[2] Horne (1994:79) too has observed that random fluctuations in demography affect the smaller settlements more than the larger ones.

crossing Malwa and Khandesh in 1780 during the first Anglo-Maratha war found several deserted villages.

Large areas of Khandesh and Malwa were often raided by the Bhils and the Kolis inhabiting the 'buffer zones' or the marginal agricultural areas surrounding the Malwa plateau and the Tapi valley. In this situation too, villages were often temporarily deserted. After 1749, in several *parganas* of Khandesh, the Peshwa began to appropriate the maintenance estates of one of his generals, Bande. A little later, the estates of Bande's entire faction were seized. As a result, a rebellion broke out, with Bande and his men turning against their own estates in order to prevent the collection of any revenue by the state officials. Crop production also suffered in the following year due to drought and the destruction of irrigation works during the rebellion. In 1751, after the Battle of Bhalke, Khandesh province was ceded to the Marathas.

Due to all these factors, villages began to be abandoned. In Adilabad *pargana*, there were 4 deserted villages in 1748, but by 1751 the number had risen to 12. In the adjacent Erandol *pargana*, 6 villages were abandoned around 1751. In Nimbait, out of 51 villages, 23 had been deserted by 1753. In the Dhulia *pargana* (with 125 villages), 31 villages were vacated in a space of about three years. Even more extreme was the case of Baglan *sarkar* in south-west Khandesh where in Songir *pargana*, all the villages had become deserted. Moreover, several *sarkars* (between Khandesh and Malwa) that were vulnerable to attacks by the Bhils were also completely abandoned.[3]

Yet this whole situation changed within a decade, with most areas being repopulated with the resumption of cultivation; many people seeking refuge with relatives in still-occupied neighbouring villages, but in areas where abandonment was on a larger scale, with state intervention. The latter included defeating the major rebels, adopting a conciliatory or punitive policy towards the Bhils, appointing officials specially for recruiting settlers, offering potential settlers favourable tax terms, and also rebuilding some of the irrigation works. Significantly, it was not a simple case of villagers returning to their ancestral

[3] We are aware that many Bhils would also have formed a part of these village communities, but there were others who would have inhabited a different niche in the forest. (I am grateful to Nandini Sinha for bringing up this point during the workshop.)

fields. In fact, we are informed that none of the repopulation documents indicate the return of the original population.

Mountstuart Elphinstone's *Report*, compiled soon after the British conquered Maharashtra and Central India in 1818, said that:

> some parts of the provinces are still in a high state of cultivation, and others, more recently abandoned, convey a high notion of their former richness and prosperity; but the greater part of Candeish is covered with thick jungle, but scattered with the ruins of former villages. The districts north of the Tapty in particular, which were formerly very populous, and yielded a large revenue, are now almost uninhabited forest (Gordon 1979 [rpt. 1994]:113-14)

W.H. Sykes, Statistical Reports to the Government of Bombay in 1820s, wrote in 1829 that some of the northern and western parts of Khandesh 'are little better than a jungle, and the whole province is miserably depopulated' (cf. Guha 1985:168).

Here are some figures for the abandonment of villages in this period. For instance, 280 villages are said to have existed in the Sultanpur division in western Khandesh. Of the 206 held by Holkar, only 37 had inhabitants in 1810; the rest had been abandoned. What is also interesting to note is that of the 280 villages of the Maratha period, the existence of the only 11 are attested to in the Mughal period others were new villages (Guha 1996:48-9).

Before we go into the details of what lay behind these events, we would like to point out that the crisis lasted for about two decades, at the end of which there were few visible signs that the area had once been inhabited. In fact, the landscape was completely transformed. We find that villages once deserted were very quickly eclipsed; scrub weeds were replaced by thorny bushes and trees; when irrigation works fell into disuse, drainage changed and large areas north of the Tapti became infested with malaria; and predatory animals fanned onto the plains and the river valleys. In such a scenario, repopulation would have required a great deal of effort. Moreover, the customary law prevalent in Maharashtra gave a *thurlkuree* (or original cultivator) thirty years in which to return and reclaim his land. As a result 'very few of the new villages were built on the exact site of older villages' (Gordon 1979 [rpt. 1994]:118).

Why is it that the crisis of 1750 was followed by a quick recovery while that of the early nineteenth century resulted in complete destruction? The devastation beginning in 1802 first saw the land being ruined by Holkar's army; this was followed by a famine; and this process of destruction was completed by Bhil raids (ibid.:113-14). So in a sense, many of the elements are common to both situations—a tussle over paramountcy resulting in warfare, then a drought, followed by Bhil raids. Gordon, however, is of the view that there are two important differences. The first is the absence of a strong central authority which could crush the revolts of the chiefs in the early nineteenth century. The second is related to the nature of Maratha armies, especially the policy of recruiting mercenary war bands of Pindaris. Often Pindaris in collusion with local landed elites raided the villages and residents were left with three options: to become marauders themselves, seek refuge with the local armed zamindar (and cultivate land around his fort), or migrate long distances to safe parts, including large towns. In 1820, John Briggs, the Khardese Commissioner in the early 1820s, found over 400 forts in Khandesh with populations living inside or outside the walls (ibid.: 115). Regarding the third option, one account, dated 1843, mentions that 'cultivators fled to Berar and Guzerat' (Guha 1996:141-2).

Thus, we find that villagers return to a settlement only in the case of short-term adversity, say, for a few weeks. But in times when adverse situations continued beyond a year, there is no evidence for their return. Moreover, the process of rehabilitation was an arduous one and could even take a century or so. It is, therefore, clear that villages may not have been as stable in the past as has been assumed.

Further south, we find that deserted villages were a regular feature of rural Tamil Nadu in the late eighteenth and early nineteenth centuries. Lardinois (1989:16-48) has undertaken a quantitative assessment of the villages deserted between 1730 and 1830, based on the censuses conducted by the East India Company. In the archival sources, three categories of villages are mentioned: *mazra* (principal or revenue villages), *majra* (secondary villages), and *be-chiragh* (uninhabited villages). Sometimes, the *be-chiragh* villages were also classified according to their principal or secondary status. The distinction between principal and secondary villages was mainly on administrative grounds and was not based on size or population; secondary villages may have been predominantly inhabited by occupational castes, while revenue villages by landowning households. Overall, the statistics collated by Lardinois covered eighty *talukas*. Out of a total of 32,993 villages, 4,288 (12 per cent) were considered as deserted or in ruins. The deserted sites were reported in the dry central tablelands as well as in irrigated lowland areas of the coastal plain. The average population of a village in the central areas was less than 100 (or 20 households), while in the coastal plains it was almost 250 (50 households). A comparison of the distribution of the deserted villages by status, principal or secondary, revealed a slightly higher desertion rate for the subordinate villages (ibid.:22). For instance, in Coimbatore, in 1846-7, about 9 per cent of secondary villages were designated as deserted, compared to just 2 per cent of principal sites; in Tiruchirapalli district, nearly 27 per cent of subordinate villages were deserted while no principal villages were so classified; in Madurai, in 1813-14, approximately 32 per cent and 28 per cent of principal and secondary villages were so described; but in North Arcot district, the desertion rates were the same (12 per cent) for both categories.

Along with the desertion of villages, there was a corresponding reduction in cultivation. Simultaneously, a large number of tanks (ranging from 30 per cent to 60 per cent in different *talukas*) have also been classed as unusable. In this case, the widespread desertion of sites was attributed to war, famine, and epidemics. Although Lardinois is not very certain whether these desertions reflect temporary or permanent migrations, in the absence of records of the establishment of new villages, he seems to hold that migration (from rural to urban areas) alone does not explain the phenomenon of deserted villages. Perhaps we must also contend with a demographic crisis, with the period 1780 to 1830 witnessing 'a decline in population of perhaps 15 to 20 per cent' followed by 'no population growth' (ibid.:32-3).

Village desertions thus appear to have been fairly common in the protohistoric period and need to be investigated. Although the picture that is emerging is far from clear, we may to draw some tentative conclusions. First, in early societies when population would have been fairly low, and output not very high, there may have been little incentive for investment exclusively in agriculture; there were multiple other subsistence options, as well as general availability of land. In times of crises due to soil infertility, political insecurities, war, epidemics, or drought, relocation may have taken place. The scale of adversity could also have been an operating condition. In case of a minor adversity extending from a few days to a few weeks, villagers may have returned but when it extended to over a year, then villages may have been permanently abandoned. We note that if desertions were a recurrent feature and villages were routinely short-lived, then they would have little visibility in the archaeological record.

Another significant factor leading to desertions could have been a demographic crisis. This is an area of research that needs to be investigated further. It is generally believed that the onset of agriculture in prehistory led to an increase in population density at the cost of reduced mobility. During the spread of early farming in Europe, there was a rapid growth of farming communities resulting in the absorption or displacement of hunter-gatherers. Moreover, with a demographic increase there is a gradual but continuous expansion of agricultural communities. Population increase at a constant radial rate has been referred to as 'diffusional', a wave of advance (Ammerman and Cavalli-Sforza 1973:343-560). However, this does not seem to be the case in Kathiawad. Instead of a demographic expansion, the protohistoric period may have witnessed a demographic crisis.

There could also have been deliberate population dislocations in connection with the colonizing movements of a state. For instance, Ratnagar (1991:94-5) suggests that the Harappan state may have 'organized movements and resettlement of people on a substantial

TABLE 1: SIZEWISE DESERTION OF RANGPUR II B–C SITES

Size (ha)	Number of sites in the II B-C period	Number of sites deserted at the end of the II B-C period
0.1 – 1.0	20	18
1.1 – 2.0	11	10
2.1 – 3.0	6	6
3.1 – 4.0	7	4
4.1 – 5.0	3	3
5.1 – 6.0	7	5
6.1 – 7.0	4	3
7.1 – 8.0	5	5
10.1 – 11.0	1	1
11.1 – 12.0	4	4
12.1 – 13.0	1	1
13.1 – 14.0	2	2
16.1 – 17.0	1	1
23.1 – 24.0	1	1
Total number of sized sites	73 +	64

Note: + Sizes of only 73 of a total of 140 sites are known.

scale'. In later periods, the practice of giving land grants would also have led to considerable relocations of populations.

With this discussion, we return to our problem of the non-existence of mounds in Kathiawad between the chalcolithic and the early historic periods.

Disjunctures in the Settlement History of Kathiawad

Apart from the long hiatus,[4] we need to recognize that at no site in Kathiawad is there continuity in occupation from the chalcolithic to the early historic periods.[5] Among the excavated site are Rangpur,

[4] However, this may not have been as protracted as it appears, for at Nagara (Mehta 1968:17-18), Prabhas Patan (Nanavati, Mehta and Chowdhary 1971:56-61), and Dwarka (Ansari and Mate 1966:29; *IAR* 1979:25-9), there is evidence for the occupation of these sites prior to the fourth century BC. While at Prabhas Patan, iron in association with black-and-red ware has been reported from pre-northern black polished ware levels (*IAR* 1955-6:7-8; *IAR* 1956-7:17), no details are known about Dwarka except the occurrence of black-and-red ware (*IAR* 1979-80:25-9). The picture is no better for Nagara even though the excavation report has been published. Here in the earliest levels (before the occurrence of northern black polished ware and punch-marked coins) have been reported a range of ceramics (plain red ware, burnished red ware, fine black-and-red ware, and coarse ware) in association with bone tools. No copper or iron artefacts were recovered in this stratum. Regarding all other artefacts (of stone, terracotta, and shell), the particular stratum in which they were deposited has not been indicated. The pre-northern black polished ware levels at this site comprise a 7 m. deposit, suggesting a substantial length of occupation. We may compare this with the northern black polished ware and the red polished ware levels which constitute nearly 6.5 m. of deposit here (Mehta 1968:Figs. 3 and 6).

Outside our region, iron objects have been reported in pre-northern black polished ware contexts from Nagal and Bharuch in south Gujarat; Nagda, Eran, and Ujjain in Malwa; and Prakash and Bahal in the northern Deccan (Banerjee 1986:19, 27-8; *IAR* 1958-9:19, 195; *IAR* 1961-2:11: Thapar 1964-5:23, 123; Tripathi 1976: 99-100). The depth of deposit below the earliest occurrence of the northern black polished ware is usually between 4 m. and 5 m. testifying to a fairly lengthy occupation. But nowhere are there clusters of radiocarbon dates relating to the early Iron Age levels.

[5] A shorter hiatus in occupation spanning 100 to 400 years is evident in the Deccan between the chalcolithic and the early historic periods at sites such as Nevasa, Songaon, Navdatoli, Maheshwar, Prakash, and Nasik (Dhavalikar 1973: 145, 147; Ratnagar 1989:299).

Lothal, Kuntasi, Vagad, Padri, Oriyo, Kanewal, and Nesadi, mostly occupied in the chalcolithic period. Nagara, Valabhi, and Amreli are early historic in date. There are three excavated sites, Prabhas Patan, Dwarka, and Rojdi, that were inhabited in both periods, but at all three sites there is a sterile layer separating the two occupations. While no details are known for Rojdi (*IAR* 1958-9:20-1) or Dwarka (*IAR* 1979-80:28-9), at Prabhas Patan, the gap in the occupation is stratigraphically represented by a 30 cm. sterile layer (*IAR* 1971-2: 13).

The sizes of 73 Rangpur II B-C sites (51 per cent) out of a total of 140 sites are known to us. They range between 0.2 and 23.9 hectares (Varma 1997:157-9). Contrary to our expectations, we find that both large and small sites were deserted at the end of the Rangpur II B-C period. Moreover, there is a high incidence of deserted sites in our region. Out of 140 Rangpur II B-C sites, only 17 continue into the next period of occupation, while out of 44 Rangpur III sites, barely 9 are reoccupied in the Iron Age. Hence, 88 per cent of the Rangpur II B-C and 80 per cent of the Rangpur III are abandoned (ibid.:348-56). It may be noted that these figures for the desertion of settlements seem to be higher than the two other areas in the subcontinent for which we could collate the data on settlement continuity.[6]

[6] For instance, in the central Tapi basin, out of 26 Savalda (2000-1800 BC) sites, 8 continue into the Late Harappan (1800-1600 BC) period; out of 21 Late Harappan sites, only 3 continue into the Malwa (1600-1400 BC) period; out of the 36 Malwa sites, 11 continue into the Jorwe (1400-1000 BC) period; and out of 47 Jorwe sites, 19 are reoccupied in the early historic (600 BC-400 AD) period. Thus, here the desertion figures are as follows: 69 per cent in the Savalda period, 86 per cent in the Late Harappan, 69 per cent in the Malwa, and 60 per cent in the Jorwe phase. These figures have been compiled from Shinde's survey (1998). In the Ganga valley, however, the patterns for settlement desertions appear to be quite different. Here, we find that out of 45 Painted Grey Ware (PGW) Culture (1300-700 BC) sites, as many as 43 continue into the Northern Black Polished Ware (NBPW) period (700-200 BC). Of the 99 NBPW sites, 91 continue into the early historic (200 BC-300 AD) period. These figures are based on Lal's survey (1984). We find a much more stable pattern in this case, with only 5 per cent and 8 per cent desertions in the PGW and NBPW periods respectively. Another point of contrast with Kathiawad and the Deccan is the absence of a hiatus in occupation in the first millennium BC in the Ganga valley.

I do not rule out altogether a catastrophic abandonment due to widespread aridity at the end of the Rangpur III occupation. Yet, when no incontrovertible evidence has been found regarding change in climate, the reason/s for the absence of mounds could lie elsewhere.

In my analysis of Kathiawad settlement patterns, several points had emerged (ibid.:11-64). We had found that in the peninsula, soils are shallow and not very productive. Moreover, Kathiawad falls in an area of high seasonality and consequently droughts and crop failures are frequent. What also came to the fore is that in the past our region has remained sparsely populated. In all probability, therefore, land-use strategies were highly flexible, involving herding, cultivation, hunting, and gathering. It is equally possible that subsistence strategies alternated between hunting/gathering, herding, and cultivation. This appears to be occasionally suggested by the archaeological record too. For instance, at the site of Kanewal, the chalcolithic habitation levels lie sandwiched between the mesolithic occupations (Mehta and Momin 1980:12-14). Another site, Ratanpura, in the Rupen estuary of north Gujarat, has both mesolithic as well as chalcolithic occupations (Bhan 1989:228, 231). Although it has been suggested that the chalcolithic settlement was subsequently occupied by hunter-gatherers, a simple sequence is not present to corroborate this view.

The reduction of the mean size of sites in the Rangpur III period (2.9 ha. as compared to 4.5 ha. in the Rangpur II B-C period) could indicate smaller aggregations of populations (Varma 1997:160). Perhaps, in the subsequent centuries, the average size of sites became even smaller. Relatively small and dispersed populations can enhance the potential of local hunting, collecting, and grazing activities. Moreover, in an area which has poor soils, fields may have become exhausted periodically and villages would have moved frequently.[7] Perhaps the absence of local elites, or state institutions, could even have encouraged such a tendency. Elsewhere, we have suggested that the earliest evidence for chiefships in our region comes from the early historic period (ibid.:275-94). If small populations had occupied

[7] If there were frequent desertions, then we cannot rule out the repeated reuse of particular sites. However, if new settlements were being established next to a site rather than on top of the earlier settlement, there would be shallow occupational deposits (Horne 1994:78).

villages for relatively short periods, mound formation would have been retarded. For instance, if sites on an average were less than half a hectare in size, were occupied for less than a hundred years, and were not overlain by vegetation or later period occupations, then perhaps such sites would not be visible archaeologically.[8]

Settlement morphology can also play a role in the formation of mounds. Horne (1994:165) has observed that compact villages with structures close together will leave a deeper deposit than those with scattered houses. A compact mass of buildings and material tends to be better protected from exposure and erosion. She has also suggested that more densely built villages will build up a deposit at a faster rate than those with a lower density. That the spatial layout of village houses in Kathiawad was dispersed has been referred to elsewhere (Varma 1997:169).

It is equally possible that there was a gradual shift from farming to herding. Earlier we had discussed that often impoverished pastoralists turn temporarily to farming. Cultivation may offer a survival strategy for pastoralists who have lost their herds. Perhaps in the insecure times that followed the collapse of the Harappan state, destitute pastoralists turned to agriculture. Animal wealth can be an easy target during raids and invasions. This could be one explanation for the increase in the number of sites in Kathiawad from 5 in the Mature Harappan period to 140 in the Rangpur II B-C. Over time pastoralists would have built up their herds, and there may have been a gradual shift from agro-pastoralism to pastoralism (see Varma 1991). Increasing nomadic incursions can also contribute to the conversion of agricultural lands into pasture. Hence, the reduction in the number of sites from 140 to 44 and, finally the desertion of all the sites at the end of the Rangpur III period. As Mace (1993:369) writes, 'pastoralists are likely to increase their chances of long-term survival by taking up agro-pastoralism if their wealth declines below a certain

[8] A similar situation could perhaps be hypothesized for the end of the Deccan chalcolithic, with large villages such as Inamgaon, Daimabad, and others being deserted. We have seen that the Ganga valley had an extremely low desertion rate. Perhaps due to the availability of better soils, a more stable subsistence strategy based primarily on agriculture may have developed here. Moreover, the emergence of states in the Ganga valley in the mid-first millennium BC could have been a contributing factor.

level; similarly, when agro-pastoralists become wealthy, they will usually do better to give up cultivating and devoting their effort to their herds'.

We cannot discount a third possibility: demographic crisis. So far we have no evidence for such a crisis from our region but negative evidence cannot preclude this possibility either. Elsewhere, Ratnagar (1989:289) has drawn our attention to the low life expectancy at Inamgaon, a chalcolithic village located on the Ghod river. Out of 243 burials, nearly 154 (or 63 per cent) were child burials. Evidence for infantile scurvy and iron-deficiency anaemia have been cited.

In this essay we have explored several possible reasons for the non-existence of mounds in Kathiawad between the chalcolithic and the early historic periods.[9] Perhaps it was a combination of three major factors: the nature of villages (small and short-lived), a gradual shift to pastoralism, and a demographic crisis. The entire discussion is based on the assumption that the field survey techniques utilized so far in Kathiawad have been accurate enough to uncover small mounds. Also, as pointed out by Runnels (1995:96), survey methods need to 'shift away from the investigation of single sites to studies of the natural and cultural history of entire regions'. Until we adopt the 'non-site' approach by recording artefact scatters and isolated features on the landscape, we will continue to have these gaps in settlement histories.

[9] This phenomenon is not unique to the period between the chalcolithic and the early historic. A similar gap in occupation has been observed in the early medieval period in the Deccan. Several archaeological sites in this region (Paunar, Nasik, Karad, Kaundinyapur, Kolhapur, and Nevasa) show a disjuncture in habitation—a gap of seven to eight centuries (Mate 1990). Yet inscriptional evidence reveals that the Chalukyas of Badami, the Rashtrakutas of Malkhed, and the Yadavas of Devagiri ruled over this region between the fifth and the thirteenth centuries AD.

Adding to this, Ajay Dandekar also brought to my notice the absence of land grants and inscriptions in the early medieval period (eighth to the thirteenth centuries) in the semi-arid zone of the area between the Godavari and the Krishna river valleys. However, the landscape is dotted with cattle-raid-depicting hero-stones. In his paper, Dandekar has argued that in this region cattle pastoralism played an important role in resource mobilization and in the state formation processes.

REFERENCES

Ammerman, A.J. and L.L. Cavalli-Sforza, 'A population model for the diffusion of early farming in Europe', in C. Renfrew, ed., *The explanation of culture change: models in prehistory*, London: Duckworth, 1973, pp. 343-57.

Anderson, D.M., 'Cultivating pastoralists: ecology and economy among the Il Chamus of Baringo, 1849-1980', in D.H. Johnson and D.M. Anderson, eds., *The ecology of survival: case studies from northeast African history*, London and Boulder, Colorado: Lester Crook Academic Publishing Westview, 1988, pp. 241-60.

Ansari, Z.D. and M.S. Mate, *Excavations at Dwarka*, Poona: Deccan College, 1966.

Banerjee, N.R., *Nagda (1955-57)*, New Delhi: Archaeological Survey of India, 1986.

Bhan, K.K., 'Late Harappan settlements of western India with specific reference to Gujarat', in J.M. Kenoyer, ed., *Old problems and new perspectives in the archaeology of south Asia*, Madison: University of Wisconsin, 1989, pp. 219-42.

Bird-David, N., 'Beyond the hunting and gathering mode of subsistence: culture-sensitive observations on the Nayaka and other modern hunter-gatherers', *Man* (n.s.), vol. 27, no. 1, 1992, pp. 19-44.

Cameron, C.M., 'Abandonment and archaeological interpretations', in C.M. Cameron and S.A. Tomka, eds., *Abandonment of settlements and regions: ethnoarchaeological and archaeological approaches*, Cambridge: Cambridge University Press, 1993, pp. 3-7.

Census of India. Gujarat, vol. V, no. 6.1, Delhi: Government of India, 1961.

Cronk, L., 'From hunters to herders: subsistence change as a reproductive strategy among the Mukogoda', *Current Anthropology*, vol. 30, no. 2, 1989, pp. 224-34.

Culbert, T.P., 'The Collapse of Classic Maya civilization', in N. Yoffee and G.L. Cowgill, eds., *The collapse of ancient states and civilizations*, Tucson: University of Arizona Press, 1988, pp. 69-101.

Dhavalikar, M.K., 'Development and decline of the Deccan chalcolithic', in D.P Agrawal and A. Ghosh, eds., *Radiocarbon and Indian Archaeology*, Bombay: Tata Institute of Fundamental Research, 1973, pp. 138-47.

Dhavalikar, M.K. and G.L. Possehl, 'The pre-Harappan period at Prabhas Patan and the pre-Harappan phase in Gujarat', *Man and Environment*, vol. 17, no. 1, 1992, pp. 71-8.

Dhavalikar, M.K., M.H. Raval and Y.M. Chitalwala, *Kuntasi: A Harappan emporium on west coast*, Pune: Deccan College, 1996.

Gordon, S., 'Forts and social control in the Maratha state', *Modern Asian Studies*, vol. 13, 1975, reprinted in S. Gordon, *Marathas, marauders, and state formation in eighteenth-century India*, Delhi: Oxford University Press, 1994.

———, 'Recovery from adversity in eighteenth-century India: rethinking villages, peasants and politics in pre-modern kingdoms', *Peasant Studies*, vol. 8, no. 4 (Fall 1979), reprinted in S. Gordon, *Marathas, marauders, and state formation in eighteenth-century India*, Delhi: Oxford University Press, 1994.

Guha, S., *The agrarian economy of the Bombay Deccan 1818-1941*, Delhi: Oxford University Press, 1985.

———, 'Forest politics and agrarian empires: the Khandesh Bhils, c. 1700- 1850', *Indian Economic and Social History Review*, vol. 33, no. 2, 1996, pp. 133-53.

———, *Environment and ethnicity in India, 1200-1991*, Cambridge: Cambridge University Press, 1999.

Hodder, I., 'Social organization and human interaction: the development of some tentative hypotheses in terms of material culture', in I. Hodder, ed., *Spatial organization of culture*, London: Duckworth, 1978, pp. 199-269.

———, *Symbols in action: ethnoarchaeological studies of material culture*, Cambridge: Cambridge University Press, 1982.

Horne, L., *Village spaces: settlement and society in northeastern Iran*, Washington and London: Smithsonian Institution Press, 1994.

Indian Archaeology—A Review (IAR) 1953-93.

Lal, M., *Settlement history and rise of civilization in Ganga-Yamuna Doab (from 1500 BC to 300 AD)*, Delhi: B.R. Publishing, 1984.

Lancaster, W. and F. Lancaster, 'Limitations on sheep and goat herding in the eastern Badia of Jordan: an ethno-archaeological enquiry', *Levant*, vol. 23, 1991a, pp. 125-38.

———, 'Tribe, community and the concept of access to resources: territorial behaviour in south-east Ja'alan', in M.J. Casimir and A. Rao, eds., *Mobility and territoriality: social and spatial boundaries among foragers, fishers, pastoralists and peripatetics*, New York and Oxford: Berg, 1991b, pp. 343-63.

Lardinois, R., 'Deserted villages and depopulation in rural Tamil Nadu c. 1780-1830', in T. Dyson, ed., *India's historical geography—studies in famine, disease and society*, London-Riverdale: Curzon Press-The Riverdale Company, 1989, pp. 16-48.

Mace, R., 'Transitions between cultivation and pastoralism in sub-Saharan Africa', *Current Anthropology*, vol. 34, no. 4, 1993, pp. 363-82.

Mate, M.S., 'The clay feet?' *Bulletin of the Deccan College Post-graduate and Research Institute*, Vol. 49, 1990, pp. 243-9.

Mehta, R.N. *Excavation at Nagara*, Baroda: M.S. University, 1968.

Mehta, R.N. and K.N. Momin, *Excavation at Kanewal*, Baroda: M.S. University, 1980.

Nanavati, J.M., R.N. Mehta and S.N. Chowdhary, *Somanth 1956*, Baroda: M.S. University, 1971.

O'Shea, J., 'The role of wild resources in small-scale agricultural systems: tales from the Lakes and Plains', in P. Halstead and J. O'Shea, eds., *Bad year economics: cultural responses to risk and uncertainty*, Cambridge: Cambridge University Press, 1989, pp. 57-67.

Pandya, S., 'Recent advances in protohistoric Gujarat', *Puratattva*, vol. 12, 1980-1, pp. 59-63.

Pesez, J-M. and E. Le Roy Ladurie, 'The deserted villages of France: an overview', in R. Foster and O. Ranum, eds. and trs., *Rural society in France: selections from the Annales: economics, societies, civilizations*, Baltimore and London: The Johns Hopkins University Press, 1977, pp. 72-106.

Possehl, G.L., *Indus civilization in Saurashtra*, New Delhi: B.R. Publishing, 1980.

———, 'The date of Indus urbanization: a proposed chronology for the pre-urban and urban Harappan phases', in A.J. Gail and G.J.R. Mevissen, eds., *South Asian Archaeology 1991*, Stuttgart: F. Steiner, 1993, pp. 231-49.

Prasad, A., 'The political ecology of swidden cultivation: the survival strategies of the Baigas in the Central Provinces of India, 1860-1890', *Tools and Tillage*, vol. 7, no. 4, 1995, pp. 206-30.

Rafferty, J.E., 'The archaeological record on sedentariness: recognition, development and implications', in M.B. Schiffer, ed., *Advances in Archaeological Method and Theory*, vol. 8, Orlando: Academic Press, 1985, pp. 113-56.

Rao, S.R., *Lothal and the Indus civilization*, Bombay: Asia Publishing House, 1973.

———, *Lothal: a Harappan port town*, vol. 1, New Delhi: Archaeological Survey of India, 1979.

Ratnagar, S., 'A chalcolithic village in a famine belt', *Studies in History*, vol. 5, no. 2, n.s., 1989, pp. 287-302.

———, *Enquiries into the political organization of Harappan society*, Pune: Ravish, 1991.

———, *The end of the great Harappan tradition*, New Delhi: Manohar, 2000.

Runnels, C.N., 'Environmental degradation in Greece', *Scientific American*, March 1995, pp. 96-9.

Schlanger, S.H. and R.H. Wilshusen, 'Local abandonments and regional conditions in the North American Southwest', in C.M. Cameron and S.A. Tomka, eds., *Abandonment of settlements and regions: ethnoarchaeological and archaeological approaches*, Cambridge: Cambridge University Press, 1993, pp. 85-98.

Shinde, V.S., *Early settlements in the central Tapi basin*, New Delhi: Munshiram Manoharlal, 1998.

Shinde, V.S. and E. Thomas, 'A unique Harappan fish-hook from Padri, Gujarat', *Man and Environment*, vol. XVIII, no. 2, 1993, pp. 145-7.

Singh, C., 'Conformity and conflict: tribes and the "agrarian system" of Mughal India', *Indian Economic and Social History Review*, vol. 25, no. 3, 1988, pp. 319-40.

Sonawane, V.H. and P. Ajithprasad, 'Harappa culture in Gujarat', *Man and Environment*, vol. XIX, nos. 1-2, 1994, pp. 129-39.

Sumner-Columbus, W. M., 'Proto-Elamite civilization in Fars', in U. Finkbeiner and W. Rolig, eds., *Gamdat Nasr: period or regional style?*, Wiesbaden: L. Reichert Verlag, 1986, pp. 199-211.

Sunder, N., *Subalterns and sovereigns: an anthropological history of Bastar (1854-1996)*, Delhi: Oxford University Press, 1997.

Tainter, J.A., *The collapse of complex societies*, Cambridge: Cambridge University Press, 1988.

Thapar, B.K., 'Prakash 1955: a chalcolithic site in the Tapti valley', *Ancient India*, vol. 20-1, 1964-5, pp. 5-167.

Tomka, S.A., 'Site abandonment behaviour among transhumant pastoralists: the effects of delayed curation on assemblage composition', in C.M. Cameron and S.A. Tomka, eds., *Abandonment of settlements and regions: ethnoarchaeological and archaeological approaches*, Cambridge: Cambridge University Press, 1993, pp. 11-24.

Tomka, S.A. and M.C. Stevenson, 'Understanding abandonment processes: summary and remaining concerns', in C.M. Cameron and S.A. Tomka, eds., *Abandonment of settlements and regions: ethnoarchaeological and archaeological approaches*, Cambridge: Cambridge University Press, 1993, pp. 191-4.

Tripathi, V., *The Painted Grey Ware: an Iron Age culture of northern India*, Delhi: Concept Publishing, 1976.

Varma, S., 'Villages abandoned: the case for mobile pastoralism in post-Harappan Gujarat', *Studies in History*, vol. 7, no. 2, n.s., 1991, pp. 279-300.

———, 'Settlement patterns in Kathiawar from the chalcolithic to the early historic period', Ph.D. dissertation, New Delhi: Jawaharlal Nehru University, 1997.

Watson, J.W., *Gazetteer of the Bombay Presidency. Kathiawar*, vol. VIII, Bombay: Government Central Press, 1884.

The Bhils in the Historic Setting of Western India

NANDINI SINHA KAPUR

THIS ESSAY highlights the processes of the interaction between the Bhils[1] and the regional states and the rural society in which they lived, in southern Rajasthan and Gujarat, in medieval times. Sources for this study are drawn from inscriptions, literary texts, bardic traditions, and the accounts of European travellers. The central theme relates to the participation of the Bhils in the processes of regional state formation, their contacts with rural peasant society, and the consequent emergence of an elite among the Bhils. I have thus tried to break the traditional academic mould (see Roy 1915; idem 1925; Elwin 1942; Majumdar 1950; Dave 1960; Das and Raha 1963) of treating tribal peoples as isolated and in a stereotyped image.

* I take this opportunity to express my gratitude to Prof. Shereen Ratnagar, Dr. Rudolf Heredia, and Dr. Ajay Dandekar for inviting me to this seminar on Nomatic Pastoralism.

[1] 'Bhil' is an outsider's name that derives from the Dravidian word *Vil* or *Vilawar* meaning a bow or a bow-man and indicates a prevalent perception of the Bhils as good archers (see Doshi 1971:32). The earliest mention of the name *Bhil* in Sanskrit literature occurs in the *Kathāsarit-sāgara* of Gunadhya (*c.* AD 600) where there is a mention of an elephant-riding Bhil chief denying a king passage through the Vindhyas. Today the Bhils of Rajasthan are classified into Gametia Bhils (who claim to be decendants of the Bhil rulers and heads of the Bhil villages and who are concentrated in the northern and western parts of Udaipur district and in parts of Sirohi district), Kataria Bhils (Dhariavad, Ashpur, and Ghatol tehsils of Udaipur, Dungarpur, and Banswara districts), and the Mama Bhils of Kushalgarh. The Bhils are the largest tribal community in Gujarat, where they are divided into major groups such as the Bhil Garasia, Vasavas, Pawra Bhil, and Tavadi Bhil (see Suresh Singh 1997:118, 125-7).

Colonial Reports and Changing Perceptions of the Bhils: A Brief Survey

W. Crooke of the Bengal Civil Service, quoting from the *Rajputana Gazetteer* of the late nineteenth century, observes that all Bhils go about armed with tribal weapons, bows, and arrows, keep quiet in the winter and the rainy season, but indulge in raiding other thereafter (W. Crooke 1896:48–9). At that time notions of a hunting-gathering group reduced to the ranks of farm servants and field labourers dominated the definitions of the Bhils (Russell and Hira Lal 1969:292; Sherring 1975). However, the ethnographer R.E. Enthoven gave a more realistic description of the Bhils of Gujarat and Khandesh as peasants, labourers, and watchmen (1920:170).

Modern anthropological studies of the Bhils then began. Y.V.S. Nath, analysing the social structure of the Bhils of Ratanmal, observes that they are primarily cultivators and their non-agricultural income accrues from labouring on timber and charcoal coupes (dumps) in forests (Nath 1960:40). T.B. Naik (himself a Bhil) rightly opines that the Bhil economy was not of primitive character. The Bhils 'show rationality in their choice for the disposal of scarce means over numberless requirements', he states (Naik 1956:70). Echoing Naik's views, Ranvir Saxena states that the study of the economy of tribes in general is a study of rural economics in which agriculture and forests form the principal and secondary sources of livelihood (Saxena 1964:279; see also Kumar 1997:40).

Yet such observations failed to inspire the vision of the latest generation of anthropologists. For instance, Ramamani and Singh feel that tribal societies being non-industrialized and non-monetized small-scale communities, 'the economy is only a part of the social setup' (Ramamani 1988:70) and 'in the absence of any mechanism for surplus appropriation, their mode of production hardly underwent any significant change' (Singh 1995:16). Neither scholar highlights the management of local resources or adaptations to alternative strategies for survival in particular historical settings as, for instance, do Chetan Singh, Supriya Varma, Archana Prasad, and Jaya Menon in this volume (see also Casimier and Rao, 1991; Lancaster and Lancaster 1997:367–78).

On the other hand, recent studies on state formation among tribes and in areas of tribal domination have not only disproved the idea of the tribe as an 'isolate', e.g. the cases of the Bhumijs of Barabhum (S. Sinha 1962:36-80), the Nagabanshis of Chotanagpur (Singh 1987:51-72), and the Ahoms of Assam (Guha 1974:65-7), but studies on state formation in Orissa (Eschmann, Kulke and Tripathi eds., 1978) and eastern and north-eastern India (S. Sinha, 1962) have also stressed the processes of tribal acculturation. Since the importance of the Rajputs as agents of change has been recognized in many areas, this process has also been aptly described as Ksatriyaization (Eschmann, Kulke and Tripathi, 1978:129) or Rajputization (S. Sinha 1962:36). Sumit Guha (1999:199) observes that forests of varying but always significant extent coexisted with and amongst the cleared lands of peasant settlement for long, and forest groups as specialists made optimal use of such niches. Forests were both political and military resources. Regional ruling elites could turn the hunter's mobility, resourcefulness, and skills in weaponry to serve their own military ends. Hence, the forest folk were early integrated into the regional political economies. Tribal integration and tribal specialization necessitate differences which, in turn, become the 'organizing principles in inter-community relations' (ibid.). Hence, studies of the historical context of tribal communities reveal that the fixed notion of the Bhil tribe as a hunting-gathering group is not always correct.

The Bhils of Mewar and Dungarpur

In this section, we shall highlight the interaction between the Bhils of Mewar and Dungarpur with states and with society at large. We will discuss similarities and differences in the experiences of the Bhils of Mewar and Dungarpur in their interaction with state and society.

The Bhils of Mewar (southern Rajasthan, comprising the districts of Udaipur, Chittaurgarh, and Bhilwara) between the seventh and the fifteenth centuries occupied regions of both politico-military importance and economic significance. The tradition about Bappa Raval (the legendary founder of the Guhila dynasty of Mewar) and the Bhil chiefs of Oghna Panarwa and Undri, Baleo, and Dewa, participating in the Rajput royal coronation ceremonies (the historic ritual of anointing the Ranas of Mewar at their accession with a *ṭīkā* of blood by the chiefs of these two Bhil settlements) points towards political alliances and negotiations of power (N. Sinha 1993:58). This custom, which continued until Jagat Simha's coronation in 1628 (Tod

1971:183), could be a symbol of the transfer of power from Bhils to Guhila Rajput, but it would be difficult to say what kind of power the Bhils could have enjoyed or could have transferred.

The state of Mewar employed Bhils as forest guards and watchmen to control hill passes and forest routes. This is evident from such popular Bhil names as Vanaputras (Children of the Forest), Mairote (Born of the Mountain), and Goind (Lord of the Caves and Lord of the Pass) (Tod 1971:39). In the medieval period, both Rajput and Bhil chiefs are known to have collected a levy called *rakhwālī* (Sharda 1922:175-6) from travellers in their dominion as a fee for their protection (Mathur 1987:138). The state of Mewar, having interacted with and realized the importance of the Bhils, would have been eager to politically contain such leaders as the chief of Oghna. The latter held the title of rana and belonged to the category of Bhumia chiefs (Tod 1971:262). He enjoyed political importance in his own territory and hence considered himself as important as the Rajput chiefs of the peripheral areas (forests and hills) of Mewar. Such chiefs might have facilitated the occasional mobilization of Bhil militias from within their own settlements for the wars of Mewar. Traditions have preserved accounts of Bhils fighting for both Rana Hammira and Rana Pratap in the fourteenth and sixteenth centuries respectively (Tod 1971:262). The military importance of the chief of Oghna-Panarwa is also evident from his title as the 'head of five thousand bows' (Tod 1987:262). The mobilization of armies by the different deities of Chittaur and the consequent victory of its maharanas is a recurrent theme in the Bhil songs recently compiled by Giridharilal Sharma (1956: I:120 and II:115-20). Bhils may have also been mobilized by rulers for state projects such as the construction of fortresses, roads, and bridges.

Limited 'peasantization' (Shanin 1987:8) and the emergence of miners among the Bhils of the core area of the Mewar kingdom is evident in the Samoli inscription of AD 646. This record dates to the period of the beginning of local state formation in Udaipur district, and refers to the opening of a mine (*ākara*) at Aranyakupagiri and the building of a temple for the goddess Aranyavasini (*EI* 19:97-8) by certain *mahājanas* (a group of migrating entrepreneurs). The opening of mines in a hill locality perhaps led to some deforestation and the expansion of peasant settlements into Bhil territory. Also, the Brahmanization of a tribal deity (Eschmann, Kulke and Tripathi, eds.

1978) that was initiated by the *mahājanas* may mark the beginning of Guhila interest in the Bhil localities. The mining centre could have been opened either in the copper belt around Udaipur or in Zawarmata, where lie zinc-lead-silver mines, about 45 km. south of Udaipur (Craddock, Freestone, Gurjar, Middleton and Willies 1989:62). It is significant that the celebrations and worship of Zawarmata are a popular theme in Bhil folk songs, indicating a long association of the local Bhils with the Zawar mines (Sharma 1956: II:31-3). The fact that Bhil people participated in the operation of mines is evident from the discovery of charcoal retort dumps (smelting) at Zawar (Craddock et al. 1989:56). Charcoal preparation has been one of the major economic pursuits of the majority of the Bhils engaged in non-agricultural activities (Gahlot and Dhar 1981:27). The Bhils also exchanged with the neighbouring rural settlements forest products such as honey, wax, gum, and *anwal* (a tanning material) (ibid.:214). (See also Archana Prasad's discussion in this volume of the role of tribal people in central India in the collection and exchange of forest produce.) The Bhils must have also been suppliers of medicines, as the forests of the Mewar hills abound in plants and herbs of medicinal value such as *safed*, *musli*, *gugal*, and *gokhmi* (ibid.:214). That the forests played an important economic role in the life of rural folk in southern Rajasthan is evident from the mention of forest routes (*vanamarga*) as the boundaries of an agricultural plot in a seventh-century record of the Guhilas of Kiskindha (*EI* XXXIV:175).

It was not the case, however, that relations were entirely harmonious. Rana Hammira and Rana Kheta are credited with military victories over the Bhils of Jilwara and the Meenas (*EI* XXII:35; Kothari, ed. 1985:142, verse no. 6). It was not easy to control either the Bhomat country (the hill and forest tracts of south-west Rajasthan inhabited by the majority of the Bhils) or even the Bhils in the heart of Mewar. Recurrent revolts by the Bhils of Bhomat are evident in inscriptional references to conquests of them by the Guhila kings. In the fifteenth century, Maharana Kumbha fortified many passes to defend the area against the Bhils of Panarwa (N. Sinha 1997:63). Hence, not only the Bhils of Bhomat but also those of the core area of the Guhila state of Mewar seem to have been in and out of actual territorial control. At the same time, the long period of contact and the settlement of a Solanki Rajput family in Oghna-Panarwa in the sixteenth century (Mathur 1987:28) could be responsible for the claim to Solanki caste (the category of Bhilalas) made by the chiefs of Oghna (Shyamaldas 1986:195). This claim may have its origins in a Bhil-Solanki marriage in the sixteenth century. (An interesting parallel can be drawn with Champakalakshmi's study of Tondai Nadu in the early historic and early medieval periods. The incorporation and encapsulation of pastoral settlements within the expanding agrarian landscape in the Pallava and Cola periods gradually resulted in a stratification of pastoralists that was based on cattle wealth, political authority and access to land resources.)

Epigraphic records of the thirteenth to the fifteenth centuries, the *Nainsī rī Khyāt* (seventeenth century), and bardic traditions all point to the formation of a regional state in the Bhil locality of Dungarpur. However, a probe into the records and traditions reveals that tribal participation in the history of the medieval state of Dungarpur was somewhat different from that of Mewar.

The earliest evidence of Bhil residents in the villages of Dungarpur comes from a thirteenth-century inscription indicating the residence of some important Bhils in rural settlements. Copper plates of Virasimhadeva (AD 1293) refer to Bhil Nadhol and Bhil Ralhua in their list of witnesses to royal land grants made in the village of Mala near Dungarpur (*EI* XXII:185). The possible presence also of Bhil cultivators-cum-watchmen and forest guards in rural settlements may indicate that, as in Mewar, members of the rural society of Dungarpur had expanded agricultural activities into the Bhil domain. As late as the nineteenth century, Bhils were employed to protect reserve forests of mahua and mango trees, to stop wasteful felling, to watch out for forest fires, and to supervise *waler* or shifting cultivation (Erskine 1908:143).

The process of regional state formation inevitably necessitated agrarian expansion. This point is evident from a series of land grants. Maharaval Virasimhadeva granted extensive land and a house to the Brahmana Talha of Bharadvaj *gotra* in the village of Mala (ibid.). Maharaval's *mahāpradhān*, Vaman, made some (unspecified) grants to a temple of Siva near the tank at Barauda (ancient Vatapadraka, the first capital of the Dungarpur state) (Ojha 1936:61, fn. 2). Virasimhadeva granted the village of Mangahadaka (Munger) to an astrologer, Bajhaditya (Ojha 1936:62, fn.1). Maharaval also donated the village of Vasvasa (modern Varvasa) to one Sri Samkara (Ojha 1936:62, fn. 2), a *purohita*. The economic and political significance of royal grants of land to brahmanas, priests, and astrologers in early medieval central India and Orissa is too well known to repeat here (Sharma 1966:34-5). Extensive tribal land was brought under cultivation through the socio-political and technological intervention of the donees—brahmanas and priests.

Interestingly, the impact of the late thirteenth-century and early fourteenth-century royal land grants on the Bhils of the Dungarpur region does not seem to have been so extensive as to ensure the 'peasantization' of the entire local tribe. Royal attempts to bring tribal land under cultivation seem to have been resisted, as is evident from the legendary association of the Bhils of Dungarpur with Maharaval Virasimhadeva and the rivalries between them. Local *khyāts* attribute the killing of Dungar Bhil to Shalashah Mahajan (a trader, who was appointed a minister in the court of Dungarpur) on behalf of Maharaval Virasimhadeva (Ojha 1936:58-9). But Virasimha never seems to have controlled the Dungarpur locality effectively, as all his records mention that he ruled from Vatapadraka (modern Barauda).

Although the *Badvā Khyāts* ascribe the foundation of the city of Dungarpur (the capital of the Guhila state of Dungarpur) to Maharaval Virasimhadeva in AD 1358, the foundation seems to have actually materialized under his grandson Dungarsimha, possibly around this date (Ojha 1936:62-3). Thus, it is only with the process of territorial expansion that the problem of the incorporation of the Bhils presented a challenge to the Guhila state of Dungarpur. Bounded by the state of Mewar on its north, hills and forests on its south-west, and the Sultanate of Gujarat on its south, the state of Dungarpur had to expand and consolidate its hold over the tribal belt, the Dungarpur locality. It became the base of the political operations of the Rajputs. Not only was there a need to increase revenues, but the Dungarpur settlement was also strategically important, as routes from Mewar to Malwa and Gujarat passed through this point (Dhabai 1975: Map of the Link Routes of Mewar). Hence, the transfer of the capital from Vatapadraka to Dungarpur was a strategic move for the closer control of the local Bhils. Maharaval Gopinath actually sent an expedition against the Bhils under his minister Salharaj, a member of the Osval trading community. The Shantinath temple inscription at Antari, of

AD 1468, credits Salharaj with the conquest of the Bhils (the inscription states that this minister rid Vagod of this trouble) (Ojha 1936:66, fn. 2).

Recurring incursions into Dungarpur by the sultans of Gujarat (Ojha 1936:66–8) necessitated the exercise of effective control by the Rajputs over the inhabitants of the forest routes and hill passes. Thus the period between the thirteenth and the fifteenth centuries seems to have witnessed a long process of territorial incorporation of Bhil groups. Undoubtedly, land grants to temples and the passage of traders through tribal territory brought many Bhils in proximity to periodic markets and fairs, facilitating their participation in the networks of local exchange. The possibility of the mobilization of Bhils as militiamen is evident from an epigraphic record of AD 1474 in Rampal (near Dungarpur). It records the bravery and death of Ratkala, son of Biliya, without being commanded by Maharaval, at the time of the sack of Dungarpur by Mandachalpati (Mandupati) Sultan Giyasuddin. Ojha (1936:69) identifies Ratkala as a Bhil, and this is quite plausible in view of the fact that in state records the political titles of Rajput chiefs were always mentioned whereas non-Rajputs were identified by their *gotra* or lineage. Ratkala does not figure in this inscription with any title, *gotra* or lineage affiliation.

Perhaps a limited form of 'Rajputization' can also be seen in the erection of memorial stones by Bhil chiefs. A memorial stone stands on a hillock (Dhanmata Ki Pahari) at Dungarpur, commemorating the death of Dhani and Kali, wives of Bhil Dungaria (Ojha 1936:59). Although the Rajputs adopted the traditions of memorial pillars from tribal peoples and transformed them into *goverdhanas* or *pāliyas* (memorial pillars of Rajput style), 'the social process which transformed the humble wooden pillars of the tribals into stone memorials with sculpted tops' (Chattopadhyaya 1994:122) underlines the social distance between Rajput and Bhil, and consequently became something to be emulated by Bhil chiefs. It is also of interest that today the Bhils of Dungarpur participate in large numbers at Brahmanical festivals such as Gokalatham-Janmashtami and the Baneshwar fair at the temple of Mahadeva at the confluence of the Mahi and the Som, and in Jain festivals at Rikhaladeva (Sehgal 1974:50, 54–5).

It is significant that the Bhil chiefs of Dungarpur, as early as the seventeenth century, claimed a 'history' of territorial predominance in the pre-Rajput period. Nainsi narrates that Dungarpur was controlled by a 'big' Bhil landlord (*bari thakurai*), Dungar, who led 5,000 Bhils. Having convinced Dungar Bhil, Raval (the first Guhila king to found a kingdom in Dungarpur) and his men settled in Dungarpur. But Raval hatched a conspiracy and exterminated Dungar and his Bhils after inviting them to his daughter's wedding (Ranawat 1987: 85-6). Equally significant is the fact that, in spite of territorial claims, the Bhil chiefs of Dungarpur, unlike those of Mewar, have never been associated with royal accession ceremonies.

What was the elite or royal response to Bhil perceptions of their past? Royal *khyāts* mention that Dungar Bhil desired to marry the daughter of the minister, Osval Shalashaha. On the other hand, Raval Virasimhadeva (the king of Dungarpur) is known to have killed the Bhil chief, Dungar (Ojha 1936:58-9). In fact, it was the *Badvā Khyāt* version which was adopted by the historians of Rajasthan in the nineteenth century (Shyamaldas 1986:1005). In other words, the Bhil traditions that reveal elements of treachery and of royal distance from the Bhil chiefs point perhaps to a closer royal control of Bhil territory. Hence, the royal dependence on the Bhil chiefs seems to have been minimal and the scope for social interaction between the Rajput ruling elite and the Bhil chiefs is likely to have been minimal. Consequently, unlike Mewar, there are no Bhils in the Dungarpur region (Sehgal, 1974:58) who have traditional claims to Rajput origin.

Although the Bhils of Mewar and Dungarpur interacted with the local Rajput states and society on similar terms, the different geo-political, strategic, and economic situations of the Guhila states of Mewar and Dungarpur brought about differences in the behavioural pattern of the Bhils concerned, as well as royal perceptions of the Bhils.

The need for control of vast expanses of Bhil territory prompted the Guhila state of Mewar to settle Solanki Rajput chiefs in the Bhil settlement of Oghna, and the proximity between the Solankis and the Bhil chiefs of Oghna seems to have resulted in a social alliance and the claim of the Bhil chiefs to a higher status—'Solanki Bhils' (the category of the Bhilalas). In contrast, better military control over the Bhils of Dungarpur seems to have offered less scope for tribal social mobility. The absence of Rajput Bhils or Bhilalas in Dungarpur is perhaps an important indication of this historical process.

The Bhils of Medieval Gujarat

A study of early medieval and medieval Gujarat also confirms some of our observations regarding developments among the Bhils in Rajasthan. Historical sources indicate participation by the Bhils of Gujarat in the functioning of the Caulukyan state. It is important to note the different patterns of relationships between the Caulukyan state and the Bhils of different localities of Gujarat. While the Bhil localities of the Ahmedabad region had economic significance, the Bhils of Panchmahal occupied hills that were of strategic importance for the Caulukyas. In this section we will explore the emergence of a new social status claimed by the Bhil chiefs of the Ahmedabad region in the medieval period.

Inscriptions of the reign of Mularaja I (the founder of the Caulukya dynasty) (Muni I:73; *IA* VI:191; *EI* X:78) point to Caulukyan control over almost the whole of Kadi district and Viramgam *taluka*. Initially, the Caulukyas faced the local Bhils as militias in opposite camps. Hemacandra, in the *Dvyasrayakāvya* (an early twelfth-century text) refers to Bhillas as allies of the Abhira chief Graharipu against Mularaja (*Dvyasrayakāvya* Canto IV:16: vv. 20-40). The *Abhayatilakagani* (a mid-fourteenth-century text) confirms this fact (Narang 1972, Chap: vv. 2-3, Chap. II: v. 83). However, the Caulukyan state in the time of Mularaja I and his successor Bhima I does not seem to have been very successful in mobilizing agricultural revenues from the Bhil settlements. This fact is evident from the last inscription of Mularaja's reign: it refers to grants of land in Satyapura-mandala or Sanchor in the Jodhpur region (Balera Grant, *EI* X, l.3) of Rajasthan. These grants indicate the limited scope of agrarian expansion and resource mobilization from areas in Gujarat under Caulukyan control, forcing expansion towards the north of Anhilwara. But Mularaja's construction of the temple of Mulesvara dedicated to Somanatha in Mandali (now Mandal) (Kadi Grant, *IA*, vol. VI: 191) in Viramgam *taluka* cannot be seen as only a religious act. The economic significance of the construction of this temple is evident from the extent of the grants. The village of Komboika was granted together with wood, grass, water, and pastures (ibid.:192, Plate II, 11.1-2). Although this early grant may not have converted Bhil settlements into 'peasant' settlements, the donee's right to natural resources is likely to have set the pace for the expansion of agriculture in a locality which did not seem to have many villages. It is significant that Komboika was not surrounded by villages on its boundaries. Unlike most of the villages granted, where boundaries were specified with reference to the neighbouring settlements, Komboika seems to have been situated in a sparsely settled area, one populated by tribes.

Bhima I of Gujarat made land grants in agricultural pockets in Koli and Bhil regions for different reasons. The Radhanpur inscription of AD 1028 records the grant of village Masura (bounded by the villages of Ghadaharika, Aikayska, Dharavalika, and Prajharika) to Bhattaraka Ajapala, a native of Navanisaka, Kutch (*IA* VI:193-4). This grant did not have much to do with agricultural expansion, as this locality was already populated with villages. It seems from Ibn Asir's account of Mahmud Ghazni's march to Kutch that the Caulukyas made this grant to a Brahmana to gain allies in a newly-annexed territory (*IA* VI:185).

Although the reference to the Bhils in Kutch is not direct, Ibn Asir states: Mahmud received intelligence that Bhim, the chief of Anhalwara, had gone to the fort of Kandahat (near Somnath, Gujarat), which is situated about forty prasangs from Somnat, between that place and the desert. He marched thither, and when he came in front of the place he questioned some men, who were hunting, as to the tide. From them he learned that there was a practicable ford, but that if the wind blew a little he might be submerged. Mahmud prayed to the Almighty and then entered the water. He and his forces passed over safely and drove the enemy out of the place. From thence he returned, intending to proceed against Mansura (Elliot and Dowson 1955: II:349). The 'hunters' who were knowledgeable about the details of the tides were possibly Bhils or Kolis. (Patel 1971:141; Deopujari 1973:61, 262-3)

The Palanpur plates of AD 1062 record the grant of three *halas* of land in village Varanavada (Idar in Mahikantha) to a mahabrahmana, Janaka. This village, too, was surrounded by others: Vara-Asavali, Padra, and Chhimdriyala (*EI* XXI:171-7).

Besides revenues, the Caulukyas needed passage through this largely tribal region for military reasons, since the Bhils guarded the forests and routes to Rajasthan. The fact that the Caulukyas had to enlist the support of the Bhil chiefs of Mahikantha for strategic reasons is evident in the problems they faced in the control of the Mount Abu region. Bhima's Mount Abu Vimala temple inscription of 1062 describes the Paramaras of Chandravati (Mount Abu) as recalcitrant elements (*EI* IX:148-58). Hence, the Bhils of Idar and

Mahikanta who guarded the forests and hill routes to Rajasthan were more important to the Caulukyas strategically than economically.

It is strange that today the Bhils of Ahmedabad district are only described as agricultural and miscellaneous labourers (Rajyagor, Tripathy and Chokshi 1984:207). A large gap seems to exist in our understanding of the distinction between the Bhils of the present day and those of the early medieval and medieval periods. The *Kumārapālacarita* (early thirteenth century) and the *Prabandhacintamani* (early fourteenth century) refer to one Caulukya Karnadeva who defeated a Bhil chief named Asa, and conquered Asapalli (SJ No. 41, 1956:39; *Prabandhacintamani* 1933:55). Asapalli is identified with modern Ashawal near the city of Ahmedabad. The fact that Asa Bhil commanded the local Bhils is evident from the bardic tradition that he led an innumerable force of archers against the Caulukyan king (Forbes 1993:103). Karna is supposed to have received an omen from Bhairavadeva and built at Asapalli a temple to the goddess Kocharba (*Prabandhacintamani* 1933:55). In fact, there is a small village named Kochharba on the western bank of the Sabarmati, contiguous to Ahmedabad (city map of Ahmedabad, 1917, Gillion 1968). Karna also built temples of Siva and the goddess Jayanti at Asapalli (*Prabandhacintamani* 1933:55).

The above account clearly reveals Caulukyan attempts at agrarian expansion in the Bhil localities of Ahmedabad, south-east of Anhilapataka. The royal construction of the temples of Siva and Jayanti is likely to have accelerated the growth of agricultural settlements. It is also significant that Karna won another Bhil ally, Bhilla Khangara (*Prabandhacintamani* 1933:55).

It is significant that Dholka (another Bhil locality near Ahmedabad), a thriving trading centre from the Caulukyan period onward, witnessed the construction of a huge water reservoir at the end of the eleventh century by the Caulukyan queen Minaladevi (Rajyagor, Tripathy and Chokshi 1984:919). The Bhils of Dholka claim that this centre (ancient Viratpur) was governed by a Bhil queen, Sudishva, in ancient days (ibid.).

The increasing need for revenue compelled the Caulukyas, like many of their contemporaries, to conduct regular raids into neighbouring states. There arose the necessity to control the marches into not only Rajasthan, but also Malwa. Routes to Malwa ran through Sabarkantha and the Panchmahal hills, the Bhil country. King Bhima confronted some of the Bhils of the Panchmahals on his way to central India (Narang 1972:16, Canto IV; vv. 41-5; 18, Canto IX: vv. 1-10). Hemacandra credits King Jayasimha (Karna's successor) with conquest over the Raksasas or the Barbaras (Narang 1972:20). Jayasimha was given the epithet *Barbaraka Jisnu* (killer of the Barbara) in his Ujjain inscription (*IA* XLII:258). The Barbarakas, Barbaras, and Raksasas have been identified as Bhil tribes inhabiting the hills and forests of Gujarat (Majumdar 1956:81-2). If Jayasimha killed a Bhil chief on the battlefield, he seems to have also incorporated others into his state as allies. Hemacandra also refers to a Barbara presenting a number of valuables, including *manikyas*, to Jayasimha (*Dvyasrayakāvya*, Canto XIII:20, vv. 104). The clash with this Barbara seems to have originated with his attacks on a temple at Sripurasthala (ibid.: Canto XII:19-20: vv. 3-15). On the request of some sages, Jayasimha proceeded against this Barbara and defeated him (ibid.). Raksasas were also entrusted with the protection of Patalaloka (forests and hills) (ibid.: Canto XIII:20: vv. 105-110). Along with their chiefs, many aboriginal inhabitants are known to have joined the army of Kumarapala (Jayasimha's son and successor) (ibid.: Canto XVI:21). Thus, two different localities of the Bhils seem to have been controlled by Jayasimha. The Bhils of Kochharba around Ahmedabad are likely to have resisted intrusion subsequent to Karna's expansion in the area. Hence, Jayasimha had to militarily subjugate the Bhils of Ahmedabad (Majumdar 1956:82). Second, as noted earlier, any expansion towards the south, Malwa, or Khandesh from Anhilapataka lay through Ahmedabad, Baroda, and the hills and forests of the Panchmahals (Parmar 1922:701, map). Therefore, the Bhil chief presenting *manikyas* to Jayasimha can perhaps be identified as a chief of Rajpipla, and his *manikyas* as the agate mined at Ratanpur in the west of Rajpipla state (Parmar 1922:33).

Other valuables would have comprised forest products that the Bhils of the Panchmahal hills exchanged with local agriculturists. These hills, especially the areas of Pavagarla, Santrampur, Ratanmal, and Devgarh Baria, are rich in medicinal plants (Patel 1972:63). In the medieval period, mahua flowers were supplied to the merchants of Surat and Khambat for the manufacture of liquor (Nath 1969:35). Whether the Bhils of the Panchmahals, like those of Khandesh, were also involved in the manufacture of liquor or the supply of mahua timber for building purposes is a matter of conjecture. It is equally noteworthy that the Bhils of the small state of Devgarh Baria (Panchmahal hills) have been anointing the local Rajas with a tika in blood at royal coronation ceremonies (Nath 1960:33).

References in the *Dvyasrayakāvya* to the protection of Patalaloka point to the royal appointment of Bhils as forest guards, watchmen and guides. Further, the 'Kiratas', who were knowledgeable about local topography and mining, and who guided Jayasimha to the banks of the Sipra river (Jayasimha's march to Malwa) (*Dvyasrayakāvya,* Canto XIV:20: vv. 14-36), may have included some Bhils. Although Hemacandra does not identify the Bhillas with the Kiratas, both social categories could have been mixed populations inhabiting the same localities in the hills and forests of the Panchmahals. The Bhillas are described in the *Abhayatilakagani* as experts in archery (ibid.:185).

The release of a 'Barbara' chief (ibid.) and his gifts of valuables to Jayasimha evidently point to the creation of military allies in the Bhil localities. It seems that Bhil chiefs repeatedly facilitated the mobilization of their kinsmen as militia in the royal army. Hemacandra refers to the army of Kumarpala's enemy, Anna, as consisting of men of the Jangala (forest) caste.

It is significant that in a list of eighteen guilds in a twelfth-century text, the *Jambudvipāprajnath* (originally a Prakrit text, the *Jambudvipāpannoti*), Bhillas figure as one of the categories of guilds (Majumdar 1956:263, n. 41). This may signify the economic identity of those Bhils who had settled in the agricultural pockets and who offered special services as archers, militiamen, watchmen, forest guards, miners, and construction labourers in the building of fortresses, roads, and bridges.

The beginnings of process of acculturation of some of the Bhils of Ahmedabad may have been possible with the royal construction of the temple of Kochharbadevi. This is likely to have set the pace for the Brahmanization of this local goddess (for a similar process in Orissa, see Eschmann, Kulke and Tripathi 1978). We also note that Asapalli-Karnavati ranked among the Jain centres of pilgrimage (*IA* VI:210).

In medieval times the locality of Ahmedabad must have continued to be an important Bhil base for Bhils, for the legend of the conquest of Asa Bhil was appropriated by Persian historians. The *Mirat-i Sikandiri*, an early seventeenth-century text, credits Ahmad Shah I with victory over Asa Bhil (Misra and Rahman 1961:72). Bhils continued to contribute to the making of militias in the post-Caulukyan period. A sixteenth-century Arabic text, the *Zafar-ul-Walih-bi-Muzaffar-Waalihi*, mentions Bhils and Kolis helping the amirs of Sultan Bahadur Shah of Gujarat in their attacks on Humayun at the Gulf of Khambat (Sandesara 1970:208). We thus infer that Bhils in different localities of Gujarat developed relationships at different levels with the surrounding state and society.

Bhils or Kolis?

As a concluding note it would be worth exploring the trajectory of social developments among the Bhils of Ahmedabad. Unlike Mewar or central India, the district of Ahmedabad does not have a population of Bhilalas or Bhils claiming Rajput descent. It is strange that in spite of long interaction with regional states and society, their chiefs did not claim a social status superior to their kinsmen. Did some of the Bhil chiefs of early medieval Ahmedabad claim the status of Kolis in the medieval period?

Hemacandra does not mention the Kolis in his list of social groups in the twelfth century. Did they emerge later in the Ahmedabad locality? Besides being a part of the agricultural population, the Kolis might have included some other social groups claiming agriculturist status. G.S. Ghurye observes, 'The overall designation of Koli, applied to a number of communities, only serves to disguise the variety of occupations and the different stages of cultural development which are met with in the different communities making up group' (1957:1). The Kolis were not good cultivators in the medieval period, and are not described as an economically homogeneous group at the end of the nineteenth century.

> The character of the Kolis, as agriculturists, varies much in different parts of the district. In the central villages their fields can hardly be distinguished from those cultivated by Kunbis while towards the frontiers they were little superior to those of the aboriginal tribes. Crimes of violence are occasionally committed among them; but, as a class, they have settled down in the position of peaceful husbandmen—a marked contrast to their lawless practices fifty years ago. (*Imperial Gazetteer* n.d.:98).

The Kolis of medieval Gujarat too figure in medieval sources more as lawless elements than as peaceful producers. Raja Vikramajit, Shahjahan's governor of Gujarat, had to conduct an expedition in 1622 against some Kolis north of Ahmedabad who had been for generations a terror to travellers (Foster 1923:153). Between 1662 and 1668, a Baluchi adventurer impersonating the late Dara Shikoh successfully gathered around himself a large number of followers, including the Kolis of Viramgam and Chunwal. The Mughal commander Mohabat Khan had to march out to drive him away and take control of the Kolis (Commissariat 1957:169).

Records of the East India Company mention that the Ahmedabad route to Surat was particularly dangerous because of the constant irruption of brigands, robbers, and highwaymen. In fact, in 1644, some Kolis attacked a caravan between Ahmedabad and Broach (Gokhale 1978:88). Kolis armed with bows and arrows and muskets attacked Fidauddin Khan's forces in the mid-eighteenth century (Sandesara 1965:597-8). Like the Bhils, the Kolis also launched guerrilla attacks on Gaikwad forces. But it is significant that the eighteenth-century Kolis of Gujarat refused to identify with the Bhils. Alexander K. Forbes, writing on the Kolis and the Bhils of Mahikantha in the period of the Gaikwads, mentions that although these two groups could hardly be distinguished, the former did not like to be equated with the latter. Hence, the Kolis of Mahikanta were possibly in a kind of transitional stage between the status of Bhil and that of Koli.

The above point indicates that the status of 'Koli' had become a respectable one for those tribal groups in Gujarat who sought to distinguish themselves from the larger mass of their kinsmen. The Kolis seem to have attained an important socio-political status by the fourteenth century, at least on Konkan coast. A Koli kingdom is known to have been founded by Jayba Popera in north Konkan in 1348 (S. Roy 1983:29). The chief of the celebrated Janjira fort was a Koli named Ram Patil in the time of Shivaji (Deopujari 1973:263). Kolis had served the Maratha army since the time of Shivaji and exercised considerable control over the Konkan coast (ibid.) The Bahmanis conferred the rank of Sardar on Koli chiefs who held charge of hill tracts (ibid.).

In contrast, we have noted that the Kolis of Gujarat were mostly perceived as a 'predatory tribe'. From the way they are described in the literature of the medieval period and in travellers' accounts, we suspect that some descendants of medieval Bhil chiefs, particularly those of Ahmedabad, could have claimed the status of Koli. Their occupations alternated between the seasonal practice of shifting cultivation and hunting, while indulging in brigandry during the rest of the year. We recall Fred Crick Barth's discussion on ethnic boundaries among the Pathans of Swat in the context of 'our' Bhils and Kolis of medieval Gujarat. If the Pathans of Swat could change their identity (Barth 1959:30) and those Rabaris serving the Rajput dynasties preferred to call themselves Raika to distinguish themselves socially (Srivastava 1997), could not some of the descendants of the Bhils have claimed the status of Koli for themselves in medieval times?

> The same group of people, with unchanged values and ideas, would surely pursue different patterns of life and institutionalize different forms of behaviour, when faced with the different opportunities offered in different environments. Likewise, we must expect to find that one ethnic group, spread over a territory with varying ecologic circumstances will exhibit regional diversities of overt institutionalized behaviour which do not reflect differences in cultural orientation. (Kuper 1981:201)

A point of comparison can perhaps be made with Archana Prasad's study of the Gonds and Baigas of central India between the Maratha and the colonial periods. There the Raj Gonds or the zamindar Gonds tried hard to achieve upward mobility amongst the Rajput and Muslim rulers.

Concluding Observations

We have outlined some historical processes through which the Bhils of western India developed their livelihood, adapting to different ecological, economic, and political conditions. These processes resulted in the emergence of an elite among the Bhils, accelerating stratification and marginalization within the community. For instance, there were the Solanki Bhil chiefs of Oghna as against the rest of the Bhils there. On the other hand, the state of Dungarpur seems to have maintained a social distance from the Bhils of that locality through careful military control. Our evidence points to similar processes of interaction between the Caulukyan state and the Bhils of the Ahmedabad locality and the Panchmahals. The fact that the Bhils played a significant role in the Caulukyan state is evident in the title of Jayasimha, *Barbaraka Jiṣṇu*. If economic reasons were important for the Caulukyan state to initiate the process of 'peasantization' in the tribal locality of Ahmedabad (Kochharba), strategic reasons were equally important in initiating an alliance with the Bhils of the Panchmahals. The latter turned out to be an indispensable militia and forest guard force, while the Bhils of Ratanpur supplied agate and carnelian from the local mines. Although the Bhils of the Ahmedabad locality initially seem to have resisted the process of 'peasantization', royal temples were likely to have set in motion a limited process of acculturation. Consequently, the possibility that some of the Bhil chiefs of Ahmedabad claimed the status of 'Koli' in the medieval period to distinguish themselves from their brethren cannot be ignored. The process of acculturation, 'peasantization', and the changing worldviews of the Bhils of western India during the medieval period were undoubtedly the natural consequences of the processes of state formation and the growth of rural society at regional levels. Hence, generalizations about the Bhils need to be reviewed and specific case studies, in the historical context, are essential to distinguish the Bhils of one region from another.

REFERENCES

Bahura, Gopalnarayan tr. and Chandramani Singh, ed., *Marathakalin Gujarat: Alexander Kinloch Forbes' Rasmala*, Jaipur: Publication Scheme, 1981.

Barth, Fredrick, *Political Leadership among Swat Pathans*, London: University of London, 1959.

Bhattacharjee, J.B., 'Dimasa state formation in Cachar', in S. Sinha, ed., *Tribal Politics and State Systems in Pre-colonial Eastern and North-eastern India*, London: K.P. Bagchi, 1987, pp.177-211.

Casimier, Michael J. and Aparna Rao, eds., *Mobility and Territoriality: Social and Spatial Boundaries among Foragers, Fishers, Pastoralists and Peripatetics*, Delhi: Oxford University Press, 1991.

Chattopadhyaya, B.D., 'Early Memorial Stones of Rajasthan: A Preliminary Analysis of Their Inscriptions', in his *Making of Early Medieval India*, Delhi: Oxford University Press, 1994.

Commissariat, M.S., *A History of Gujarat: With a Survey of its Monuments and Inscriptions*, II, Bombay and Calcutta: Orient Longman, 1957.

Craddock, Paul T., Freestone, Gurjar, Middleton and Willies, 'The Production of Lead, Silver and Zinc in Early India', in A. Hauptmann, E. Pernickna and

G. A. Wagner (eds.), *Old World Archaeometry*, Bochum: Selbstverlag des Deutschen Bergbau-Museums, 1989, pp. 51-69.

Dave, P. C., '*The Grasias*', *also called Dungri Grasias a Scheduled Tribe in Bombay and Rajasthan States*, Delhi: Bharatiya Adamjati Sangh, 1960.

Deopujari, Murlidhar Balkrishna, *Shivaji and the Maratha Art of War*, Samshodhan Mandal Series XVIII, Nagpur: Vidarbha (1st edn.), 1973.

———, *Shivaji and the Maratha Art of War*, Samshodhan Mandal Series XXVIII, Nagpur: Vidarbha (1st edn.), 1973.

Dhabai, R.K., *Regional Structure of Mewar*, M.Phil. Dissertation, Centre for Studies in Regional Development, Jawaharlal Nehru University, New Delhi, 1975.

Dikshit, K.R., *Geography of Gujarat*, New Delhi: National Book Trust, 1970.

Doshi, S.L., *Bhils: Between Societal Self-awareness and Cultural Synthesis*, New Delhi and Jullundur: Sterling Publishers, 1971.

Elliot, H. and John Dowson, eds., *History of India, as told by its own historians*, II, Allahabad: Kitab Mahal, 1955.

Elwin, Verrier, *The Agaria*, Bombay: Oxford University Press, 1942.

Enthoven, R.E., *Tribes and Castes of Bombay*, I, Bombay: Government Central Press, 1920.

Erskine, K.D., *Rajputana Gazetteer*, IIA, Ajmer: The Mewar Residency, 1908 (rpt. 1922, Gurgaon: Vintage Book).

Eschmann, Anncharlott, Hermann Kulke and Gayacharan Tripathi ed., *Cult of Jagannath and Regional Traditions of Orissa*, New Delhi: Manohar, 1978.

Forbes, Alexander Kinloch, *Rasmala: Hindu Annals of the Province of Goozerat in Western India*, ed. H.G. Rawlinson, Gurgaon: Vintage Books (rpt. of 1921 edn.), 1993.

Foster, W., ed., *English Factories in India: 1661-64*, Oxford: Clarendon Press, 1923.

Gahlot, Sukhvir Singh and Banshi Dhar, *Castes and Tribes of Rajasthan*, Jaipur: Jain Brothers, 1989.

Gazetteer of the Bombay Presidency, I, I: History of Gujarat, Government Central Press, 1896.

Ghurye, G.S., *The Mahadev Kolis*, Bombay: Popular Book Depot, 1957.

Gillion, Kenneth L., *Ahmedabad: A Study in Indian Urban History*, Berkeley and Los Angeles: University of California Press, 1968.

Gokhale, B.G., *Surat in the Seventeenth Century: A Study in Urban History of Pre-modern India*, Bombay: Popular Prakashan, 1979.

Guha, Amalendu, 'Tribalism to Feudalism in Assam: 1600-1750', *Indian Historical Review*, vol. 1, no. 1, 1974, pp. 65-76.

Guha, Sumit, *Environment and Ethnicity in India, 1200-1991*, Cambridge: Cambridge University Press.

Kothari, Dev, ed., *Amarakavyam of Ranachod Bhatta*, Institute of Rajasthan Studies, Udaipur: Sahitya Sansthan, 1985.

Kumar, Bachchan, *The Bhils: An Ethno-Historic Analysis*, Delhi: Sharada Publishing House, 1997.

Kuper, Adam, ed., *Process and Form in Social Life: Selected Essays of Fredrik Barth*, I, London-Boston: Routledge & Kegan Paul, 1981.

Lancaster, William and Fidelity Lancaster, 'Indigenous Resource Management Systems in the Badia of the Badia of the Bilad ash-Sham', *Journal of Arid Environments*, vol. 35, 1997, pp. 367-78.

Majumdar, Ashok Kumar, *Chaulukyas of Gujarat: A Survey of the History and Culture of Gujarat from the Middle of the Tenth to the End of the Thirteenth Century*, Bombay: Bharatiya Vidya Bhavan, 1956.

Majumdar, D.N., *The Affairs of a Tribe: A Study in Tribal Dynamics*, Lucknow: Lucknow University, 1950.

———, *Races and Cultures of India*, Bombay: Asia Publishing House, 4th revd. and eng. edn., 1961.

Mathur, Tej Kumar, *Feudal Policy in Mewar (1750-1850)*, Jaipur: Publication Scheme, 1987.

Merutunga's Prabandhacintamani, Singhi Jain Granthamala, Santiniketan: Viswabharati, 1933.

Misra, S.C. and M.L. Rahman, eds., *The Mirat-i-Sikandari by Shaikh Sikandar Ibn Muhammad Urf Manjhu Ibn Akhar*, Baroda: Faculty of Arts, Maharaja Sayajirao University, 1961.

Muni, Jinavijaya, ed., *Bharatiya Vidya*, I. Kadi Grant ofV.S. 1043, *Indian Antiquary*, VI, and Balera Grant of vs 1051, *Epigraphia Indica*, X.

Naik, T.B., *The Bhils: A Study*, Delhi: Bharatiya Adamjati Sevak Sangh, 1956.

Narang, Satya Pal, *Hemacandra's Dvyasrayakavya: A Literary and Cultural Study*, New Delhi: Munshiram Manoharlal, 1972.

Nath, Y.V.S., *Bhils of Ratanmal: An Analysis of the Social Structure of a Western Indian Community*, Baroda: The M.S. University of Baroda, 1960.

Ojha, G.H., *History of Rajputana*, III, I, *Dungarpur Rajya Ka Itihasa*, published by the author Mahamahopadhyaya Raibahadur Gauribahadur Gaurishankar Hirachand Ojha, Ajmer: Vaidic Yantralaya, 1936.

Parmar, Ladhabhai Harji, *The Rewakantha Directory*, Rajkot: Chakubhai Vakhatchand & Dhanji Ramji, Parmar Press, 1922, endpaper.

Patel, G.D., *Gujarat State Gazetteer*, Kutch District, Ahmedabad: Gujarat Government Publications Depot, 1971.

———, *Gujarat State Gazetteer*, Panchmahals District, Director, Ahmedabad: Government Printing, Stationery & Publications, 1972.

Rajyagor, S.B., S. Tripathy and U.M. Chokshi, eds., *Gujarat State Gazetteer: Ahmedabad District Gazetteer*, Ahmedabad: Gujarat Government Publication Depot, 1984.

Ramamani, V.S., *Tribal Economy: Problems and Prospects*, Allahabad: Chugh Publications, 1988.

Ranawat, Manohar Singh, *Muhonot Nainsiki Khyat*, vol. I, Sitaman: Shrinatnagar Shodh Sansthan, 1987.

Roy, S.C., *The Oraon of Chota Nagpur: Their History, Economic Life, and Social Organization*, Ranchi, 1915.

Roy, Shibani, *Koli Culture: A Profile of the Culture of Talpad Vistar*, New Delhi: Cosmo Publications, 1983.

Russell, R.V. and R. Hira Lal, *The Tribes and Castes of the Central Provinces of India*, II (rpt. of 1916 edn., Netherlands), Delhi: Cosmo Publications, 1969.

Sandesara, B.J., ed., *Zafar ul Wallih Bi Muzaffar Wa alihi: An Arabic History of Gujarat*, by Abdullah Muhammad Al-Makki Al-Asafi Al-ulughkhani Hajji Ad-Dabir, Baroda: Oriental Institute, 1970.

Sandesara, B.J., *Mirat-i-Ahmadi: A Persian History of Gujarat of Ali Muhammad Khan*, Gaekwad Oriental Series, 146, Baroda: Oriental Institute, 1965.

Saxena, Ranvir Prakash, *Tribal Economy in Central India*, Calcutta: Firma K.L. Mukhopadhyay, 1964.

Sehgal, K.K., *Rajasthan District Gazetteers*, Dungarpur Directorate, District Gazetteer, Jaipur: Government of Rajasthan, 1974.

Shanin, Teodor, 'Peasantry as a Concept', in *Peasant and Peasant Societies: Selected Readings*, 2nd edn., Oxford and New York: Basil Blackwell, 1987, p. 8.

Sharda, Harbilas, *Maharana Kumbha*, 1922.

Sharma, Giridharilal, ed., *Rajasthan Bhil Geet* (1st edn.), Udaipur, n.d., vols. I-II.

Sharma, R.S., *Indian Feudalism*, Calcutta: Macmillan, 1966.

Sherring, M.A., *Tribes and Castes of Rajasthan*, first published in London, 1881, Delhi: Cosmo Publications, 1975.

Shyamaldas, Kaviraj, *Vir Vinod*, I, New Delhi: Motilal Banarsidass, 1986.

Singh, C.S.K., *The Sound of Drums: Tribal Movement in Rajasthan*, New Delhi: Manak Publications (P) Limited, 1995.

Singh, K. Suresh, 'Chhotanagpur Raj: Mythology, Structure and Ramifications', in Surajit Sinha, ed., *Tribal Politics and State Systems in Pre-colonial Eastern and North-Eastern India*, Calcutta: K.P. Bagchi, 1987.

Singh, K. Suresh., *The Scheduled Tribes: People of India Series*, III, Delhi: Oxford University Press, 1997.

Singhi Jain Granthamala, no. 41. *Jinavijayanmuni's Kumarpalacaritra-samgraha*, Bombay: Bharatiya Vidya Bhavan, 39, 1956.

Sinha, Nandini, 'State and Tribe: A Study of the Bhils in the Historic Setting of Southern Rajasthan', in *Social Science Probings*, vol. X, nos.1-4, 1993, pp. 55-67.

Sinha, Nandini, 'State Formation in Mewar: AD 10th-15th Centuries', Ph.D. thesis, Jawaharlal Nehru University, New Delhi, 1997, Ch. IV, Section: Kumbha and the Bhomat (published as *State Formation in Rajasthan: Mewar during the Seventh-Fifteenth Centuries*, New Delhi: Manohar, 2002).

Sinha, Surajit, ed., *Tribal Politics and State Systems in Pre-colonial Eastern and North-Eastern India*, Calcutta: K.P. Bagchi, 1987.

Sinha, Surajit, 'State Formation and Rajput Myth in Tribal Central India', in *Man in India*, vol. 42, no. 1, 1962, pp. 35-80.

Spate, O.H.K. and A.T.A. Learmonth, *India and Pakistan: A General and Regional Geography*, London: Methuen and Company, 1967.

Srivastava, Vinay Kumar, *Religious Renunciation of a Pastoral People*, Delhi: Oxford University Press, 1997.

The Tribes and Castes of the North Western Province and Oudh, Calcutta, 1896 (rpt., Delhi: Cosmo Publications, 1974).

Tod, Col. James, *Annals and Antiquities of Rajasthan*, 1st edn., London, 1920, Indian rpt. in three volumes edited with an introduction and notes by William Crooke, Delhi-Varanasi-Patna: Motilal Banarsidass, 1971.

———, *Travels in Western India*, Delhi: Oriental Publishers, 1st Indian rpt., 1971.

Reinterpreting Tribal Survival: The Baiga of the Central Provinces, 1730-1900

ARCHANA PRASAD

THIS ESSAY attempts to revise dominant notions about tribal livelihoods and their changing relationship with the wider political economy. Like other essays in this volume, it argues that the stability of the subsistence economies of tribal groups was embedded in multiple seasonal strategies, related to one another through semi-sedentary lifestyles or lifestyles that required a great amount of seasonal mobility from one form of production to another. Supriya Varma and Jaya Menon have explicated the issue of mobility, while the question of multiple livelihood strategies has been illustrated in this volume by Chetan Singh and Nandini Sinha for the Himalaya and medieval central India, respectively. This essay attempts to extend the argument to the context of the Baiga and the Gond economies, and to show that the semi-sedentary lifestyles and the multiple survival strategies of tribal forest dwellers endured until about 1800.

One of the main features of such a system was that each of the seasonal strategies was associated with a set of production linkages that were, in turn, manifested in relationships of cooperation and conflict between peasants and tribal communities, artisans and graziers. Hence, the multi-occupational arrangement was an open-ended system firmly integrated into the local and regional economy. It was not, as some anthropologists and historians have suggested

* A portion of this paper is being published in *Studies in History* under the title 'The Baiga: Survival Strategies and Local Economy in Colonial Central Provinces'. I am grateful to Neeladri Bhattacharya, Shereen Ratnagar, and Dinesh Abrol for comments on this paper at various stages.

(Gadgil and Guha 1992), a stable and self-sufficient system. Neither were these societies isolated from or perennially in conflict with other local and regional economies as some scholars (Singh 1983; Haimendorf 1985) have implied.

In the light of the above propositions, it is also logical to assert that the nature of the subsistence systems was such that upheavals in the political economy at the local, regional, and national levels had a profound impact. Environmental historians of modern India have argued that colonialism was a watershed in the life of the tribal communities, initiating processes that led to their marginalization, because of state control over forests and the introduction of scientific forestry (Guha 1990; Gadgil and Guha 1992; Rangarajan 1996). This proposition needs to be modified, since scientific forestry and monopoly control over forest lands were only symptomatic of a wider process of tribal destitution through the spread of industrial capitalism during the colonial period. Tribal societies in forested regions were transformed into underdeveloped adjuncts of imperial capitalism when forest produce was linked to global markets. This led to the disruption of local production linkages that were essential for sustaining the tribal economy, limiting the scope for economic growth, and resulting in a loss of tribal livelihood.

Multiple Survival Strategies Amongst Gonds and Baigas

The changing nature of Baiga and Gond subsistence is outlined in this section. In the main, I show that these tribes depended on a multiple occupational structure for their subsistence. However, the latter was not merely a matter of ecological adaptation. It also reflects the political marginalization of the tribes in the forested highlands of the Gondwana region. If we view the Gond and the Baiga survival patterns in this context, it is hard to characterize the Baigas as exclusively swiddeners or gatherers or hunters depending on any one kind of these activities for their daily needs throughout the year (Elwin 1939; Rangarajan 1996, Gadgil and Guha 1992).

Until the mid-eighteenth century, Gond livelihood was intrinsically linked to movement between plains and forests. The English records of the pre-colonial era used the term 'Gond' for almost all tribes who lived in the principalities of Garh Mandla and Deogarh, the original abode of the Gonds and the Baigas. An example of this is provided by Richard Jenkins when he records the origin myths in his 'Memoirs of the Nagpur Rajah'.[1] He records these myths, learnt from a Gond informer, in the following way:

> A certain woman by the name of Moolaee having come to Mahadeo from the distant part of the country [name unknown] became his wife by whom she conceived and bore a son by the name of Goand [*sic*]. The woman afterwards gave birth to a number of children and the family increased considerably. The eldest son was called Koettoor Gond, the rest of the children had no names.[2]

The abode of Mahadeo that Jenkins's source refers to is in Chhindwara district in the heart of Deogarh, and this leads us to infer that some Gonds may have originated in Deogarh and settled in Chhattisgarh. This is explained by Jenkins' informant thus:

> On a certain day Mahadeo with his large family sat down at meals which were composed of dal, rice and of bread and . . . after finishing their meals they got up and when the last person left there it rained and the deo nadee swelled. At that time the person [stranded in the rain] prayed to his deo, by means of which a large tortoise appeared to him swimming by the water by which he landed the Gond [later known as Khuttola Gond] on the other side of the river where others had already secluded him from society and he cooked for himself and went to reside in Garh Katangee as far as Chhattisgarh.[3]

There are similar stories narrating the reasons why the Gonds settled in Malwa and describing how they became fishermen or pujaris of Mahadeo (now known as Korkus). All of them reveal the mobility of the Gonds and their perception that their community was scattered all over Deogarh, Chanda, Malwa, and Chhattisgarh. In another instance, the informant also talks of a section of the Gonds (the Bhuriyats or the Binjawar Gonds who were later known by the name of Baigas) going up to the hills to guard the earth and never coming down.[4]

[1] These memoirs are contained in MSS Euro. F. 34, pp. 315–30 and my analysis of Gond life is based mainly on these.

[2] MSS Euro. F. 34, p. 315.

[3] Ibid., p. 316.

[4] Ibid., pp. 316–18.

Although there is no mention of the Baiga in the early records, the origins of the Gonds as recorded by Jenkins leads us to conjecture that the history of the Gondwana influenced both Baiga and Gond livelihood patterns. Early colonial accounts of the conflict between Deogarh and the Maratha armies suggest that Raghojee's invasion and conquest of Deogarh resulted in the organization and settlement of Gond zamindaris inside the forests. Gond perceptions of movement and migration as a result of military conflict are highlighted in the fact that Jenkins' informant refers to the displacement of Gonds by Gowalees in Deogarh after the 'Great War', in which they were slaughtered. Thereafter, he notes that the Gonds went and settled in Chanda.[5] He further tells Jenkins that Raghojee's invasion led to a Gond migration into the Vidarbha region. Jenkins quotes his source as follows:

> Originally [the Gonds] were in the country. Afterwards they went below the Ghats to Chanda . . . there were considerable numbers of Gonds in this country but very few below the Ghats. When Raghojee Bhonsla took possession of the Gadee of Deogarh the inhabitants both from the top and below the Ghats went as far as Wurda and now very few Gonds of the Koetoor caste remain below the Ghats.[6]

Although Jenkins' authority is not very certain about the dates when the Gonds were displaced from what he calls 'their original abode', it is amply clear from his oral evidence that the Ghats and the highlands were hardly the first place that a large section of the Gonds had inhabited. In fact, he points to two types of Gond migration: one before the Maratha occupation and the other after the conquest of Gondwana by Raghojee Bhonsle. In either case, the mid-eighteenth century habitations of the Gonds were migratory in character. Their patterns of movement usually depended upon the nature of political conflict in their regions.

Gond memory is also accompanied by recall of the days when the Gonds were wealthy. These days are traced to the period of Bukht Bulund, the father of Chand Sultan, who ruled Deogarh in the seventeenth century. As Jenkins' informant tells him:

> Formerly in this country almost everyone used to bring up cows and buffaloes and all the inhabitants possessed great wealth—kodo, kutki, mandya were in

[5] MSS Euro. F.34, p. 318.

[6] Ibid., p. 320.

abundance—in the country and none of them were without gold and silver . . . in this state the country continued till the reign of Bukht Bulund.[7]

Jenkins' source is probably referring to the loss of livelihood in the Maratha period when Bukht Bulund's son, Chand Sultan, went into the service of Raghojee Bhonsle. There is a clear indication that the Gonds of Deogarh were farmers who grew small millets on tracts that were fertile. They also owned livestock and practised a form of agro-pastoralism, about which Supriya Varma and Chetan Singh offer some discussion in their papers in this volume.

Both the English records as well as Jenkins' sources tell us about the displacement of Gond families and the loss of their livelihood after the 1740s. Jenkins notes that Raghojee left no stone unturned to secure his dominions by replacing petty Gond and Gowalee families 'who were opposed to regular Government' with 'more industrious inhabitants'.[8] By giving non-Gond people rights of permanent cultivation in these lands, Raghojee ensured that the Gonds were not able to resettle on them or use the tracts seasonally for cultivation; they were forced to depend primarily on the forest and uncultivated lands at the periphery of the forest. Other tribes such as the Bhils, as described by Nandini Sinha in this volume, also went through similar processes of marginalization.

Thus in the late pre-colonial period Jenkins' informer noted that the Gond *dhurm* was: 'that they should live in the jungle, cut trees and level the ground and make cultivation and through the labour of their own hands provide themselves with their provisions. This is their principal Dhurm.'[9] This passage is important because it reveals key facets of Gond life in the period after Raghojee displaced them. It shows that the production strategies of the Gonds now involved living in the jungle and engaging in semi-permanent cultivation with the plough. This form of cultivation is mentioned in later colonial records as *burra* cultivation. Though Jenkins' source does not mention the existence of hunting and gathering here, in another instance he asserts that food gathering and hunting were important supplements (Jenkins' interpretation) to cultivation which were provided by their

[7] Ibid., pp. 330-1.

[8] Ibid., p. 88.

[9] Ibid., p. 321.

God, Pharsee Pen.[10] The coexistence of food gathering, hunting, and *burra* cultivation is also recorded in the mid-nineteenth century, and clearly shows that the occupational structure of the Gonds had been altered by about 1800. Most Gonds lost their occupation of animal husbandry and others were pushed out from fertile *haveli* tracts into lands with laterite and sandy soils of low productivity. Others were forced to depend on forests for their livelihood in a major way, since seasonal mobility between the forests and fields was curtailed by the settlement of lands in the Sagar and Narmada Territories.

As for Baiga subsistence, it depended on a combination of gathering, hunting, and swidden cultivation in the early nineteenth century. Of these, swidden cultivation was considered the cornerstone of Baiga livelihood. To this end, the debate over the ecological and economic viability of *bewar*, a Baigani term for shifting cultivation, dominated discussions on Baiga ecology. However, swidden cultivation or *bewar* cannot be studied in isolation from other modes of food procurement.

The success of *bewar* cultivation depended intrinsically on the linkages between the Baiga production and the rest of the agrarian economy of the region. There are very few nineteenth-century sources for the reconstruction of the structural parameters of such seasonal activities. Verrier Elwin's *The Baiga* (Elwin 1939), is the best source because it provides us a thick description of Baiga livelihood. However, despite its value, it is also problematic in that it assumes that all Baiga practices were eco-friendly in character in the pre-colonial era. On the other hand, an uncritical use of colonial sources also gives us a lopsided picture. These sources often project the strategies as 'destructive' of forest. Unpublished proceedings of departments, settlement reports, and other records betray a general bias towards sedentary permanent cultivation. However, this is not the only limitation of these nineteenth-century sources. Their distinguishing feature is their confusion over the classification of *bewar* practices.

The attempt to wish away the problem of agricultural land classification in forested areas is reflected in the confused images of Baiga swiddening in nineteenth-century official records. Most of

[10] Ibid., pp. 330-1.

these use the terms *bewar* and *dhya* for both the field as well as the system of cultivation. Reports of officials such as Richard Temple often use these two terms interchangeably. There is also a third angle to this classification: the word *dhya* is also used for shifting cultivation in general, without making a distinction between Baiga *bewar* and Gond *burra*. The difference between Gond cultivation forms and the practices of the Baigas is only mentioned in the reports of some forest officials. The centrality of *bewar* in late nineteenth- and early twentieth-century Baiga society reveals that the mobility of the Baigas had become an impediment to the achievement of colonial aims in the forested areas. In the light of this, any reconstruction of the Baiga system has to look at the sources critically, if not skeptically.

In Baiga livelihood, gathering, hunting and *bewar* were bound together in a precarious balance by a fragile seasonal rhythm, whose success as a whole was dependent on the success of the *bewar* cycle. Unlike other forms of permanent cultivation, *bewar* was only cultivated on the same field for three consecutive years, the cropping patterns and agricultural cycle differing from one year to the next. In the periods when no cultivation took place, gathering and hunting became the basis of Baiga survival. For example, in the first year the Baigas prepared the *bewar* field and, therefore, their dependence on hunting and gathering was likely to be greater than in the second year, when the fruits of the first crop were available. Gathering and hunting were seasonal, and undertaken when *bewar* was not possible. Consequently, the periods of hunting and gathering were determined by the *bewar* agricultural cycle shown in Table 1.

Two periods of hunting and gathering are prevalent in the given *bewar* cycle. Women gather mahua, roots, sal seeds, and fuel wood, while men are busy firing, preparing, and working on the fields. The men engage in different kinds of gathering activities when the lac cocoons need to be picked or when the *ral*, tan, or dye-tapping season arrives. Scholarship on the Baigas and other forest communities has not taken due account of these hunting and gathering activities as an intrinsic part of seasonal production. Instead, they have considered them as auxiliary or supplementary activities (see Forsyth 1889; Russell and Hiralal 1910, vol. 2; Rangarajan 1996). Yet if we analyse the linkages between these three activities we find that the shifting cultivation system is difficult to sustain without the existence of hunting and gathering.

TABLE 1: THE AGRICULTURAL CYCLE UNDER BEWAR

Indian Calendar	English Calendar	Nature of Work
Chait	March-April	Clearing fields of undergrowth and large trees.
Baisakh	April-May	Firing of the *bewar* field.
Jeth	May-June	Broadcasting of seeds.
Asad	June-July	Men work in fields.
Sawan	July-August	Men work in fields.
Bhadon	August-September	Men work in fields.
Kuar	September-October	Beans ripen and are harvested.
Kartik	October-November	Kodon and kutki ripen.
Aghan	November-December	All crops are harvested.
Pus	December-January	Winnowing takes place.
Magh	January-February	Shift to new *bewar* fields.
Phagun	February-March	Mostly festival time.

The example of the Khonds of Orissa, a tribal community whose subsistence strategies are similar to those of the Baiga, can be used to make this connection more explicit. There, in Chait, women went to clearings to pick castor and cut stalks that were ripe. The women gathered forest products such as sago, tamarind, and mushrooms. Baiga women gathered only roots and mahua (*Madhuca Latifonia*) seeds at this time.[11] Both Khond and Baiga women did the gathering, while the men cut large trees and prepared the *bewar* fields. Men of both communities also went on their ritual hunt that began at full moon. In this context, Elwin notes that the Baiga were known as the best hunters amongst all the forest communities in the Central Provinces. They used bamboo bows, arrows, and spears. The spears were usually made of a bamboo shaft with an iron head. The bows and arrows were generally made of the *dhamin* (*Grewia elastica*) wood. Traps were only used to protect the fields (Elwin 1939:87).

In Baisakh, the firing of the forest took place, and the Khond women gathered unburned wood for fuel. Men continued to hunt,

[11] Verrier Elwin Papers, Number 165, Notes on the Khond, Nehru Memorial Museum & Library, New Delhi, p. 89 (hereafter Khond Notes). Here Elwin uses some valuable nineteenth-century monographs to make his case. He makes a similar case using his anthropological experience in *The Baiga*. Since the connections in that monograph are ambiguous, I use the Khond experience to show the dynamic nature of the swiddening cycles.

but only in nearby forests. The seeds were sown in Jeth, and hunting continued. From Asadh to Bhadon, men worked in the fields. In Kuar, the first beans ripened and in Kartik, small millets or *kutki* became ripe. In Aghan every crop was ready and in Pus winnowing took place. Pus was also the time for dancing and weddings. In Magh, shifts were made to new *bewars* and hunting-gathering was the main source of food. This was the agricultural cycle of the first year. In the second year, there was more time for hunting because fewer crops had to be sown and harvested, but since there was enough food, the people lived on the *bewars*. It was only in the third year that the diet had to be supplemented with forest produce and game from hunting.[12]

The Khond case shows the dynamic nature of seasonal adjustments in non-sedentary cultivation practices. It indicates that the dependence of the community on forms of production other than cultivation was maximized in the first year. *Bewar* was prepared for the first time in that year, and cultivators were occupied in clearing the fields. Therefore, dependence on hunting and gathering activities was almost total. The interaction between *bewar* and other seasonal activities was minimized in the second year. This was primarily because the community could depend on the crop of the first year. During this period, hunting and gathering was important for both ritual purposes and for supplementing the diet, unless there had been a crop failure in the first year. In the third year, a combination of both cultivation and hunting-gathering was the basis of survival. The communities depended on the crops of the second year and on fruits, roots, etc., from the forest. Thus, the three-year cycle of survival was intrinsically dependent on the success of the crop of the first year. If that failed, the precarious balance between these three modes of production would be disturbed.

It is therefore evident that the importance of *bewar* in the Baiga livelihood system varied from year to year and from one season to the next. This was true even as *bewar* formed the fulcrum of the seasonal cycle and enjoyed a dialectical relationship with hunting and gathering. Without these, *bewar* itself would become unsustainable. If it were to be practised on its own, either its fallow cycles would become shorter, or the Baiga would have been compelled to move

[12] Khond Notes, p. 109.

to other places to cut more fields. Furthermore, hunting and gathering provided important inputs to the diet, such as meat, roots, and food during times when there was either a drought or when the crops failed. Therefore, it was important that these activities coexist with shifting cultivation practices. The need for ensuring against risk was also met through a system of production relations and exchanges that are described in a later section.

Forest Diversity and the Ecological Viability of Bewar

Given the precarious nature and dynamism of the Baiga economy, it is pertinent to reconsider some of Elwin's frequently-quoted contentions. Regarding the nature of *bewar* he writes: 'I have quoted enough to show . . . that given proper conditions the forest always recovers itself in time, that given a small tribe like the Baiga the effect on erosion and rainfall was not a very serious danger' (Elwin 1939:129).

The claim that *bewar* was eco-friendly and did not hinder the production of timber trees involves an inquiry into several questions. What does Elwin mean by the term 'forests'? Does his perception of the forest match that of the forest officials? Do the Baigas see the forest in the same way as Elwin? The answers accrue from an analysis of the relationship of *bewar* fallows with the regeneration of timber trees such as sal and the role of these trees in Baiga survival.

The north-eastern Maikals, the principal locus of *bewar* cultivation, had an abundance of dense mixed forest. Early travellers to the area described it as a 'wild' environment characterized by undulating plains and laterite soil. A combination of slope, soil, and forest provided the setting for *bewar*, gathering, and hunting. The viability of these activities was crucially dependent on the nine-year fallow period that each field was allowed after one year of cultivation. The main reason for these fallow cycles was the need for the regeneration of forest undergrowth in order to replenish the nutrients of the soil. If the undergrowth failed to appear, it was impossible for the cultivator to do *bewar* cultivation on the field (Prasad 1995). What swiddening did not require was the growth of large timber trees. In fact, there is sufficient evidence to show that the cultivation cycle often interfered with the natural regeneration of sal trees that had been felled in the preparation of the *bewar*. The frequent complaint of colonial foresters that *bewar* resulted in the replacement of mature trees with young trees of a stunted growth was sometimes justified.

Early surveys of the region by foresters show that good sal trees were found on gentle, undulating slopes of the Mandla district. Foresters described the maximal conditions for the regeneration of the sal tree as rainfall between 40 and 80 inches and good subsoil drainage. This was possible on a surface with permeable rocks. Slopes in places where the soil was not very good ensured the penetration of the surface soil. But where the soil drainage was good, the best sal would grow also on low-lying plains (Ostmarton 1928: 569-70). The rainfall in the Maikals was about 56 inches, and lush grasses helped to retain some moisture in the ground hardened by the thick canopy of the sal. Trees such as bamboo and sal had a high rate of natural regeneration, which protected the soil from erosion and leaching (ibid.: 654).

The dangerous effects of drought, forest fires, and the growth of thick bamboo and grasses for the natural regeneration of sal were realized by the foresters as early as the late nineteenth century. As the foresters saw it, the relationship between the density of the forest and the growth of sal was an adverse one. At any rate a 'good sal tree' would take about fifteen years to reach its full height of 25 to 40 m. It is only after this height that coppicing would be possible for it to shed its seeds and this would, in turn, lead to its natural regeneration (Champion and Seth 1968:121). In this way, the temporal cycle of sal regeneration, as the foresters wanted to practice it, and that of *bewar* conflicted with each other.

However, pure sal tracts could only be found in the low-lying valley of the Narmada and the foothills of the Maikals. On the higher elevations, small sal clumps were interspersed by tracts where sal grew with a variety of other species, and where *bewar* was practised (Forsyth 1889:365). The main trees in the Maikals are shown in Table 2.

Sal grew with drought-resistant trees such as *saj*, *salai*, and *aoula*. It was also surrounded by a variety of grasses such as *khel*—the principal grazing grass—and *sukra* in the western Maikals (*Mandla DG* 1909). John Nisbet, an official of the Indian Forest Service, enumerated the advantages of a forest where sal grew with other trees. He said that such forests had a greater density and better retention of the soil. The forester argued that the natural reproduction of these forests was easier than that of forests with a single species. Last, such forests were

TABLE 2: FOREST TREES AND GRASSES IN THE MAIKALS

English (Latin) Names	Local Name	Uses
Sal (*Shorea robusta*)	Surye or Rinjal	The seeds are used for food and the resin is used for medicines.
Black Eyne (*Terminalia tomentosa*)	Saj	Used for breeding lac and its resin is sold to local craftsmen for dyes.
Butea frondosa	Palas and Dhak	Useful for dyes and tans needed by local craftsmen and its flowers are used by local people for ornaments.
Bosewellia thurifera	Salai	Drought-resistant tree used by the Agarias to make charcoal.
Scheilchera trijuga	Kosum	Oil is generated from its bark and the lac insect prefers this tree.
Embilica officinalios	Aoula	Its fruit is eaten during famine.
Grewia elasica	Dhamin	Used for making bows, arrows, and traps.
Madhuca indica	Mahua	Used for liquor and food.
Dichanthium caricosum.A	Khel	Principal grazing grass.
	Sukra	Medicinal grass.

Sources: Abstracted from *Mandla DG* 1909; and Forsyth 1889.

less prone to natural disaster than pure forests (Nisbet 1894:5). They thus helped to neutralize the onslaughts of *bewar* on sal forests, and also helped to protect the tribal communities such as the Baiga from scarcity and famine.

The official sources of the nineteenth century reveal that *bewar* and the natural regeneration of pure sal forests were mutually exclusive. In the progress reports of the 1860s, foresters often referred to the depletion of timber in the *bewar* areas. Both contractors and the Baigas were blamed for the poor condition of sal in the low-lying areas of the Maikals. For example, Colonel Ward wrote that the Baigas had 'destructive propensities' and their cultivation had destroyed the sal on the hillsides, laying the land absolutely bare (Ward 1869:35). Similarly, Forsyth spoke of the Baigas as the 'most terrible enemy of the forest', their biggest crime being the felling of large trees during *bewar*. As he noted, short stumps in *bewar* tracts replaced large sal trees. Neither officials like Ward and Pearson, nor travellers like Forsyth, however, denied the existence of thick undergrowth and bamboo in the *bewar* areas (Ward 1869; Forsyth 1889: 304; *FRCP* 1864-90).

In 1939, Elwin selectively quoted from these sources to make a case for *bewar*. He argued that *bewar* cultivation had not led to the 'destruction of forests'. But the evidence that he provides is thin and he focuses on the rapid regeneration of undergrowth rather than of large trees. In fact, Elwin confirms Forsyth's opinion when he quotes J.B. Fuller's statements of 1898 and 1901:

> I am under the impression that in the past rather exaggerated ideas have been entertained of the injurious effects of bewar, especially in a country of heavy rainfall where its effects seem to be not of permanent denudation of the land, but of the substitution of one kind of forest growth for another . . . it is of much more importance that a tribe of people should live in peace and comfort, than a certain area should have trees of one sort or another or that trees should grow at all. (Quoted in Elwin 1939: 129)

The foresters of the nineteenth century objected to precisely this replacement of forests. By the 'destruction of forests' they implied the destruction of full-grown and valuable sal trees. The term 'forest' signified totally different things to Elwin: serene, harmonious, and beautifully 'wild' surroundings inhabited by the forest communities. For this reason, Elwin was unable to counter the claim that banning of *bewar* was essential to the successful regeneration of timber forests. Contrary to Elwin's contention, the interests of *bewar* cultivation were often in conflict with the processes that led to the growth of large sal trees in a natural forest. In this situation, the Baigas were left with no option but to practice *bewar* in mixed forests. Thus, issues related to the ecological viability of *bewar* were, in fact, more complex than Elwin's text portrays them to be. It needed the support of other seasonal livelihood strategies which, in turn, required a forest with a diversity of species.

Baiga Life and the Local Economy

So far I have argued that Gond and Baiga subsistence involved interrelated and multiple occupational structures. I have also hinted that this was only possible in a forest with diverse forest species which made seasonal gathering possible, as well as provided a market for some of this produce. This is so because forest gathering was undertaken, not merely as a supplement to other occupations, but also as a seasonal livelihood. It required the Baigas and the Gonds to have local linkages with peasants and artisans who either visited the forests or used forest produce. Let us now consider the nature of some of these networks and the ways in which they brought about the integration of Baiga and Gonds into the widei local political economy.

An examination of gathering activities in forests shows that the Baiga economy was connected with that of peasants, graziers, and craftsmen who were important users of the forests. The Baigas believed that the forest had everything they needed for sustenance. Since their primary source of survival was the forest, and the Gonds, Pankas, and lower-caste Hindus considered them superior to the other tribes because of their important ritual rôle, the Baiga saw themselves as kings of the forests.

This image was firmly grounded in a material reality. The Baiga used the forests for gathering food, sal seeds, and other minor forest produce. Both women and men undertook gathering activities. Women gathered roots, fruit, leaves, mahua, and sal seeds. Root and fruit gathering were important sources of food in periods when the *bewar* crop was ripening. Men also gathered roots in times of drought and famine. According to Russell and Hiralal, a Baiga could collect a full basket of roots in a single day (Russell and Hiralal 1910, vol. 2: 91). Mahua and sal seeds were collected by women and used as food or for brewing *tadi* (country liquor). Apart from this, the collection of leaves was useful for household use and bamboo was collected to make baskets and mats that were sold in the markets.

Gathering was not a gender-specific task. Men and women engaged in gathering for the local agrarian market. This brought them in contact with people who did not live in the forests but who depended in one way or another on them. The nature of the contact was, however, gendered in at least some respects. Men sold the more lucrative honey, lac sticks, silk cocoons, and tans to local craftsmen. In contrast, the women sold flowers, leaves and seeds of trees like the sal, as well as fuel wood, to peasants. These were presumably less lucrative than the produce sold by the men and this could have led to the exercise of male control over any surplus in the household income.

The domination of male members over the more profitable exchanges is mirrored in other work relationships. The male members of the community controlled the technology and the means of production. For example, women were not allowed to even touch the axe. The father was the head of the family, but the son could own his own axe after marriage. Once he married, his father gifted him an axe. The gift of the axe was an important gesture that recognized the son as an equal producer. At the same time, it also created a hierarchy between households—the domination of the patriarch continued until the son attained that position himself. The male child's access to the axe, bows, and arrows gave him power. The same was not true of the women (Elwin 1939:78-9, 273).[13]

The Baiga patriarch reinforced his position vis-à-vis the women in relationships with the peasants. Even as the Baigas considered cultivation by the plough a sin, and most peasant castes as socially inferior, the structure of the regional political economy ensured that peasants were wealthier and had more social influence than the Baigas. Apart from excluding the women from the decision-making process, the self-image of the Baiga men as protectors of Mother Earth had little effect on their social and economic position within the wider economy. They continued to eke out their existence from the precarious combination of swiddening and gathering. But by refusing to work as wage labourers, the men forced the women to do the bulk of the work and perform the tasks of transplantation and harvesting, especially during times of scarcity when *bewar* crops had failed. Men only hired their labour out for one specific task: the uprooting of rice seedlings before transplantation (Russell and Hiralal 1910, vol. 2: 91). In this way, the Baiga men refused to be integrated into the local agrarian economy as oppressed servants.

The relationship of the Baiga with the Agaria iron smelters and grain traders was more clearly indicative of the differential integration

[13] Elwin argues that Baiga society is morally and socially superior to the modern one because of the freedom it grants its women. As he wrote: 'In Baiga society the women enjoyed an excellent position. Theoretically, in so patriarchal and priestly a tribe man should be in the ascendant: actually women have great freedom and no little authority. She may go about on her alone; she generally chooses her own husband, and changes him at will, she may dance in public; she may take her wares to a bazaar and open her own shop there, she may own property and she may drink and smoke in her husband's presence' (Elwin 1939: 235). But his evidence does not bear out this conclusion regarding the position of the Baiga women. In fact, the precarious survival strategies of the Baigas were held together in a loosely structured system of survival by collective male authority that denied the women many rights in property and land (Prasad 1995).

of men and women into the local society. In Mandla, the main job of the Agarias was to repair old sickles and axes and to supply new ones. For this they received an annual fee of grain from the villagers, called *jewar*. Then they got food grain in the month of Asad known as *bij phutti*, and finally they received grain at the time of the harvest of both spring and autumn crops, known as *kainhari*. The Agaria rates depended on the nature of the soil. In the zamindaris of Bilaspur, all trade took place through the medium of iron. Instances of exchange between the Maria and the Agaria were common in Bastar and Chanda (*Mandla DG* 1909:179-80; Elwin 1942). The presence of the Agaria linked the Baiga to the wider agrarian economy. In times of famine, the Agaria played an important part in sustaining the Baiga economy. They sold them food, oil, and salt for everyday needs.

Despite this linkage, the Baigas considered the Agarias outcastes. The latter lived in settlements outside the villages they visited. They were only called into a village when they had to repair implements or perform rites on a newly-born child with red-hot iron (Russell and Hiralal 1910, vol. 3:122). The women of the two communities hardly met each other and contact was maintained largely by the men. Since the Agaria were mobile smelters and traders, they would have carried information about the outer world to the forest dwellers.

The Baiga economic system was thus one in which men and women not only performed different tasks, but were also linked to the local society in different ways. Though both men and women found themselves at the lower end of the local relations of production, the men were in a slightly better position as they supplied valuable raw materials to local industry. Nevertheless, the burden of production did not fall entirely on women, as men also did gathering and partook of the tasks for cultivation. As we shall see later, this pattern changed in the colonial period.

Local Economy and Gathering of Forest Produce Amongst the Gonds and the Baigas

In the early and mid-nineteenth century, the fate of lower-class Gonds and Baigas was sealed together by the networks of commodity exchange in forest items. The forests saw a convergence of different occupational interests that supported the artisan and the peasant economies. The mobility of the artisans between towns, villages, and forests ensured the development of wider linkages of forests with other economies. The lac jewellery and toy makers were good examples of this development. The craftsmen who worked with lac did not necessarily live in the forest, because upper-caste peasants and craftsmen regarded lac propagation with a certain superstitious repugnance. Therefore, these craftsmen bought stick lac from the Gonds, the Korkus, and the Baigas (ibid.: vol. 3:122).

The lac seed swarmed twice a year. The Baisakh crop was collected in June-July and the Kartik in October-November. The lac was then sold in the markets by forest dwellers to craftsmen. The main lac market near Mandla was Seoni where lac was in great demand.[14] After collection, stick lac was cleared of the wood and the encrusted twigs and barks were placed in long cotton bags. These bags were heated and the lacquer gum was squeezed from the sticks and mixed with clay and other materials to make toys and bangles (Russell and Hiralal 1910, vol. 3:106). The main markets were in the small towns such as Mandla and Seoni, but lac bangles were also sold in the villages. Since the best business for the Lakheras was during festivals, incomes was seasonal and any transaction of the forest communities with the Lakheras would have needed to take into account the seasonal imbalances in demand and supply.

The presence of lac artisans in the suburbs of towns and the mobility of the Korku, Gond, and Baiga lac sellers created wide-ranging linkages between the urban, agricultural, and forest societies. The tribes found themselves at a disadvantage in these exchanges. They had to walk long distances to get to the markets and were compelled to sell at prices acceptable to the artisans. The Lakheras who moulded lac were superior to the Baigas in the social hierarchy, claiming that their ancestors were Kayasthas who had established friendly social relations with the Rajputs and the Banias. In some societies they were ranked above the Kunbis. The Kunbis on their part considered the tribal people to be outcastes (ibid.).

Similar linkages between urban centres and forests were evident in the case of the dyers. The main dyers of the province were the

[14] Central Provinces Secretariat Records, Nagpur (henceforth CPSR), Forest Department, Case File No: 22, 'B' Progs, April 1919 (henceforth Lac 1919), p. 3. Also see CPSR, Forest Department, Compilation No. 50(6), 1875 (henceforth Lac, 1875), pp. 85-6.

Koshtis, Chippas, Nillars, Rangaris, and Rangrez. They dyed in traditional colours, mainly reds and yellows, obtained from the roots of trees such as the *al*, *kusum*, and *rohun*. Resin was extracted by tree tapping, and in, some cases, by pounding roots. Forsyth does not record whether resin or gum was extracted by the dyer or was bought from the forest dweller. Rangrez and Rangaris wove silk-bordered cloths and dyed their own thread with lac or *palas* flowers. Since they are said to have abhorred manual labour, it is likely that they bought stick lac and *palas* flowers from forest people. Apart from this, the tussar silk industry and the silk weavers were dependent on the collection of silk cocoons by the Gonds. Silk weavers such as the Koshtis bought cocoons from the forest communities and boiled them, and wound the thread on reels. Dyers used myrabolan flowers to obtain blue or black colours. Other cotton weavers such as the Chippas, the Nillars, and the Rangrez also bought flowers to make dyes for cloths (Russell and Hiralal 1910, vols. 2 & 3). The dyers did not necessarily develop close social relations with the forest communities. Those like the Koshtis lived in towns and enjoyed a good income. The class difference gave them an economic advantage over the forest communities. Conversely, the reluctance of these artisans to go into the forest to collect their own resins also made them dependent on mobile forest dwellers.

There was also a close relationship between the forest economy and the rural agricultural economy. Graziers like the Ahirs and seasonal pastoral traders like the Banjaras came in regular contact with tribal people when they grazed their animals in the forests that lay on the fringes of ryotwari villages. Peasants, forest dwellers, and specialist herdsmen such as the Ahirs, the Gowaries, and the Banjaras shared forest lands in such fringe areas. The Ahirs kept and grazed cattle in the forests for individual peasant families. Their intimate relationships with the Gonds and others living in the forests were a result of these daily excursions. Russell notes that in Chanda, the Ahirs had developed intimate links with the Gonds. They not only employed the Gonds to graze their cattle but also admitted them within the Ahir caste. In fact, the origins of the Gowarie community of Chanda were traced to intermarriage between Gonds and Ahirs. In Mandla, it was thought that the Ahirs were scarcely Hindus as they lived in Gond villages (Russell and Hiralal 1910, vol. 2:24).

The relationships of the Banjaras with the peasant and forest communities followed a different pattern. An early study of the migratory people of India describes the Banjaras as grain merchants whose wares were carried on pack oxen. They traversed the most difficult terrain to get supplies, which they took into districts where scarcity prevailed, and later moved to large army camps where they supplied grain. Thus, they established a considerably important status in the political economy of the Central Provinces (Balfour 1844: 2-3). The Banjaras made their living from the sale of salt and oil to forest dwellers and from the transportation of goods. Ethnographers have given instances of the Charans and the Banjaras carrying loads for the Rajput and the Maratha armies (Cumberledge 1882; Mackenzie 1881; Russell and Hiralal 1910, vol. 2:163-92). Banjara seasonal movement spanned a large territory. Their ability to negotiate thick forests and 'rugged' terrain made them indispensable as messengers and carriers of arms. Due to this the British often condemned them as robbers and bandits. Their activities were essential for their counterparts in the forests, but their utility to the peasant economy was minimal. Though they sold a few milk products to the peasants, they never grazed peasant cattle. This was done by more 'trusted' graziers and residents of the village, such as Ahirs and the Gowaries who, even though of low caste, were certainly included in the system of exchanges within the village community.

The multiple networks described above resulted in defining the framework of the local economy, with the Gonds and the Baigas playing an important role in the lives of the graziers, artisans, and peasants, depending on the nature and location of the forest. But in all cases the tribes of the Central Provinces found themselves at the lower end of the social and economic scale. Their access to productive resources and land became restricted with the changing nature of the state in the eighteenth and nineteenth centuries.

Tribes, the State, and the Local Economy

For the environmental historians of modern India, the colonial period is an ecological watershed. They have argued that the creation of state monopolies by colonial regimes over forest resources was primarily responsible for the marginalization and oppression of tribal people in modern India. Further, this led to dependence and the erosion of local knowledge systems (Guha 1990; Gadgil and Guha 1992; Rangarajan 1996). In this section I show that this proposition needs to be modified in some respects.

First, marginalization of tribal people was not a solely colonial phenomenon but began with the territorial conflicts between the Marathas, the Gonds, and the British in the late pre-colonial era. Second, the large-scale introduction of industrial capitalist interest in forest produce was the main feature of the transformation of the tribal economy from a pre-colonial to a colonial one. Finally, this industrialization of the forest economy led to the disruption of local production linkages and economic marginalization. Since the tribes were already at the lower end of the economic scale, they suffered the most from the consequences of this process.

Gondwana Before the British

In the seventeenth century, Gondwana formed a part of the Mughal Empire. The chief principalities within Gondwana were Khatola, Magadh, Mandla, Silwani, Deogarh, Kherla, and Lanji. Its main seats of power were in Chanda, Deogarh, and Garh Mandla. In 1645, the Gond Raja of Deogarh, Chand Sultan, conquered Garh Mandla and made it a principality of Deogarh (Habib 1982:34-5 and sheet 9A). This principality was ruled like an independent kingdom so long as it paid tribute to the Mughals and made pledges of loyalty to them. The *subedar* collected tribute and dues from the chieftains, who, in turn, enjoyed relatively autonomous control over their resources.

In this situation, the mobility of the tribal people was maintained because the political structure did not involve centralized control over resources. The Raja allowed his people to migrate seasonally and extract minor forest produce as long as they gave a portion of it to him as a symbol of their subordination. Interference in land-holdings was minimal as neither the *subedars* nor the emperor showed any interest in settling Hindu castes on the tracts that were occupied by the Gonds. This situation changed markedly with the beginning of Maratha rule in the early 1730s. In 1731, Raghojee became the ruler of the *suba* of Berar with the help of the Raja of Deogarh. The Gond Raja paid ten lakh rupees a year as *chouth* and *sirdeshmukhee* to him as acknowledgement of his political subordination. But from

1737 onwards, both Chanda and Deogarh territories were subject to frequent Maratha attacks.[15]

Early colonial accounts of the conflict between Deogarh and the Maratha armies suggest that Raghojee's invasion resulted in the organization and settlement of Gond zamindaris in the forests. Jenkins notes that Raghojee left no stone unturned to secure his dominions by replacing petty Gond and Gowalee families 'who were opposed to regular Government and replacing them with more industrious inhabitants'.[16] For this reason, Raghojee followed the Gonds and the Gowalees into the forest. By giving non-Gond people rights of permanent cultivation in these lands he ensured that the Gonds were not able to resettle or visit these tracts seasonally for cultivation.

Jenkins' records show that even in this period the Gonds were not tenants or people with land grants like the Brahmins and other castes. They were probably people who cultivated land at the pleasure of their chieftain, as is reflected in the piece of iron given to him every year. Access to land and forest was, thus, a result of a privilege granted in return for assistance whenever the ruler required it.[17] This assistance was, more often than not, in the nature of serving in the Gond Raja's army or providing agricultural or household labour. Though the English records tell us little about the organization and the revenue settlements of Gond villages, there is sporadic evidence to suggest that these villages enjoyed some kind of autonomy as far as their use of land and forests were concerned. While zamindars did not restrict access to forests, they extracted certain dues from the tribal people in their territories, including labour time and a portion of the extracted forest produce (Grigson 1936:14, 18, 141-3; Glasfurd 1876). Gond peasants were also exempted from taxes such as the Pandree (toll tax collected from cattle carrying merchandise or grain) or the Kosa Baree (collected on tussar worms) because of the services they rendered to the Gond Raja (Agnew 1830:14-29).

But the services rendered by the Gonds to their rulers was also a source of potential conflict that arose out of the Gond zamindar's tendency to extract revenue and destroy the villages in order to

[15] MSS Euro. F. 34, pp. 13-17.

[16] Ibid., p. 88.

[17] Ibid., p. 321.

escape the enemy. The alliances between the lower-class Gonds and their immediate rulers, whom they still perceived as the Rajas, were a result of the wider political conflicts that arose over the control of land and revenue. The differential integration of the zamindars and the Gond peasants and tribesmen was seen in the way in which the zamindars perceived themselves. The zamindars, often referred to as the Raj Gonds, tried hard to emulate the Rajputs and to achieve upward mobility amongst the Rajput and Mughal rulers. (This calls to mind Nandini Sinha's discussion of the Bhils and the process of their upward mobility and differentiation in this volume. Her discussion shows that the patterns in Western Madhya Pradesh were similar to the ones in Eastern M.P. where the Gonds and Baiga lived.) Many of them changed their names to end with 'Shah'or 'Khan' or even 'Singh' (S. Sinha 1962).

The zamindaris themselves suffered a great deal in the wider conflict, and this, in turn, led to the social and spatial marginalization of the Gonds. They were repeatedly uprooted and driven into the forests after every military conquest. They, in turn, ravaged their subjects who tried to defend themselves against the warring parties. In the unequal relationship between the zamindars and their subjects, the biggest casualty was the flexibility of Gond subsistence, which was dependent upon mobility between the forest and the non-forest tracts. Even so, the political structure of both the Mughal and the Maratha regimes allowed them some local control over their natural resources, and did not interfere with the system of linkages in times of peace. That was not so under the subsequent British regime.

The First British Colonisers and the Gonds

We have seen that changes in the livelihood patterns of the Gonds began with the invasion of Raghojee Bhonsle in the eighteenth century. The permanent confinement of these zamindaris to the forest areas took place with the consolidation of territorial control under the early British regime.

The British, however, saw themselves as benefactors of the Gonds. They wanted to cure the Gonds of their habitual depredations, as they believed that these tendencies were born out of the insecurity and 'wild'. disposition of the Gond people. The cause of the insecurity was perceived to be conflict with the Marathas. The British saw themselves as the saviours of the Gonds from Maratha mismanagement. Keeping this in mind, Jenkins asserted that dependencies like Garh Mandla, such as Sohagpur, Bastar, and the Banjara tracts of Chanda would benefit from British rule. They would be willing to put up with British governance because of their 'knowledge of the equity of [British rule] and their experience of the oppression of the Rajah' (Agnew 1830:434).

The Gond chiefs incurred the wrath of the British Resident in Nagpur by making the escape of Appa Sahib possible after the Maratha War of 1817. The British officers claimed that leaders such as Chyne Khan of Hurrye Jagir, the most powerful Gond zamindar, had assisted in the escape of Appa Sahib and this intensified the conflict between the Gond chiefs and the British, who wanted to bring the territories of Nagpur under their direct control.[18] The campaign was also designed to maintain the tranquillity of the ceded districts and the districts of Nagpur State from the 'ravages of the wild and hitherto lawless tribes' who plundered fertile tracts with impunity.[19]

By 1819, the British Army had defeated the first and the most formidable Gond chief, Chyne Shah,[20] and other chiefs surrendered soon thereafter. Those who did not, migrated further into the hills, carrying on their freebooting on the western side of the Narmada and in the territories of the Nawab of Bhopal.[21] From then onwards, the British government began settling their estates and determining the conditions of the surrender.

The first condition on which zamindari rights were to be settled was that the Gonds should make promises of fidelity both to the British Empire and to Nagpur State which was now a British Residency. Most Gond chiefs had been obliged to serve the Nagpur Raja after their estates has been settled by Raghojee in the pre-1819 period. Unlike the Marathas, the British claimed that they did want to neither humiliate nor ill-treat the Raj-Gond chiefs. Their objective was to 'civilize' them and to accustom them to 'regard the govern-

[18] Board Collection, F/4/755/20541, p. 138.
[19] Ibid., pp. 136-7.
[20] Ibid., p. 122.
[21] Ibid., p. 142

ment with confidence and respect'.[22] By this Jenkins meant that the Gonds should be taught how to obey government orders and not loot or plunder. As long as the zamindars did not challenge British authority and paid tribute, they would get the right to control land and resources according to the guidelines laid down by the colonial government. The submission of the Gonds to the British was accompanied by a change in the official perceptions: Gonds were now 'timid' and shy people, as against Jenkins' 'ravaging and wild' people.

The consolidation of territorial control was the most important aim of the settlements. The British wanted all fertile tracts of the Narmada valley, places of pilgrimage, and trading routes under their control. Zamindaris such as Hurrye had very fertile haveli tracts and trade routes that connected the eastern with the western part of the province. The zamindari of Pachmarhi continued to be with the zamindar Mohan Singh, on the condition that he let the British collect the pilgrim tax and maintain a military base there. (Formerly this tax was collected by Mohan Singh and distributed amongst different Gond chiefs, giving rise to conflict). The British thought that their taking charge of the Pilgrim Tax would allow them to maintain law and order.[23]

The British recognized that the question of the settlement of zamindaris was complex. Through these settlements the British wanted to maximize revenue and minimize political instability and dissent. In order to achieve this, it was proposed that a portion of the zamindari estates may be given as the *nankar* allowance for ancient rights. In the remaining estates, the assessments should be carried on in the 'normal course' by the village patel.[24] Many British officials wanted to bypass the zamindars' right to assess their own lands and to create a system of settlements of the sort that prevailed in British-ruled territories. It was suggested that *obarree* or quit rent should only be paid on 'hilly tracts which are unproductive'. The rest of the lands should be assessed on the basis of a five-year *malguzari* tenure, in which cultivating zamindars would be given preference. Since hardly any Gond zamindars cultivated land, this principle was bound to

[22] Ibid., p. 150.

[23] Ibid., pp. 158-60.

[24] Boards Collections, F4/796/21428 of 1824, pp. 66-8 (IOL).

benefit non-Gonds. Finally, hereditary patels and *goantias* (including zamindaris) should be incorporated into the colonial system of agrarian settlements in all areas.[25]

It was also proposed that in Garh Mandla tenure would continue only in places which were either inaccessible or where the farmers could carry out improvements on their lands. All land of 'superior' quality should be under periodic assessment. According to this criterion, there was no need to show leniency to farmers in Garh Mandla, as the productivity of its land would be high if monsoons were good.[26]

The conclusion of Gond settlement along these lines thus led to the reduction of the territorial power of the Gond zamindars. Zamindari tenures were confined to hill and forest tracts, and this development severely curtailed the movement patterns of those who were earlier exempt from taxes and who had enjoyed free mobility in zamindari tracts. Because of this, it is possible to surmise that the flexibility of the Gond subsistence economy was severely curtailed. Statements by Richard Jenkins' Gond informants show us that the process of the marginalization of Gond rights began in the late eighteenth century, when Raghojee Bhonsle expanded his territorial control over Gondwana. The Gond settlements of the 1820s intensified the pace of this process and diminished the fiscal, political, and military power of the Gond zamindars in a more permanent and severe way. This was reflected in the changed status of the zamindars in the colonial era.

The extension of Gond zamindaris into forests affected the livelihood of the tribal people. Most of them lost their occupation of animal husbandry and were pushed out from fertile *haveli* tracts into lands with infertile laterite and sandy soils. Others were forced to depend on forests for their livelihood in a major way since their seasonal mobility was curtailed by the settlement of lands in the Sagar and the Narmada Territories. This also led to the disruption of networks in the local economy, and there lay the main contribution of colonialism to the process of marginalization.

[25] Ibid., pp. 1-11.

[26] Ibid., pp. 191-2 and 265.

Baiga Chak and the Exclusion of Bewar from the Local Production Linkages

After a considerable amount of upheaval in the Gondwana, Baiga subsistence could only remain in a precarious balance under limited physical and demographic conditions. Until the middle of the nineteenth century, the forests around the Baiga Chak were extensive and the pressure on forest land was limited. However, with the implementation of the colonial agrarian policy, the pressure on these forests and pasture lands increased significantly, and, therefore, the tensions between gathering and *bewar* activities were greatly accentuated. This was a result of two interrelated processes: the reservation of forest lands since 1865 and the formation of the Baiga Chak.

Nineteenth-century perceptions of *bewar* cultivation were marred by confused classifications of this form of cultivation. These perceptions can be identified in early forest and revenue surveys. Swiddening by the Baigas was classified either as *dhya, dhaiya,* or *bewar.* Thus Richard Temple wrote: 'One great cause of the wastage and destruction of the forest is called Dhya cultivation . . . . This Dhya cultivation is practically a substitute for ploughing and a device for saving trouble of that operation. It is resorted to by the hill people who are averse to labour and have practically no agricultural capital' (*FRCP* 1863-4:84).

Temple, using the standards of capitalist agrarian economy, classified the *dhaiya* economy as 'primitive' or 'backward'. Its traits were laziness and wastefulness, both dispositions that refuted the virtues of hard work and thrift that informed the behavioural patterns of capitalist societies. The most significant feature of this perception was that it was not based on any topographical or ecological survey of the region. But the perception of the cultivation system of the forest communities was based on the strong conviction that it harmed sal forests. For example, Forsyth wrote:

> The Byga is the most terrible enemy to the forests we have anywhere in these hills. Thousands of square miles of sal forests have been destroyed by them in the progress of their dhya cultivation, the ground being afterwards occupied by dense scrub of low sal bushes springing from the stumps. In addition to this, the largest trees every where have been girdled by them to allow the gum resin of the sal to exude. (Forsyth 1889:304-5)

As I have shown, such opinions were not entirely wrong. The

argument against the Baiga cultivation techniques was formulated from the standpoint of the official need to preserve large sal trees. In this context, the first settlement report of Mandla pointed out the need to control *dhaiya*. By the mid-1870s, all officers of the eastern Central Provinces started linking the efforts to control *bewar* with forest conservancy. For example, the Chief Commissioner of the Provinces, Croswaithe, wrote: 'There are only two courses open to the Baiga: either he be induced to give up bewar and take to plough cultivation or we make it impossible for them to practice bewar in these valuable jungles.'[27]

Croswaithe expressed this view at a time when the reservation of forests had already been put in place by the Forest Act of 1865. The fact that the statement was made right before the Forest Act of 1878 only accentuated its significance. This Act detailed the rights of the local population in the forests. However, by doing so it also restricted the mobility of the local population in the forests. It was this feature of the forest laws that posed problems for the Baiga.

Movement from one field to another was the basis of the success of *bewar* and was necessitated by the long fallow cycles. This meant the utilization of large forest tracts over a long period of time. When the Baigas moved from one field to another, their huts remained in the village. Thus, they controlled at least two or three fields at a time. This conflicted with the British need for forest conservancy, and the expansion of plough cultivation. So determined were the colonists to take over the territorial control of the forests that they wished away the natural constraints that affected the practice of plough cultivation in thick tropical forest conditions. Thus Forsyth opined:

> As for the obstacles supposed to be presented by the rank vegetation and noxious animals, they are chiefly imaginary. Immense plains lie ready for the plough, if merely the coarse natural grasses were cleared away, there being no brushwood or heavy timber to speak of. The luxuriance of grasses is only evidence of the fatness of the land that lies below; and a torch applied in the month of May will, over large tracts, remove all obstacle to the immediate application of the plough. (Forsyth 1889:309)

Like many other officials of the late nineteenth and early twentieth

[27] Madhya Pradesh Secretariat Records, Bhopal (henceforth MPSR), Forest Compilation No. 178, 1878, p. 18.

century, Forsyth believed that the forest communities used the axe for social and cultural reasons. Some administrators also felt that they wanted to use the plough but did not have the requisite knowledge or means to do so. In 1869, the settlement officer of Chanda reported that the Maria wanted to use the plough but did not know how. The officer also highlighted the nexus between the moneylender who lent the plough and the Maria's desire to use it. He thus expressed the need for the 'improvement and the protection' of the Marias (*FRCP* 1862-3).

The colonial project of protection was integrally connected to forest conservation, its main aim being to curtail the mobility of the local communities. The first serious attempts to 'improve' Baiga agricultural methods and wean the Baiga away from the axe and their migratory habits came after Ward's note of 1868-9. As regards his progress, Ward reported:

> I had many a talk with the village panchayat as regards the manner of their cultivation, and was rather put in to reply to some of the pertinent questions of the shrewd old men occasionally. My efforts to persuade them to take to the plough were quite unsuccessful and after hard pleading I could only induce them to confine their depredations on the forest and take up land accorded to them in regular rotation. (Ward 1869:160)

In the 1860s, the elders of the Baiga community asserted that 'they were Baigas, their fathers had been born Baigas before them; that they had for generations cut bewars and would continue to do so. Let the sirkar do whatever it pleases to try and prevent it.'[28]

In response to this, the Chief Commissioner of the Provinces, Croswaithe, took a hard line and ordered that the Baigas should not be allowed to take the law into their own hands. Other officials such as the Deputy Commissioner of Mandla, Major General Miller, favoured the establishment of a separate Baiga settlement. This would help confine *bewar* to a specified area, if not eradicate it altogether. In July 1878, Miller reported that 200 Baiga families were willing to settle under such a scheme.[29] In 1890, two villages and four *tolas* or settlements of houses were chosen to form a 'Baiga reserve'. Originally comprising 362 families, these villages were in the Dindori

[28] CPSR, Forest Department, Compilation No. 178 of 1878, p. 47.

[29] Ibid.

and Karanjiya forest reserves. Tracts were to be allotted only to the Baigas and were to be available for further colonization by them.

Miller's stance shows that colonial officials at the district level realized the need for providing an alternative means of survival to the Baiga if their mission was to be successful. In part, the officials hoped that the latter would provide labour for the departmental forest works if they were allowed to practise *bewar* in a limited area. For this reason, the first efforts to curtail *bewar* were made in Balaghat in 1878. *Bewar* was to be allowed in a few chosen villages in the Baihar tahsil of this district. These villages were within the limits of the reserved forest. The Commissioner of Balaghat reported that eighteen Baiga families had given up *bewar* cultivation and had settled with the Gonds in the upland villages. By inducing such a settlement, the government hoped that the Baigas would be introduced to a 'civilized' life and the use of the plough. For this the government was willing to provide the Baigas with cattle, seeds, and a plough in every village (Ward 1868-9: 160).

Early results showed that the Baiga had obliged the government by making attempts to give up *bewar* and pursue other subsistence activities such as rope making, fruit gathering, and undertaking labour for the Gonds. The administrators thus evolved more stringent and exacting measures to keep them away from the axe. In the same year, the Commissioner issued instructions under which the Baigas were to be only settled on leased land and new clearings would be discouraged. The most coercive measure was that *bewar* crops were to be destroyed if the Baigas were caught at it. In addition, all cultivators were to pay a rent of two rupees for every plough, along with forest and grazing dues. The government retained the prerogative to enhance the rent by four rupees. Each cultivated strip was equivalent to one plough.[30]

In the mid-1870s, Colonel Fischer, the District Commissioner of Balaghat, contended that the Baiga had 'largely improved' in terms of taking to the plough and had migrated to Kawardha or Sakh Tehri, with only about 250 families left in Balaghat district. Of these, 15 or 20 families had turned to plough cultivation.[31] However, time was to show that this assessment was premature. By 1880, the scheme had

[30] CPSR, Forest Department, Compilation No: 178, 1878, pp. 47-8.

[31] Ibid., p. 36.

faced certain reverses. All the village elders appealed to the government to lift restrictions on *bewar*.[32] This appeal was linked to the fact that Baiga priests and elders had lost control of a large measure of forest land by the mid-nineteenth century when the first forest laws were implemented. Baiga institutions could not play a role in the distribution of land to individual families. Nor was the labour process based on the interpretation of the old Baiga myth. The rhythm of seasonality was broken by the very act of the reservation.

By the 1880s, the foresters themselves realized that plough cultivation was not the most suitable alternative to *bewar*. In a statement made in 1880, the Conservator of Forests implied that the officials promoting the introduction of the plough in these areas had not thought carefully about its ecological assumptions. He further stated that the abandonment of fields was not merely a form of protest, but was also a way of avoiding declining productivity. The schemes to exchange *bewar* lands held by the Baigas for other cultivable lands also failed miserably. The plan was abandoned since the Baigas refused to move from the forest. Further, the government restrictions of granting land rights to the Baigas who had been cultivating the same piece of land for at least thirty years would leave them destitute, since hardly any Baigas had remained in one place for long. By 1881, the officials reported that most Baigas had attained the status of squatters on their *bewar* lands.[33]

The harsh measures taken by the British government to introduce the plough had led to the indebtedness and destitution of at least 485 Baiga families. Major Bloomfield pointed out that only seventy-five Baiga families had received any kind of government assistance to survive, and about forty families had been able to fend for themselves. The rest were living either in indebtedness or abject poverty.[34] It was admitted that the produce of *bewar* cultivation coupled with the gathering and sale of minor forest products had helped the Baigas to survive so far. Thus, if the Baigas could not take to regular permanent cultivation, alternative forms of livelihood should be created for them, such as labour in forest works and in fisheries.[35]

[32] CPSR, Forest Department, Compilation No. 178, 1881, p. 7.

[33] Ibid., p. 3.

[34] Ibid., pp. 11-16 and Compilation No. 178, 1880, p. 61.

[35] Ibid., p. 22. Also see Compilation No. 178, 1878, pp. 63-79.

By the turn of the century, the aims of the forest department changed from the complete eradication of *bewar* to containing it to a limited area. The Baiga Chak was formed in 1890 with this objective in mind. It extended over 22,858 acres and was reserved for *bewar* cultivation by the Baigas. It consisted of five villages and nine clusters, put under the jurisdiction of the District Collector and the *tahsildar*.[36] There is little information about how many *bewars* were granted during this period. But there is a record of the Baiga protest at the insufficient allocation of land for their *bewars* and the displacement that they suffered due to the formation of the Chak. Dharmu Baiga of Mouza Oudhar wrote to the *tahsildar* about the sixty *Baiga* families that were to be removed to Dhurukota:

> I am residing in Mouza Oudhar and I am cutting bewar in this village for the past three years. Sixty families of the Baigas inhabit these villages and they all live upon Dhya cultivation. We have now been ordered to leave this village and remove to Dhurukota . . . It has very little jungle and most of it was cut down by old Baiga settlers; and consequently it cannot support other Baigas of different village . . . . We therefore pray that we may be allowed bewar cutting in adjoining villages.[37]

Many Baigas were unwilling to leave their homesteads and move into the Chak. Dharmu Baiga and the people that he represented were only one such example. The Conservator of Forests then ordered that Baiga families were to be deported into the Chak. By 1891-2, only eighty families were living outside the reserve and had willingly taken to the plough in Ramgarh *tahsil*. For those Baigas who did not either want to go to the Chak or take up the plough, the government decided that four villages would be set up at Karadih, Udhan, Pandpur, and Duldul for the supply of labour to the forest department. These villages were not to be solely Baiga villages but were also to house Gond and Agaria inhabitants.[38] In 1895, the Gond and the Agaria people were allowed to take up land inside the Chak, furthering the policy of acculturation that was first started in Balaghat.

[36] Mandla District Records, Mandla Collectorate, Mandla, Forests, File No. 37, 1937, p. 105.

[37] CPSR, Forest Department, Compilation No. 178, 1890-2, pp. 11-12.

[38] Ibid., pp. 22-3.

The formation of the Baiga Chak started the process of the marginalization of Baiga society and economy in the colonial and post-colonial political economies. It ensured that the Baigas could not sell their labour to anyone but the forest department and that they could no longer cultivate the land in the same manner as before. Most importantly, the Baigas' links with the local economy were severed and they were forced to enter the labour market provided by the operations of the forest department.

Tribal Life and Local Economy under Colonialism

The collapse of networks had a detrimental effect on the livelihood of the artisans and the gathering practices of the tribal people in a crucial way. The first evidence of the rising demand for 'minor' forest produce in the international market was found in the case of lac in 1875. The industrial uses of lac were many. It was an insulating agent chiefly used as varnish. It was also used as stiffening material for felt and straw and as a preservative coating for wood or metal. Lac was also utilized as an adhesive. For this purpose it, was in demand mainly in America, England, and Germany.[39]

In 1875, the government debated whether it should grant Messrs Jardine and Skinner, an international managing agency, a contract for lac propagation in the Loisinga and Barapahar forests of Sambalpur. The District Commissioner of Sambalpur, Bowie reasoned that:

> The propagation of lac is only carried on by Gonds, Binjiwars and other jungle tribes who are poor and always require advances to survive. While they propagate lac the government can only give advances if it has the lease of the jungle. By taking a royalty interests of the government and the firm will be kept identical.[40]

This official assertion of the compatibility of Gond, official, and industrial interests was one of the first steps towards the inclusion of the Binjiwars into the world market. These developments showed that the European managing agencies had entered the forest economy.

In the wake of the growing world demand for lac, the government

[39] Lac 1919, p. 5

[40] Lac 1875, p. 8.

began to lease out forests for lac propagation in return for a minimum royalty (to be fixed at 25 per cent) from the lessee. Under this system, the government would fix the wages of the lac cultivator as well as the price at which the lessee could sell lac in the market. By fixing the price the government attempted to narrow the gap between the lease holder's profit and the price he paid to the lac, cultivator.[41] Laying down the basis of the future policy on lac the Commissioner of the Province asserted:

> It would be better if the lac was produced without human aid and the only labour used was for collecting it for then labour would make its bargain before entering the forest. The fact is that the lac produced by the Bhumia whose work it has been for generations and the present system of leasing works very badly as far as they are concerned . . . . To remove the defects it is essential that the producer has a right to produce in the open market to get a better price . . . . But free trade can only be granted in two ways: 1) By making the producer pay a certain sum on the quantity produced or the number of trees used, 2) To give passes to each producer to collect lac from its jungles.[42]

It would also help the Gonds to strike a better bargain with the representatives of the managing agencies. In order to maximize production and assess the value of lac, several government-sponsored experiments were carried out. Several techniques were tried to improve the quality of the seeds, minimize labour, and reduce the injury to trees. But the reported failure of all efforts, according to the special lac officer, proved that the methods used by forest dwellers and the peasants were more effective.[43] Before the government could implement a change of policy, the world demand for lac fell[44] and it was only in the first decade of the twentieth century that it rose again.

From 1912 onwards, there was another determined effort to promote the export of lac, tans, and other oils and gums to Europe. In 1913, the Chief Conservator of Forests wrote: 'Upto now there is only one form of preparing tan extract in India, and that too from Myrabolans. The business however has great possibilities, for the

[41] Ibid., pp. 26-30.

[42] Ibid., pp. 85-9.

[43] MPSR, Forest Department, File No. 114, September 1920.

[44] CPSR, Forest Compilation, No. 1278, 1877.

availability and supply of tan barks in Europe is already insufficient. . . . There does not seem to be any likelihood of any great demand in India for the product.'[45]

Officials felt that 'native industries' such as tanning, dyeing, etc., were on the decline, but that these could be rescued from an adverse trend by the influx of European capital.

The penetration of European capital in the propagation of lac helped to create labour opportunities for the Bhumias (another name for the Baigas in Chhattisgarh) and the Gonds. These opportunities were important for tribal survival in the wake of the restrictions imposed on gathering activities and other subsistence forms. But the interlinkages between the artisans and the forest dwellers were broken. The forest dwellers started supplying lac to the agents of the European firms instead of to the artisans. The leasing system created monopolies for firms, pushing out smaller lac artisans from the market.

While this was true in the case of lac, the situation of the silk industry was somewhat different. From Table 3 it is possible to gauge the sharp decline in the number of weavers and dyers in the ten years between 1891 and 1901.

It is important to note that in the case of silk the decline was just a regional one, mainly in Raipur district. But there was, in fact, a marginal increase also in the number of weavers in Sambalpur and Bilaspur. This was accompanied by the increase in the import of silk

TABLE 3: SHARP DECLINE IN THE WORKFORCE OF THE COTTAGE INDUSTRY, 1891-1901

Name of Industry	Number of Workers 1891	Number of Workers 1901
Tussar Silk Weavers	699	451
Silk Dyers	154	39
Cotton Dyers	15,444	6,960
Cotton Printers	2,577	289
Dye Shift Growers and Makers	522	587

Source: Compiled from Low 1908.

[45] CPSR Chief Conservator's Correspondence, File No. 207, 1913-14.

cocoons from Bengal (Low 1908:112).[46] Despite the increase in silk production in the Chhattisgarh region, Low insisted that the number of silk producers had declined. In fact, he said that the increase in the weaving population (i.e. 9,966 persons in 1891 to 23,034 persons in 1901) was due to the provincial increase in cotton weavers in the southern part of the province. But we can see that Low was mistaken about a general decline in the silk industry. His own evidence proved that the mechanization of the industry was taking place in order to increase production, the market for which was mainly in Nagpur. He showed that the silk workers were using the power loom. Perhaps this resulted in the decline of the makers of gold and silver threads as well as the dyers (Low 1908:11-13, 17).[47]

It is, therefore, difficult to make a case for a general decline in the local industries of the province. However, with the influx of urban capital, the production processes of family industries underwent a change. The efforts to mechanize the propagation of lac were confined to rearing the cocoon and not to the collection of produce. Thus, an attempt was made to increase the productivity of lac cocoons by improving the propagation methods of lac. The influx of European capital in the production of lac provided the tribals seasonal employment in the forest areas. In the case of silk too, mechanization was attempted. But the survival of the local industry due to the investment of urban capital did not mean that artisans felt no pressures in a changing situation. Local lac artisans, silk dyers, and printers lost their subsistence due to changes in the production process.

Conclusion

This essay has attempted to investigate the nature of certain transformations in tribal subsistence patterns in the late eighteenth and

[46] The number of weavers in Raipur declined from 282 to 111 in ten years but the number of weavers in Bilaspur and Sambalpur rose marginally by 26 and 91 respectively. Further, the import of silk cocoons rose from 740 maunds to 3,251 maunds between 1892 and 1905. The provincial decline shown by these figures was thus an artificial one as these three areas (especially Sambalpur) were the main silk-producing regions. Other declines were shown in Mandla, Balaghat, and other regions with minor silk production.

[47] Low's explanation for the decline in the silk industry was the influx of goods from Manchester and restricted access to forests.

nineteenth centuries. In the case of the Gonds and the Baigas, it has shown that tribal subsistence was fluid, multi-occupational, and seasonal in character. The systems depended on mobility between different eco-zones for the fulfilment of daily needs, and hence were open-ended and precariously balanced, dependent on forest diversity and local production linkages. The issue of eco-friendliness and the stability of traditional subsistence practices is complex and needs to be analysed in the context of the changing relationship between tribes and the larger political economy.

If we look at the changes within the tribal subsistence forms in this context, we find that the distinctive feature of late pre-colonial political systems was that they succeeded in pushing the tribal zamindaris from the plains into the forested highlands. This process of marginalization was intensified in the colonial period. It was also qualitatively different in that colonial intervention created centralized and monopolistic control over land and forest that resulted in making tribal economies an adjunct to the global world market. This resulted in the transformation of the tribal economy from a pre-capitalist, pre-colonial economy to an underdeveloped colonial economy. Artisans lost their jobs and markets; global markets and agencies that managed global networks increasingly replaced the local markets for minor forest produce. Finally, the division of labour in the gathering economy underwent a drastic change. The forest department stopped the gathering of all commercially valuable minor forest produce and put the burden of subsistence on the shoulders of the tribal women. In the days before colonialism, when all types of gathering was prevalent and shifting cultivation was practised, men and women had shared the work even though most of the income-generating produce and technology were controlled by the men. With forest reservations and the severing of local networks, shifting cultivation ceased, and the local market for commercial produce was restricted. The men only got seasonal employment with the managing agencies and the forest department, and thus put the main burden of everyday survival on the women. Thus, the inequalities between local and non-local economies and within the community and the household increased with the disruption of local networks. This is evident in the way in which the local artisans lost both their employment and their market when tribal people began to work for European managing agencies.

Scientific forestry and monopoly control of forest land were, thus, symptomatic of a larger process of tribal marginalization—a process that concentrated on destroying the local economy.

REFERENCES

Agnew, Col., *Report on the Administration of the Subah of Chhattisgarh*, Nagpur, 1830.

Balfour, Edward, 'On migratory tribes of the natives in Central India', *Journal of the Asiatic Society of Bengal*, 1844, vol. 1, no. 1, pp. 2-10.

Champion, H.G. and S.K. Seth, *Forest Types of India*, Delhi: n.d., 1968.

Cumberledge, N.F., *Monograph on the Banjara Clan*, Nagpur, 1882.

Elwin, Verrier, *The Baiga*, Delhi: Oxford University Press, 1939.

Elwin, Verrier, *The Agaria*, Delhi: Oxford University Press, 1942.

Forsyth, J., *The Highlands of Central India: Notes on their Forests and Wild Tribes, Natural History and Sport*, London, 1889.

Gadgil, M. and R. Guha, *This Fissured Land: An Ecological History of India*, Delhi: Oxford University Press, 1992.

Gazetteer of Mandla District (Mandla DG), vols. I-II, Bombay: Government Press, 1909.

Glasfurd, Col., *Report on the Bustar State*, 1876, n.d.

Grigson, W. V., *The Maria Gonds of Bastar*, London: Oxford University Press, 1936.

Guha, Ramchandra, *The Unquiet Woods: Ecological Change and Peasant Resistance in the Himalaya*, Delhi: Oxford University Press, 1990.

Habib, Irfan, *An Atlas of the Mughal Empire: Political and Economic Maps with Detailed Notes and Index*, Delhi: Oxford University Press, 1982.

Haimendorf, C.V.F., *Tribes in India*, Delhi: Oxford University Press, 1985.

Low, C.E., *Preliminary Report on Cottage Industries*, Nagpur, 1908.

Mackenzie, Col., 'Notes on the Banjaras', *Berar Census Report*, Bombay: Government Press, 1881.

Nisbet, John, 'On Mixed Forests and Their Advantages over Pure Forests', Appendix in *Indian Forester*, 1894, vol. 20, pp. 5-6.

Ostmarton, R.C., 'Sal and its regeneration', *Indian Forester*, vol. 54, pp. 230-74, 639-54, 1928.

Prasad, Archana, 'The Political Ecology of Swidden Cultivation', *Tools and Tillage*, vol. II, no. 4, 1995.

Rangarajan, Mahesh, *Fencing the Forest: Conservation and Ecological Change in India's Central Provinces, 1860-1919*, Delhi: Oxford University Press, 1996.

Reports of Forest Administration, Central Provinces (*FRCP*), Calcutta: Imperial Press, 1864-90.

Russell, R.V. and R. Hiralal, *Tribes and Castes of the Central Provinces of India*, 4 vols., Nagpur, 1910.

Singh, K.S., *Birsa Munda and his Movement*, Delhi: Oxford University Press, 1983.

Sinha, Surajit, 'State Formation and Rajput Myth in Central India', *Man in India*, vol. 42, no. 1, pp. 3-80, 1962.

Ward , Col. H.E.C., *Report of Land Revenue Settlements of Mundlah District, Central Provinces*, Nagpur: Government Press, 1869.

From Pastoralism to Agriculture: Tondai Nadu, a Tamil Sub-Region in the Early Historical and Early Medieval Periods

R. CHAMPAKALAKSHMI

TWO REGIONS of intensive pastoral activity in early historic Tamilakam were the Tondai Nadu and the Pandi Nadu. Of these, the northern region, Tondai Nadu, is conspicuous in terms of its physiography, with short, non-perennial river systems and low hills, and its semi-dry climatic conditions. It is not particularly conducive to intensive agriculture, except in the southernmost parts, represented by modern South Arcot district. The agricultural rhythms of this region differ considerably from those of the more monsoonal rainfall regimes. On the west, on the shelf below the Mysore Ghat, the land is still under forest cover, rather open, and used mainly for grazing. A predominantly tank-irrigated area, this zone of Tamilakam has preserved age-old memories of pastoral tribes and their early organization into pastoral-cum-agrarian units, called the *kottam*, believed to have been inhabited in the protohistoric and the early historic periods by a tribe called the Kurumbar. An early colonization by agriculturists, traditionally known as the Velala, by the decree of Karikala (an early Cola king), brought 48,000 Velala families to the region from the Kaveri valley, and is yet another persistent memory suggestive of a gradual transformation of a predominantly pastoral region into an agro-pastoral one even before the end of what is known as the Sangam period (which some scholars date between 300 BC and AD 300).

This tradition remains largely unsubstantiated for the early period, except for portions concerning the lineage of a chief called Ilam Tiraiyan of the Tiraiyar or Tondaiyar clan ruling over Kacci (Kanci-puram) and accepting the overlordship of Karikala, and some later legends associating the Tiraiyar with descent from a Cola prince.[1] The tradition about the 48,000 Velalas curiously persisted in the later Cola inscriptions; these refer to the 48,000 as the nomenclature given to the families of those agriculturists who participated in the temple-based agrarian production of the region.[2] Thus, the only resource the historian has is to look for evidence of pastoralism of the early period in the Iron Age or in the megalithic archaeological remains, and in the early corpus of Tamil literature, the Sangam texts.

The evidence from the megalithic sites of the first millennium BC being more often imprecise and inconclusive, with excavated sites forming a disproportionately small percentage of the total number of explored sites, such evidence needs to be used only as supplementary to the literary texts. The latter do not lend themselves to easy interpretation without semiotic analysis, as Rajan Gurukkal has shown.[3] However, the Sangam texts still form the only major source for the study of early Tamil society and economy.

The concept of the *tinai* as explained by the grammar of the Sangam literature, the *Tolkappiyam* (*Porulatikaram*, 5:5-6), provides the clue to different forms of land use in different eco-zones, such as the *mullai* (pastoral, forest tracts), *marutam* (agricultural plains), *kurinci* (hunting hill tracts), *neital* (fishing coastal tracts), and *palai* (dry zones where brigandage occurred). The *mullai* was not merely a forest tract, for in Tamilakam thick rain forests were meagre and were generally confined to the higher hill slopes. It would be appropriate to identify *mullai* as forest (*kadu*) around or peripheral to the plains (*marutam*), along with pastures, meadows, and scrubland, especially those on the cultivable lower slopes of the Tamil Nadu hills, the Kerala hills, and the Coimbatore plateau. Here cattle rearing was the predominant activity. These tracts were peripheral to the regions of expanding agricultural activity, either undergoing a slow transition from a dominant pastoral to an agrarian economy, or being integrated into an expanding agrarian system by the end of the sixth century AD. The

[1] See T.V. Mahalingam, *Kancipuram in Early South Indian History*, Bombay: Asia Publishing House, 1969, p. 16.

[2] See *Annual Report on Epigraphy* (hereafter *ARE*) 1909-10, no. 319, an early thirteenth-century inscription from Tirukkachchur, Chingleput district.

[3] Rajan Gurukkal, 'Forms of Production and Forces of Change in Ancient Tamil Society', *Studies in History,* vol. 3, no. 2, 1989.

mullai tracts of the Coimbatore plateau were located on major trans-peninsular routes linking the western coast with the eastern. Hence, the early pastoralists of this region may well have been involved in overland trade and oceanic trade (which began in the first century BC), as the region is rich in beryl and other semi-precious stones that were exported westward. Hoards of Roman coins have been discovered in this region. Megalithic sites of the region, such as Kodumanal, are found to have survived well into the early historic (Sangam) period (ibid.), and the exchange circuits of the megalithic context could also have continued to become part of the expanding trade network of the subsequent period. Neither archaeology nor literature provides direct testimony of such links. Yet, the uniform occurrence of the articles of one eco-zone in others (*shankh* shell and semi-precious stones, for example) indicates some exchange at a rudimentary level (drift trade?) between the different regions. And the Sangam texts refer to inter-*tinai* exchanges (ibid.)

The *mullai* region, named after its characteristic flora (*Jasminum aurichulatum*), was predominantly populated by pastoral communities referred to variously as Itaiyar, Andar, Kovalar, Ayar, Toluvar, and Potuvar.[4] The Andar and the Ayar were cowherds, and the Itaiyar were shepherds. The latter are described as *atutai-itaimakan*, or *itaiyan* who possessed sheep and goats. The Kovalar (probably derived from the Sanskrit Gopala) were cowherds (*pal-ankovalar*).[5] The dominant groups were the Ayar and the Kovalar, and are the pastoral communities more frequently mentioned in the Sangam texts. While these pastoralists tended cattle and goats, some form of shifting cultivation was also practised by them. The pastoralists were more or less sedentary, their thatched huts built close together in a circle around an open space, within a thick fence of thorny bush that kept wild animals away.[6] Huts were often made of millet straw,[7] or else of clay and wattle, with bamboo or palm posts, the upper ends of which

[4] *Kuṟuntokai*, 117:3; *Tolkāppiyam*: *Poruḷ.*, 23; *Puranānūrṇ*, 54:11, 390:1; *Neḍunalvāḍai*: 3; *Akanānūaṟu*, 14:7; *Maturaikkānñci*, 290; *Kalittokai*, 150:51; *Perumpāṇāṟṟuppaṭai*, 175.

[5] *Naṟṟiṇai*, 87:1; *Kuṟuntokai* 221:4; *Ainkuṟunūṟu*, 87:1; *Puṟanānūṟu*, 265:4; *Patiṟṟuppatu*, 21:20.

[6] *'yiḍu-muḷ-paḍappai'*—*Puṟanānūṟu* 197:10.

[7] *kavinan-vēynta kavinankuḍi-ciṟūr'*—*Perumpāṇāṟṟuppaṭai* 148.

were held together by being inserted into a broken pot, and covered with palmyra-leaf thatch. Palmyra leaves were thrown on a frame of dried sticks propped up by a few shortened bamboo pillars.[8] Such settlements of pastoralists were called *kurumpai, kuti, kollai, palli*, or *ur*.[9] The term *kuti* is particularly significant as it stood for clan as well as settlement, as for instance, Kovalar *kuti*[10] and Aykkuti or Andiran (a chief) near the Potiyil hills.

The term *puravu* meant pasture land, and it was probably owned by the community. The herdsmen (*kurumakkal*, younger members) took the herds to the pastures early in the morning, and returned with them to their settlements in the evening.[11] During the rainy season they took the animals to the highlands near by, probably for a seasonal migration.[12] The flocks comprised cows (*a*), bulls (*erutu*), buffaloes (*erumai*), sheep (*turuvai*), and goats (*vellai*). The women of the community played an important role as vendors of milk and milk products. They milked the cows and buffaloes, churned butter, and made ghee.[13] That the Sangam tribes were organized as kin groups is reflected in references to the *kuti*, which, as we have said, means 'clan' as well as 'settlement'. Cowherd settlements are referred to as *cirukuti* (small settlements), and stock expressions such as *ilaiyor* and *mutiyor* (the junior and senior members of the clan) and *kilai* meaning branch (of the lineage) indicate that the production process was jointly carried out by kin, and that the extended family was the unit of labour in all eco-zones.

References in the Sangam texts to pastoral chiefs such as Ay Antiran of the Potiyil hills, and the Aviyar of Avinanluti in the Palni hills of the Madurai district, associate them with the Velir lineages, of which eighteen are known to tradition as having migrated to the south with the well-known sage, Agastya, and the Muventar (Cera, Cola, and Pandya), and settled in the Tamil region; they claimed descent from Krishna of the Yadava clan. Other chiefs claiming Yadava

[8] *'kaunkal-kurampai'*—*Perumpāṇāṟṟuppaṭai* 148.

[9] Ibid., 148, 166; '*kollaikkōvalar*'—*Malaipaḍukaḍām*, 419.

[10] *Perumpāṇāṟṟuppaṭai*, 166.

[11] *'nar-puravu'*—*Porunarāṟṟuppaṭai*, 20; *Puṟanānūṟu*, 257: 7-8; *Naṟṟiṇai*, 69: 8-9.

[12] *Neḍunalvāḍai*, 4—*'erudai-ina-veru-pulam-parappi'*.

[13] *Perumpāṇāṟṟuppaṭai*, 153, 156-60, 165; *Ciṟupāṇāṟṟuppaṭai*, 189; *Neḍunalvāḍai*, 4.

lineage were the Irunkovelir of Kodumbalur, the Pari of Parambumalai, the Kunrur velir of (Coonoor) the Pekan of Vanamali, and the chiefs of Kodaikanal. It would appear that in literary tradition both the *kurinci* and the *mullai* chiefs, as also the chiefs of the *marutam* plains, claimed common descent. And if the conventional belief of the migration of the Velir is established in fact, Iron Age sites may be associated with the settling of tribes or clans in different parts of Tamilakam and their pursuing different economic activities, pastoralism included. The *kurinci* and the *mullai* zones often overlapped, but were generally peripheral to the *marutam* agricultural areas, and hence saw shifting agriculture for subsistence. A semi-nomadic existence may also be attributed to the pastoralists on the fringes of the *kurinci* and the *marutam* zones.

Cattle lifting and retrieving were an inevitable part of pastoral life,[14] and those who risked their lives while defending or retrieving cattle were honoured by a memorial stone and venerated as heroes. The practice of erecting hero-stones (*natu kal*) is mentioned in the Sangam texts and could well have been known even earlier, that is, in the megalith-building context. That it continued well into the period of the Pallava overlordship in the Tondai Nadu is attested to by the discovery of several hero-stones dating to the reign of the Pallavas (the seventh to the ninth centuries). Sangam poetry has many verses describing the erection and worship of the *natu kal*.[15]

Concerning evidence regarding subsistence practices, the archaeological material is not directly illuminating. We may cite the recovery of the bones of cattle and sheep/goat from excavated sites in the Tondai Nadu, such as Sanur (Chingleput district). Literary evidence mentions the use of dogs to protect grazing cattle, and to substantiate this, we find sculpted reliefs on Pallava-period hero-stones that show dogs along with the figures of the heroes who died defending or retrieving cattle.[16]

References to slash-and-burn cultivation of *varaku* (millet),[17] excavated remains of pulses at Paiyampalli, rice from the Muttrpalion site

[14] Fourteen *tuṟais—Tolkāppiyam, Poruḷ.*, 59:3, 61, 63:14.

[15] *Puṟanāṉūṟu*, 221, 223, 232, 260; *Akanāṉūṟu*, 67, 131, 297; *Ainkuṟunūṟu*, 332; *Paṭṭinappālai*, 79; *Malaipaḍukaḍām*, 388–9.

[16] Hero-stone at Eduttanur, Chengam *taluka*, North Arcot district. See R. Nagaswamy, ed., *Cengam Naḍukaṟkaḷ*, no. 1971/59.

[17] *Puṟanāṉūṟu*, 159.

(in Pondicherry) and Panduvaram Dewal (North Arcot district), stone implements such as pestles, mortars and querns from Odugattur, Kodamalaiputtur, Sanur, and Perumbair, all in the northern zone of Tamilakam, as well as some agricultural implements, indicate that slash-and-burn and dry rice cultivation prevailed. Pastoralists had to maintain contact with cultivators for grain, or else cultivators were more or less parts of the pastoral groups. In the foothill regions, opportunities for hunting would also have been used. Thus, both the *kurinci* deity, Murukan, and the *mullai* deity, Mayon (Krishna), would have been worshipped by the pastoralists, despite the distinct classification of *tinai* deities by the *Tolkappiyam*,[18] suggesting that the dark-hued Mayon was the pastoral god and Murukan of the hill tracts was the hunters' deity. It may be of interest to add here that in the Sangam literature the Pullis, a Kallar family of the Venkatam hills (Tirupati-Tirumalai), seem to have worshipped Mayon as their tutelary deity, and to this day the gates of the sanctum in the Venkatesvara temple on the hill are opened during the morning awakening of the deity by a cowherd.

This survey of data on pastoral activities in the early historic period shows that regional and environmental factors shaped and conditioned the human-nature relationship, particularly the pastoral economy. The Tondai Nadu thereafter provides an interesting example of the transformation of the kin-based, pastoral organization into a stratified agro-pastoral society, with spatial organization presenting a spectrum ranging from the *kottam* of the pastoralists to the *kottam-nadu* complex of the early medieval Pallava-Cola periods, that is, from the seventh to the thirteenth centuries.

In the early medieval period, settlements of the herding community were interspersed with the agrarian villages, called *ur*, *grama*, and *mangalam*, as a result of a steady agrarian expansion and institutional growth of the *brahmadeya* and the *agrahara* villages and the *ur* or non-*brahmadeya* villages. Pastoral settlements also appear on the fringes of big towns/cities such as Kancipuram, Madurai, and Tanjavur. Terms such as *padi*, *irukkai*, and *kollai*[19] continued to denote such settlements, which, however, were no longer independent clan

[18] *Tolkāppiyam*, *Poruḷ.*, 5:5-6.

[19] *Cilappatikāram*, XVI:46; *Maṇimēkalai*, XIII:85.

settlements but were increasingly made a part of larger village units administered by Brahmanas and the Velalas, the landowning or controlling groups. Thus, *irukkai* has the connotation of 'quarters' rather than a separate settlement. *Kollai* similarly would mean a 'backyard', the fringe of a settlement rather than a separate one. *Padi* (Ayarpadi) by now had come to represent an area set aside for different caste and occupational groups such as the Sankarappadi and where mixed caste and professional groups lived. These included pastoralists and those entrusted with the supply of ritual items such as oil to the temple. The grazing area for cattle is referred to as the *ur-pal* and the *kanru-mey-pal* (waste land used for grazing cattle).[20] In other words, grazing areas were also now part of the larger agrarian settlements.

The hero-stone inscriptions of Tondai Nadu are the largest in number so far discovered in Tamilakam (and here we see a distinct parallel to the geographic and cultural zoning of early medieval Maharashtra worked out by Dandekar in this volume). Hero-stone inscriptions are most concentrated in the North Arcot district and the contiguous Dharmapuri district. The Javadi, Sheveroy, and Pachchaimalai hills west of Tondai Nadu have, on their southern and eastern flanks, cultivable land that borders on the pastoral zone. On the shelf below the main Mysore Ghat much land is still under open forest, used mainly for grazing. This region is geographically and also historically an appendage of the famous cattle-breeding zone of Mysore. Today the Dharmapuri-Krishnagiri-Salem cattle markets are the main sources of heavy draught animals for an area stretching from Malabar to Chittoor, while the best animals are sold as far afield as Madurai and Tirumelveli as coach bullocks. Hence, the concentration of inscribed hero-stones in North Arcot and Dharmapuri indicates the important role of pastoralists from very early times. In the Pallava period, however, to which forty-five of the sixty-three hero-stone inscriptions belong, the region was gradually integrated into a new agrarian order, of which the *brahmadeya* and the temple were the major institutions. Large agricultural villages came to be founded anew and by bringing together pre-existing agricultural and pastoral settlements. Pastoral settlement was now marginal in both

[20] *Thirty Pallava Copper Plates* (Tamil Varalāṟṟu Kaḻavam), pp. 243, 271.

the economic and the geographic sense, pastoralism becoming secondary to agriculture. Yet the Pallava inscriptions abound in references to gifts of cattle, goats, and livestock in general; these are more important than land in areas of pastoral production. Land (sometimes entire settlements with their cultivated tracts) as a gift item is more frequently bestowed and in larger area by the ninth century, to become a major item by the tenth, under the early Colas, particularly Parantaka I (AD 907-55).[21]

Hero-stones decrease by the end of the tenth century, and this could be attributed to organized protection of cattle wealth in the larger settlements, in which the *sabha* and *ur* assemblies administered the villages and established *kaval* or protection of different areas (*padi*) within and on the outskirts of the villages. The term Cevakan that had been used in the Pallava-period hero-stone inscriptions to refer to the hero protecting cattle now came to denote either a watchman appointed by the livestock keepers, or a village soldier appointed by the assembly, or even a functionary of the royal or the chief family controlling the region. Henceforth, the communal duty of the pastoralists to protect cattle became a collective responsibility of the corporate assemblies, or of the ruling authority. Interestingly, the integration of the pastoralists into the larger temple society is attested to by several Cola temple inscriptions. For instance, the Tanjavur records of the early eleventh century refer to separate streets where the Idaiyar lived, the *anaikkadavar teru*, *kantarva teru*, *madappalli teru*, *villikal teru*, and so on.[22] In the thirteenth century, they were assigned privileges like the construction of brick houses, implying that hitherto they had no such status in the larger agrarian settlement.

Pasture lands existed in different geographical contexts as indicated by the terms *kurinci medu*, *mullaippuravu*, *marutat-tandalai*, and *neital marunku*. Provisions were also made by rulers for the maintenance of pasture land by the purchase of occupied land (*kudi-kadu*), or by gifts of gold for maintaining pastures for buffalo herds. *Tirunamattukkani*, or land purchased in the name of the temple deity, was also set aside for pasture, and a Pandya inscription of AD 1258 reveals that the area was demarcated by stones marked with the trident. Waste land, land reverted to the village commons (*ur-p-potu*) as escheat, and land

[21] *South Indian Inscriptions* (hereafter *SII*), vol. XIII.

[22] *SII*, II, 94,95.

abandoned or relinquished due to floods or drought were auctioned for outright purchase or leased on the highest rental bid to maintain pasture land.

Contemporary literature and inscriptions provide evidence of the role of herdsmen in looking after cattle, sheep, and goats of the village community and of the temple. The well-known story of the Bhakti saint Anaya Nayanar, employed by the village community to look after the cattle and graze them in the pasture near by, assisted by a group of *kovalar*, as narrated in the *Periya Puranam*, extols his devotion despite the severe tests to which he was subjected: losing cows and recovering them through God's grace. Here the caste status of the cowherd is based on the brahmanical norms of *varna-jati*, and as such a lower status is implied in relation to the others. Hence the importance of the Bhakti ideal that places religious devotion above caste considerations.

The Cola-period inscriptions record gifts of cows, ewes, buffaloes, and goats to the temples by many people for acquiring religious merit or for expiating a sin. The herdsmen were entrusted with the animals thus endowed, often on condition of supplying a prescribed quantity of ghee for burning sacred lamps in the temples. A group of such animals was called a *cava-muva-p-peradu*,[23] literally meaning that the animals would neither age nor die, and in reality implying that the number of animals thus endured should be maintained for ever, by replacement.

The *kaval* system of cattle protection became a regular feature in the Cola period, and special privileges and honours were conferred on those who defended village cattle. Yet, cattle lifting continued, as cattle remained an important economic asset. The properties of those who stole cattle or caused injury to them were confiscated and made into temple property, as, for instance, in Mangalam in Salem district in AD 1020.[24]

The terms used for cattle breeders in the Sangam texts were also used in later works such as the *Cilappatikaram,* without any distinction being made between one or another group. However, new terms such as *manradi* and *kon* appear from the ninth century onwards in Pallava and Cola inscriptions and in contemporary literature. The

[23] *SII*, VIII, 6.

[24] *ARE, 1915-16*, no. 157.

term *manradi* denotes the herdsman in charge of the *manru*, meaning cattle stall. The manradi often rose to high positions in the social and political organizations of their regions, with some even acquiring control over land at a later stage. Subgroups among them were named after their respective functions in temple service: the *deva-variyarana-manradi*, *tiruvilakku manradi*, and *surabi-manradi*.[25] The largest number of such manradis are known from the inscriptions of Tondai Nadu. The number of titled persons among them is high, indicating that they enjoyed considerable influence in society. Some manradi in temple service were given special privileges such as the right to allotted house sites on land belonging to the temple. They could also be exempt from payment of taxes such as the *irai*, *eccoru*, *vetti*, and *vetanai*,[26] all of which are associated with unpaid or compulsory service to the village or to royal functionaries who visited their settlements. Many of these groups emerge as castes in post-Cola times, and continue to be so. Other terms like Padaittalaivar and Srigopalar[27] seem to denote high status groups of the pastoral communities.

Stratification within pastoralist groups, based on cattle wealth, political authority, and access to land, is generally indicated in Cola-period inscriptions. Those who were attached to temples as service groups or as suppliers of milk and milk products, or as minders of temple flocks were called *devar-itaiyar* or *devar-itaiccanrar*, *tiruvilakku-itaiyar*, *surabi-itaiyar*, and *vetti-k-kuti-itaiyar*. The last-mentioned may have been those who provided forced or unpaid labour. The *itaiyar*, to whom references are more numerous, could well have been the middle-level herdsmen whose role as supervisors and service personnel in temple society was a significant feature of the pastoral organization, although their caste/class status was lower in relation to the manradi, the Ayar, and the Srigopalar.

Corporate bodies of herders came into existence during the Cola period, one of which was the *manradi kalanai*. The most notable of such organizations was, however, the *tiruvayppadi nattar*, which undertook to organize services in the temples or endowments to temples. They are conspicuous in Tondai Nadu from the twelfth

[25] *SII*, VII, 987; VIII, 119; XII, 158.

[26] *SII*, XIII, 149.

[27] *SII*, XIV, 131; XXIV, 136.

century,[28] suggesting the presence of a large pastoral population with a long historical past in this region.

Taxes on pastoral production are in evidence from the time of the Pallavas, when nine taxes on cattle, sheep, and goats, as well as on the *itaiyar* are mentioned in inscriptions. The number increases to over twenty by the end of the Cola period, which points to the economic importance of pastoralism, second only to agriculture. Temples were the major consumers of ghee, for lamps and food offerings, and we notice that gifts of livestock were made by pastoralists and also by others. Such endowments were made on the basis of accepted standard herds of ewes, cows, and buffaloes (*cava-muva-perumpacu, peradu, pererumai*) together with calves, bulls, etc., for lamps to shine in perpetuity.[29] The *srikaryam*, a temple official, or other functionaries, entrusted animals to herdsmen as *kani-madu* and *kudi-ninga-cava-muva-peradu*, for the tending of cattle and the supply of ghee. These were treated as the *kani* of the herdsmen, just as the land gifts entrusted to the *Velalas* were *kani* that bore the right of possession and cultivation. Herdsmen produced surety for the livestock and supplies entrusted to them, and also for the taxes.[30] They gradually became entitled to possession and rights of cultivation, especially so the manradis and the Srigopalars. The number of such entitlements had greatly increased by the end of the Cola period.

Without going into the details of the commercial transactions in which herdsmen came to be involved, it may be pointed out that the pastoralists entered into day-to-day as well as larger commercial activities, by barter, or with gold or money.[31] But until the thirteenth century, what they sold was largely milk and milk products; later, animals also came to be exchanged.[32]

Thus, it can be said that 'from pastoralism to agriculture' was not a change that completely did away with pastoral production in the economy. The change was gradual, and the process involved the transformation of a predominantly pastoral economy on the drier

[28] *ARE, 1936-7*, Ins. No. 165.
[29] *SII*, VI, No. 230; VII, No. 880.
[30] *SII*, XIV, No. 184; XIX, No. 116.
[31] *ARE*, 302 of 401; 100 of 421; 328 of 1924; *SII*, II, No. 6.
[32] *SII*, XVII, No. 232.

hill slopes and scrub land to an agro-pastoral economy in which the upper strata of herdsmen turned into controllers of land without, however, giving up the breeding of animals. They became as much a part of the new and developing agrarian order as the peasants, weavers, and Brahmanas, and often enjoyed privileges that marked their new and enhanced status which, in its turn, was brought about by internal stratification in pastoral communities.

Tondai Nadu illustrates this process much more clearly that other regions in southern India, as it was here that the distinctive *kottam* zone pre-existed agrarian expansion, representing an initial stage of specialized pastoral production with only limited land cultivation, but turning into a pastoral-cum-agricultural unit during the Pallava and the Cola periods. The transformation began as the Pallavas introduced several *brahmadeyas* and temples in the *kottam*, thereby increasing agricultural activities, expanding an agrarian system by incorporating pastoral and small agricultural pockets. Thus were created several *nadus* within the *kottams*, each with a new irrigation project. The early Colas, particularly Parantaka I (tenth century), built temples for the *tiruvayppadideva*, the deity of the pastoralists, in key centres throughout the kingdom, and endowed such temples liberally with land, cattle, and gold. The integration of the pastoralists into the new order became complete by the twelfth century.

Concluding Summary

SHEREEN F. RATNAGAR

IN THIS summary I briefly touch on the themes that connect the papers in the book. The first such theme is environment and ecology.

This topic is central to the discussion of specific pastoral cultures by Chetan Singh and Ajay Dandekar. In both discussions, map zones figure prominently, awaiting more detailed research that will point to the mountain passes, watering points, river crossings, and seasonal routes that actually grid any such map and are the key to the geography of pastoral movements (Waller and Sobania 1994:49–50). (Also Dandekar, in the absence of other kinds of data, relies perhaps too heavily on annual rainfall figures to delineate his ecological zones. The incidence of rainfall over the four monsoon months is equally significant.) Jaya Menon sees craft production amongst pastoralists against the background of the materials they produce, perhaps the most spectacular of these being the tribal Turkoman carpet. Archana Prasad provides fascinating details about the conditions of crop raising in forested hill tracts. Champakalakshmi shows that the cultural landscape of northern Tamilakam was a variegated one with many kinds of economic pursuits being followed.

While the environment is to an extent an independent variable, as are the biological characteristics and grazing/browsing behaviour of cattle and small ruminants, it is not merely the background to cultural development, a fact which is amply demonstrated in Supriya Varma's paper. The environment is dynamic, and Varma has to contend with the effects of major interruptions in rainfall or soil fertility and in the ensuing land use patterns.

Nevertheless, it is true that in the semi-arid zones of the world—in contrast to the central Indian forested hills where cultivators must be mobile—it is not agriculture that is mobile. Here agriculture gives low and unpredictable returns and instead of investing only/largely in fields, you invest in livestock. However large a herd, one can move it to take advantage of varying conditions within the semi-arid zone and on its fringes. Hence, an essential aspect of pastoral nomadism is that, once successful and the owner of large flocks, an individual does not own land or invest in land. This ecological feature has an obvious bearing on the marginalization of pastoral peoples, which is discussed below.

It needs to be reiterated that ecology is a systemic framework in which one makes sense of mobile pastoralism or shifting cultivation or the flexibility of Bhil livelihood, but that this does not mean that ecology is a 'cause'. It cannot be, when pastoralists and shifting cultivators are still regularly blamed for overgrazing and forest denudation! As we have seen, Vasant Saberwal (1999) has presented a critique of the 'alarmist discourse' and he asks whether pastoralists can be expected to both expand their herds and fail to regulate grazing. Hence, as he demonstrates, it is not only the vegetational and climatic mosaic of the mountains that counts in the serial utilization of pastures, but also the social institutions: how one accommodates kinsmen in one's area when they have fallen on hard times, how grazing associations are made and changed, how pastoralists can change their pasture grounds if they have good social networks.[1] Thus, pastoralists are able to gain access to resources to which they do not necessarily have formal or legal entitlement. (See also Bhattacharya 1995:66.) So too Madgulkar in his novel *Bangarwadi* mentions an interesting social practice to which people resorted when they wished to start a herd (p. 36). A man who wishes to start breeding sheep can approach an owner of sheep and offer him a half-coconut smeared with *haldi*, and express his desire. Tradition demands that the owner give the person a good sheep. In this way, the new shepherd starts with a herd of ten to fifteen animals, and they begin to breed. The interests of the community prevail in the rule that the new owner can neither slaughter nor sell the animals so given to him.

[1] Although discussions like that of Jodha (1994) on common property resources are valuable, these still require to be fleshed out with details about the social parameters and modes of access that village residents have to them.

The second interconnecting theme is what one might call flexibility. As stated in the Introduction, this theme has been studied and explicated by other scholars, but it does receive more attention here than it did in 'Pastoralism I'. Even though Dandekar finds a general pattern in which entire sub-regions opened to different kinds of economies in the medieval period, Varma gives importance to flexibility between agriculture and the rearing of animals and she and Chetan Singh refer to agro-pastoralism; Prasad finds that in any year the food intake from swidden fields was variable and was adjusted to other subsistence quests, and that no group could be called exclusively swidden cultivators; Sinha reports the various roles that the Bhils can be seen to have played in historical record and oral tradition; and Menon refers to flexibility between different craft pursuits in the context of simple tools and techniques. The latter implies that a shift, say, from ivory to sandalwood did not bring about great upheaval in the craft workshop or in the transmission of knowledge from mother to daughter or father to son. Menon also finds that mobile craft producers move between different sets of customers, so that we can infer flexibility or adjustment to different sets of tastes and needs.[2]

It has also recently been observed that all members of a particular group were probably never fully nomadic all at the same time, even though that may have been the image the group had of itself and others of it. Individual families instead would have repeatedly shifted their labour between fields and herds, so that the sedentary dwellings of some members at certain places in the landscape gave their mobile kinsmen access to water, field stubble, or shelter there (Wilson 1995). Kavoori (1999:189) goes so far as to describe the groups he studied as 'a generally distributed society who move in and out of pastoralism as circumstance and opportunity dictate'. Agro-pastoralism, he finds, was always the Indian pattern (ibid.:55), and he does not regard these two as exclusively mutual occupations. Champakalakshmi's paper in this volume prompts us to suggest that this seemingly simple pattern

[2] It would be well not to assume uncritically what we call 'flexibility'. The pastoral groups we observe today are adjusting to very recent conditions, restrictions as well as new opportunities, in their daily lives, the most significant of which are modern transportation and urban employment. Also crucial are urban facilities such as schools and, perhaps the most important, marked increases in birth rates (see Kamal Sultan 1998).

of land use took centuries to evolve. More detailed studies are necessary on the economic factors that make this evolution possible.

Something of a puzzle arises from the fact of this level of flexibility. Group identity, we know, accrues as much from livelihood as it does from language, dress, social customs, and other factors. When we consider the history of the Bhils in Sinha's study of the medieval states of Rajasthan and Gujarat, for example, we wonder how the Bhils remained 'Bhil' in the course of taking to many different kinds of economic life. Iravati Karve's lucid introduction (1961) to this 'people' also voices this problem. She finds it hard to describe the Bhils as 'a tribe', for they have no distinctive patterns of clan organization or marriage rules; there are Hindu and Muslim Bhils; for long they have intermarried with other groups such as the Rajputs; their language is modified according to where they live (scattered across four linguistic zones); and there is no one place or single deity that brings all Bhils together. Another enigma is that the camel-herding Raika of Rajasthan have absorbed into their culture vegetarianism and the religious practice of renunciation, presumably in the course of their interaction with Jains and Hindus, and this even while their settlements remain segregated by a couple of miles from the villages of the peasantry (Srivastava 1997:2, 21).

Let us now discuss mobility. Chetan Singh (this volume) notes the skill with which the shepherds of Kinnaur move between different habitats and different social worlds. Mobility, in other words, is not only about ecology and moving between seasonally available grazing resources. Also important are the agricultural cycles of the region concerned, and the social relationships with agriculturists. Sometimes political issues may be involved; people choose to move far from a chief who makes excessive demands, or because of intra-group conflict. McCabe points out (1994) that when we investigate individual family movements and schedules, we realize the importance of the social relationships, and find that the broad ecological patterns are no longer self-evident. On leaving his village base, says Kavoori (1999:137), a nomad 'enters an ever-changing social environment that is as important . . . [for] his well-being as is the availability of grazing and water. Not only are there a wide variety of relationships that he must negotiate . . . there are also different levels at which negotiations have to be conducted.' Das (2000:4339, 4343), for his part, makes the important point that seasonal transhumance over different altitudinal zones in the Himalaya prevents the depletion of pastures; it was probably less a factor of ecology than of the shortage of labour in pre-modern times; mobile herding enables communities to increase their herds without additional labour inputs, i.e. increasing the returns on labour.

Mobility can be an asset in the sense that craftsmen can gain access to dispersed raw materials and different markets, and also be exposed to the ideas, knowledge, art motifs and information of others (Menon, this volume). This process is accompanied by the development of social skills. Another advantage is that when members of a group are mobile, the community councils meet more often, members get to know one another, endogamy is feasible at the group level, and oral traditions circulate, all leading to a stronger sense of community than if the members led busy lives all the year long in their own villages (Misra 1992:222-3; Srivastava 1997:23). Groups that are constantly on the move are hard for states to track down either for military conquest or to enumerate and record for the purposes of taxation. Besides, Varma's paper here shows that mobility is a major strategy of survival during natural calamities and political crises.

Misra (1992:218-19) finds that mobile smelters, genealogists, and entertainers fill the economic and social interstices of peasant society. Ruhela (1999:145ff), for his part, finds the annual migrations of the iron-repairing and bullock-trading Gaduliya Lohars to be fine-tuned to the needs of settled villagers. Just as Sinha in this volume has observed the Bhils of medieval Mewar coming in and out of state affairs, so too Misra finds that his mobile groups are in and out of village society.

What, then, are the connections between mobility and social marginalization? Margins are not simply geographic frontiers. The Kinnauras as described by Chetan Singh took advantage of their frontier location for trade and have received cultural influences from the heartland of India as well as from Tibet.

But it is said that a high degree of mobility makes for fluid clan/tribal membership or identity whereas colonial predispositions to fix peoples to limited or designated territories meant that identities became land based when they in fact had not been so. The cultural valuation of land amongst a wide range of settled societies and hunters and gatherers across the world has been documented, but less so the attachment of pastoral nomads to their habitat. We can assume that since the line between mobility and group dispersal is a thin one amongst nomadic groups, identities have through history been forged, relocated, and have even disappeared. Waller and Sobania (1994:55-9) find that when families with small herds have to disperse, they cannot easily reunite, and inevitably merge with other groups in their new locations.

Mobility can also be the outcome of oppression and alienation, when people are forced into the urban wage-labour system or are recruited by states for construction or mining work and seasonal agricultural labour. The stigmatizing of several groups by the British as 'Criminal Tribes' in the Act of 1871 (extended in 1921) and by 'denotification' by the Government of India in 1952 is the most horrendous case in point. Perceived to be prone to armed rebellion in the early colonial period, and actually believed, within the framework of caste, to practise crime as an inherited profession, such groups were deprived of their land and taken to seventy-two different settlements to provide cheap labour in mills and mines. Denotification only changed the brand; as Laxman Gaikwad has put it, the 'denotified tribes' and the 'nomadic tribes'—about 126 groups of pastoralists, pedlars, minstrels, acrobats, snake charmers, craftsmen, etc., and numbering about two crore altogether today—still have no land to call their own, and no place to bury their dead. For most of them there is no place in the Schedules and thus no reservation of any sort, except perhaps in Maharashtra. It may not be an exaggeration to state that these scattered and rootless people are the most degraded and brutalized in India (see Abraham 1999).

Our last theme is the connection between marginalization and tribal social organization. There are a few traces of the marginalization of groups other than pastoral nomads in the historical record. As the caste system took its shape, the Candalas, perhaps originally forest dwellers and a non-Aryan group dwelling on the fringes of Aryan settlement, gradually became disadvantaged, were granted low ritual status, and ultimately were condemned as untouchables (Jha 1987). So too the Sudras; Sharma (1990) says they were originally a distinct ethnic group or tribe, who gradually became the labouring class even though they were not totally degraded. A different kind of marginalization is studied by Parasher-Sen (1991) in the case of the

Mlecchas. This was essentially a category of people who were culturally excluded because they did not speak the pure language of the ritual, and were non-*arya*. In time the term 'Mleccha' came to have connotations of location/abode and was associated with tribal regions. In the *Akbarnama*, the Gonds of the forest were considered to be beyond the pale of civilization (Chetan Singh 1995:31). So too mobile pastoralists faced a social stigma in the colonial period (Bhattacharya 1995:77ff). Meanwhile, even though the image of the Bedouin is a kind of ideal in Arab culture—noble, inured to hardship, leading a pure life under the open skies—the harsh reality is a life under the sun, wind, and rain, day after day, a sparse diet, long distances to be covered in order to survive, and an existence generally dogged by thirst and hunger (Kamal Sultan 1998).

Thus, even though the pastoralists of Kutch and Kathiawad provide a select clientele for the urban goldsmiths, we cannot naively assume that groups outside the peasant and caste structure have suffered alienation only in recent times. True, the Rajput rulers of Rajpipla did not proceed with the investiture of a new king without making a journey to Juna Rajpipla, and receiving formal ratification for the succession from a Vasava (Bhil) elder there. And the role of the Bhil chiefs at the investiture of Rajput rulers in Mewar is described here by Sinha and in a number of other studies. It could be argued that these were only token gestures of recognition or co-option, or a means of acknowledging the perceived indigenous status of a people. Deliege (1985:50-63), however, shows that the *tika* is known to have been made by sovereign lords, fathers, paternal uncles, yogis, and other figures of authority as well. In each case, the incumbent was invested with authority, or power was symbolically transferred. Deliege's strongest argument, however, is that the *tika* performed by a Bhil elder reflects that the Bhils had lost out but yet were honoured, and, more important, that Bhil groups were co-opted by the Rajput state but were not integrated into it; tribalism persisted even as state structures were imposed from above. The *tika* symbolized a kind of contract between a ruler and a community.

Therefore, from what we have seen about pastoralists and shifting cultivators and their place in the larger world around them, we can predict that in times of rapid urbanization, the clustering of settlements, agricultural colonization, or changes in flora in the archaeological record, pastoralists in the relevant region would have felt multiple pressures on their survival or else, as in Champakalakshmi's study, they were absorbed into the rural economic and social order. Perhaps pastoral people were well placed only when they were able to gain military advantage, or when they were established across vital trade routes, as in medieval Maharashtra. Traces of this development are seen in the traditions recorded by Ktesias in the fourth century BC (and preserved by a ninth-century writer) (McCrindle 1882:23-4) about mountain people on the north-western frontier of India who bred huge flocks of sheep, goats, and donkeys and who also conveyed high-altitude products to the plains. Apparently their mountain terrain could never be conquered by the armies of the plains, and the rulers of the plains periodically sent them huge quantities of weapons to maintain them as a military buffer against their enemies.

Conditions of subordination mainly lie in the fact of tribal social organization.[3] There is, as Heredia has argued, a kind of starting disadvantage. It is not just that tribal society is small-scale and structured around the relations and morality of kinship. The major distinguishing feature of tribal society is the common entitlement to the major natural resources, agricultural land, ground water, water courses and tanks, cremation grounds and cemeteries, market-places, pastures, and forests. Moreover, it is not the formality of common resources that counts so much as the reality of individual access to them. This, in turn, is feasible when a community functions as a true collectivity. It is as much against the morality of kinship to trade in the produce of the land that is inherited by the group from its ancestors, as it is for one member to enrich himself at the cost of others. It is also important to recall that a non-hierarchical society like the tribe does not have the social wherewithal to incorporate cultural difference. Orality is a secondary feature, as is the lack of an institutionalized leadership that speaks for the group to the outside world, in the case of acephalous tribes.

Communal tenure in basic resources requires a brief discussion. It has mistakenly been said that tribal societies are not egalitarian. But the term egalitarian in the tribal context does not refer to equal prosperity or social standing. People are always different, some are

[3] It needs to be said that we cannot assert that all mobile pastoralists everywhere are tribal people. The Bhotiya described by Farooquee and Nautiyal (1996) are today peasants in that they own land as individual property.

more industrious than others and therefore more prosperous, some have the qualities of leadership and others do not. What counts is that this does not give the few superior rights to pastures or to the labour of others. Salzman (1999) has, to my mind, successfully refuted this revisionist view of tribal society. So too the morality of kinship does not rule out manipulation of genealogies, lines of descent, or ancestral proximity according to situations when people have to share the same resources.

When a group loses its communal land, the importance of genealogy dwindles as the corporateness of the group ceases to be important. The significant point, however, is that less productive lands from which groups may have to make their living as herders or swidden cultivators require group tenure and communal control to ensure flexibility of usage between members and between different parcels of land. The needs of families change over time, and people need to be able to relocate their fields or flocks with ease according to natural conditions and changing circumstances. To put it another way, private property in demarcated plots of land, or legally recorded individual proprietorship, does not make transhumant or nomadic pastoralism, or shifting cultivation, viable.[4] I had briefly touched on the social institutions described by Saberwal that are connected with mobile herding; it is such (tribal) institutions that provide buffers against individual and group misfortune or natural disasters. Famine is now believed not to be a function of climate and population increase alone; also involved are failures of group cohesion and customs such as sharing, collective decisions, restraint from over-grazing, controlled tree felling, cooperation, and the minimization of risk rather than the maximization of profit. Such institutions in their turn are hard to preserve if modern administrations recognize only private and individual property in land. While tribal organization is thus of great value in the long endurance of pastoral and shifting agriculture systems, it is not advantageous under conditions of rising population densities or emerging state power. States do not easily

[4] Pouchepedass (1995:149) states that shifting cultivation 'is not incompatible with property in land', but does not flesh out his argument. Instead he seems to think that surplus production, market exchange, and social stratification are indicators that shifting cultivation is a kind of advanced or respectable mode of production. Such signifiers may not be valid marks of 'progress' at all.

tolerate mobility, the absence of spokespersons, or the lack of individual ownership.

Thus, in the medieval and modern—but not the prehistoric—periods, tribal society needs to be viewed in the context of the larger social formation, with its stratification and state institutions and the interests of its ruling elite (as Varma, Sinha, Chetan Singh, and Prasad are well aware). As Balland has said (1991:205-6), pastoralism is not self-reproducing in its own environmental and ecological contexts. 'Historically adaptive', it evolved—though not in the prehistoric periods, I would add—within the overall development of state societies. Here the question of marginalization appears in a new form: success in herding depends much on relationships with the agrarian society at large. Political independence is thus easier to attain when a group moves beyond the frontiers of a state.

Parasher-Sen (1998) finds that in the Mauryan period there was a conflict beween (forest) tribe and state/peasant society on the grounds that by then the process of agrarian settlement was well advanced, and on a certain reading of the edicts of Ashoka and relevant passages in the *Arthashastra*. So too in S. Guha's view (1999), forest and the agrarian order seem to be separate, the one receding before the other (forest tribes would spill over into abandoned agrarian tracts, or would, in turn, be forced to retreat before the advancing frontier of cultivation), forest being sometimes the abode of 'specialists in the optimal use of this niche' (ibid.:199-200) and sometimes a refuge.[5] We had also referred above to Bhattacharya's concern (1998) with the parting of ways in recent historiography between 'nature' and the agrarian order. While we would agree that forest does not invite military campaigns or attract visits of tax collectors from state capitals, the field-forest dichotomy may be overdrawn. It could not only have been tribes and 'specialists' who regularly exploited the forest; there were also the needs of the peasantry—especially smallholders—to hunt, collect firewood and

[5] So too Guha may be interpreting the archaeological evidence for site abandonments in too literal a way, viz., as 'depopulation' (1999:24). It is specific towns and villages, albeit in large numbers, that were abandoned after the Harappan period, but other villages were founded, and, as Varma shows in this book, the absence of sites does not translate automatically into the absence of inhabitants.

building logs, make charcoal, and move herds out to graze/browse. Perhaps therefore it is more significant that Sinha in this volume finds that the incorporation of the Bhils as important players in the ambits of certain medieval states of western India sometimes involved changes or the shading off of ethnic identities, 'peasantization', and 'Rajputization', but sometimes not. Last, mobile pastoralists may have been pushed into confrontation only when denied the option to move away beyond the control of states.

Heredia set the workshop participants a difficult task. We have not reached the stage when we can place the historiography of shifting cultivators or nomadic pastoralists at the centre of our research. But it is hoped that the academic point is made that some Indians do not have to give up their way of life and their social practices just because they happen to be in a minority or are as yet unable to participate as equal members in what we optimistically call our democracy. The decade of the 1990s, with its massive displacements of populations, may represent a deterioration within the short history of the republic. In 1961, Iravati Karve in a monograph on the Bhils (1961:62 ff) had reported that many Bhils were unhappy with handouts. In her opinion, they were not the poorest section of rural society, and could put their hand to many crafts in contrast to the Maratha peasant, who, because of the caste and *balutedar* systems, was in reality 'an unskilled worker'. She found that Bhil teachers were eager to be posted outside Bhil areas, questioning why they were expected to teach only Bhil children and wanting full participation in the life of the country. Karve warned that setting tribal populations apart 'creates minorities with vested interests' and that the bureaucracy had a vested interest in the creation of autonomous departments for the administration of tribal areas, and the creation of states within states. Karve argued that tribal peoples, the Bhils in this case, 'must not be set apart from and against the rest of the population' (ibid.:64). We seem to have missed the boat.

REFERENCES TO INTRODUCTION AND CONCLUDING SUMMARY

Abraham, Susan, 'Steal or I'll Call You a Thief', *Economic and Political Weekly*, 3 July 1999, pp. 1751-3.

Arnold, D. and R. Guha, eds., *Nature, Culture, Imperialism*, Delhi: Oxford University Press, 1995.

Audouze, F. and C. Jarrige, 'Nomadic Pastoralists and Sedentary Agriculturists in the Kachi Plain, *Studies in History*, vol. 7, no. 2, 1991, pp. 231-54.

Balland, D., 'The Case of the Afghan Nomads in the Indian Subcontinent', *Studies in History*, vol. 7, no. 2, 1991, pp. 205-29.

Bhattacharya, N., 'Pastoralists in a Colonial World', in D. Arnold and R. Guha, eds., *Nature, Culture, Imperialism*, Delhi: Oxford University Press, 1995, pp. 49-85.

Bhattacharya, N., ed., 'Forests, Fields, and Pastures', *Studies in History*, vol. 14, no. 2 (Special Issue).

Butzer, K.W., 'Ecology in the Long View', *Journal of Field Archaeology*, vol. 23, 1996, pp. 141-50.

Dandekar, A., 'Landscapes in Conflict: Flocks, Hero-Stones, and Cult in Early Medieval Maharashtra', *Studies in History*, vol. 7, no. 2, 1991, pp. 301-24.

Das, Jishnu, 'Institutions and Incentives in a Garhwal Village I: Common Property Regimes in Traditional Societies', *Economic and Political Weekly*, 2 December 2000, pp. 4337-44.

Deliege, R., *The Bhils of Western India*, Delhi: National Publishing House, 1985.

Farooquee, N. and A. Nautiyal, 'Livestock Ownership Patterns among Transhumants in High-Altitude Villages of the Central Himalaya', *Nomadic Peoples*, vol. 39, 1996, pp. 87-96.

Ferdinand, K., *Bedouins of Qatar*, London: Thames and Hudson, 1993.

Galaty, J.G., 'Rangeland Tenure and Pastoralism in Africa', in E. Fratkin, K.A. Galvin, and E.A. Roth, eds., *African Pastoralist Systems: An Integrated Approach*, Boulder: Lynne Rienner Publishers, 1994, pp. 185-204.

Glantz, M., ed., *Drought and Hunger in Africa*, Cambridge: Cambridge University Press, 1987.

Guha, Sumit, *Environment and Ethnicity in India, 1200-1991*, Cambridge: Cambridge University Press, 1999.

Gupta, A.K., 'Pastoral Adaptation to Risk in Dry Regions', *Studies in History*, vol. 7, no. 2, 1991, pp. 325-41.

Gurukkal, Rajan, 'The Beginnings of the Historic Period: The Tamil South', in R. Thapar, ed., *Recent Perspectives in Early Indian History*, Bombay: Popular Prakashan, 1998, pp. 246-74.

Habib, I., 'Merchant Communities in Precolonial India', in J.D. Tracy, ed., *The Rise of Merchant Empires*, Cambridge: Cambridge University Press, 1990, pp. 371-99.

Hardiman, D., 'Small Dam Systems of the Sahyadris', in D. Arnold and R. Guha, eds., *Nature, Culture, Imperialism*, Delhi: Oxford University Press, 1995, pp. 185-209.

Holy, L., ed., *Comparative Anthropology*, Oxford: Blackwell, 1987.

Jha, V., 'Candala and the Origin of Untouchability', *Indian Historical Review*, vol. 13, 1987, pp. 1-36.

Jodha, N.S., 'Common Property Resources and the Rural Poor', in R. Guha, ed., *Social Ecology*, Delhi: Oxford University Press, 1994, pp. 150-87.

Karve, Iravati, *The Bhils of West Khandesh*, Bombay: Bombay University Press, 1961.

Kavoori, P.S., 'Transhumance in Western Rajasthan', *Studies in History*, vol. 7, no. 2, 1991, pp. 255-78.

———, *Pastoralism in Expansion*, Delhi: Oxford University Press, 1999.

Little, P., 'Maasai Identity on the Periphery', *American Anthropologist*, vol. 100, 1998, pp. 444-57.

Madgulkar, V., *Bangarwadi* (*The Village Had No Walls*, tr. R. Deshmukh), Bombay: Popular Prakashan, 1994, 1st published 1958.

McCabe, J.T., and M.S. Mate, 'Mobility and Land Use Among African Pastoralists: Old Problems and New Interpretations', in E. Fratkin, K.A. Galvin, and E.A. Roth, eds., *African Pastoralist Systems: An Integrated Approach*, Boulder: Lynne Rienner Publishers, 1994, pp. 69-88.

McCrindle, J.W., *Ancient India as Described by Ktesias the Knidian*, Calcutta: Thacker Spink, 1882.

Misra, P.K., 'Oral Strategies among Nomadic Peoples', *The Eastern Anthropologist*, vol. 45, 1992, pp. 215-26.

Munshi Saldanha, I., 'The Political Ecology of Traditional Farming Practices in Thana District', *Journal of Peasant Studies*, vol. 17, no. 3, 1990, pp. 433-43.

Nugent, J.B. and N. Sanchez, 'Tribes, Chiefs, and Transhumance', *Economic Development and Culture Change*, vol. 4, no. 2, 1993, pp. 87-113.

Parasher-Sen, A., *Mlecchas in Early India*, Delhi: Munshiram Manoharlal, 1991.

———, 'Of Tribes, Hunters, and Barbarians', *Studies in History*, vol. 14, no. 2, 1998, pp. 173-91.

Pouchepadass, J., 'British Attitudes towards Shifting Cultivation: South Canara District, 1800-1920', in D. Arnold and R. Guha, eds., *Nature, Culture, Imperialism*, Delhi Oxford University Press, 1995, pp. 123-51.

Ratnagar, S., ed., 'On Pastoralism', *Studies in History*, vol. 7, no. 2 (Special Issue), 1991.

Ruhela, S.P., *Society, Economy and Folk Culture of a Rajasthani Nomadic Community*, Delhi: Indian Publishers Distributors, 1999.

Saberwal, Vasant K., *Pastoral Politics: Shepherds, Bureaucrats, and Conservation in the Western Himalaya*, Delhi: Oxford University Press, 1999.

Salzman, P.C., 'Is Inequality Universal?', *Current Anthropology*, vol. 40, no. 1, 1999, pp. 31-61.

Sharma, R.S., *Sudras in Ancient India*, 3rd revd edn., Delhi: Motilal Banarsidass, 1990.

Sharma, S. and H.C. Rikhari, 'The Bhotias', *Nomadic Peoples*, vols. 36-7, 1995, pp. 167-74.

Singh, Chetan, 'Forests, Pastoralists and Agrarian Society', in D. Arnold and R. Guha, eds., *Nature, Culture, Imperialism*, Delhi: Oxford University Press, 1995, pp. 21-48.

Skaria, A., *Hybrid Histories: Forests, Frontiers and Wildness in Western India*, Delhi: Oxford University Press, 1999.

Spooner, B., 'Weavers and Dealers', in A. Appadurai, ed., *The Social Life of Things*, Cambridge: Cambridge University Press, 1986, pp. 195-235.

Srivastava, Vinay K., *Religious Renunciation of a Pastoral People*, Delhi: Oxford University Press, 1997.

Sultan, Kamal A., 'Towards a Continuing Pastoralism in Oman', *Oman Daily Observer*, 2 February 1998.

Swanson, T.M., 'The Economics of Environmental Degradation', in T.M. Swanson, ed., *The Economics of Environmental Degradation*, Cheltenham: E. Elgar, 1996, pp. 1-28.

Varma, S., 'Villages Abandoned: The Case for Mobile Pastoralism in Post-Harappan Gujarat', *Studies in History*, vol. 7, no. 2, 1991, pp. 279-300.

Waller, R. and N.W. Sobana, 'Pastoralism in Historical Perspective', in E. Fratkin, K.A. Galvin, and E.A. Roth, eds., *African Pastoralist Systems: An Integrated Approach*, Boulder: Lynne Rienner Publishers, 1994, pp. 45-68.

Wilson, W., 'The Fulani Model of Sustainable Agriculture: Fulbe Nomadism in a Systemic View of Pastoralism and Farming', *Nomadic Peoples*, vols. 36-7, 1995, pp. 35-52.

Index